THE LIVING GARDEN

George Ordish

THE LIVING GARDEN

THE 400-YEAR HISTORY OF AN ENGLISH GARDEN

Illustrations by
Alison Claire Darke

Houghton Mifflin Company

BOSTON • NEW YORK • LONDON

To my grandson Martin Dockery II

For more information about permission to reproduce
selections from this book, write to Permissions,
Houghton Mifflin Company, 215 Park Avenue South,
New York, New York 10003.

Library of Congress Cataloging-in-Publication Data
Ordish, George
The living garden : the 400-year history of an English garden /
George Ordish : illustrations by Alison Claire Darke.
p.   cm.
Includes bibliographical references (p.   ) and index.
ISBN 0-395-63770-8
1. Gardens — England — Weald of Kent — History.
2. Gardening — England — Weald of Kent — History.   3. Garden
ecology — England — Weald of Kent — History.   4. Weald of Kent
(England) — History.   I. Title.
[SB451.36.G7073   1992]   92-12435 CIP

Printed in the United States of America

MP 10 9 8 7 6 5 4 3 2 1

Contents

Illustrations

Foreword

In 1959 I wrote a book called *The Living House* that described a farm-house, typical of its kind in the Kentish Weald, and all the different kinds of life that had been in it from its construction in 1555 to the present day.

The farm was called Bartons End because Richard Barton, a prosperous farmer, built a house for his second son, John Barton, in 1555, in preparation for John's coming marriage to Mary Halstead in 1556. The house's life over the years that followed was very varied: there were mites, insects, worms, spiders, snails, birds, toads, and mammals—cats, dogs, mice, bats and humans. The present book gives a similar account of the garden of that typical house: in the garden the life was even more varied because there was a big range of plant life as well as the numerous animals.

The garden was started in 1556, when it was no more than a bed by the front door growing a few medicinal herbs. Over the centuries it has grown to be a fine, well-kept garden covering five acres of ground, including an orchard and a small part of the original copse. Naturally it has seen many changes throughout its history as the twenty owners in succession tended it, neglected it or entirely abandoned the property, according to their bents for gardening, their social position and the money or time—much the same thing—available for gardening. The occupiers of the house and garden are given in tabular form after this foreword, together with some notes on the main developments in the garden over the four hundred years.

This book then is the story of the biological changes in the garden at Bartons End and the effects on the balance of life on the site. We will follow the fortunes of the people who, with varying degrees of intensity and knowledge, gardened there. Though the garden was man-made and man-maintained, yet the life there in its turn influenced man from time to time, as will be shown as the story unfolds.

Basically the book goes forward in historical sequence, but each chapter deals with some particular garden interest, which may mean going ahead to a later stage and then, in the following chapter, coming back to the earlier time.

The method I have used for naming the various plants and animals is to use the popular name in the text except where some confusion might arise, when both popular and scientific names are given. In the Appendix is a list of the plants and animals mentioned in the book, with both scientific and popular names.

I am grateful to a number of authors, living and dead, for much information, also to libraries and research stations, particularly the Penzance (Morrab) Library, the Penzance Public Library, the British Library, and the East Malling and Henry Doubleday research stations. A number of individuals have also been of great assistance, among them John and Kay Charlton, Edna Orton, Caroline White, and Barbara Plank for the careful preparation of the typescript. I offer them my thanks. Finally, I am grateful to my wife for much help and for reading and correcting the manuscript.

GEORGE ORDISH
Nancledra, 1984

Nature is full of these wonders, dear cousin;
we are admitted to the view of a very small
portion of it only; there is little hope then
that we should be able to understand its relations
fully, or to unravel all its mysteries.

J-J Rousseau

The People

John Barton   m. 1556   Mary Halstead
b.1537 d.1599   b.1537 d.1610

John	Jane	Elizabeth	*Thomas Barton*	Five other
b.1557	b.1558	b.1559	b.1560 d.1629	children
d.1558	d.1632	d.1559		

m.1584 Elizabeth Standish

Mark Barton m.1604   Margaret Stead   Six other
b.1585   b.1586   children
d.1631   d.1645

2 died in infancy   *Elizabeth Barton* m.1626   Robert Onway
                       b.1608 d.1688   b.1605 d.1660

Mark Onway m.1648 Prudence Sefton   2 daughters
b.1627
d.1665 of
the plague

James Onway b.1652, sold the property   Prudence
to a retired merchant 1689   b.1654

Joseph Munroyd m.1689   Ruth Breadman
b.1640 d.1705   b.1665

Isaac Munroyd m.1711   Anne Cobb   2 other children
b.1690 d.1752   b.1691

Charles Munroyd m. 1752   Susannah Aylesford,   2 other children
b.1716 d.1764   an heiress
                      b.1729 d.1800

Charles	*George Munroyd* m.1784	Sophia Holberg	Susannah
b.1752	b.1754 d.1808	b.1760 d.1809	
d.1752			

Charlotte Munroyd
b.1786 d.1817
Unmarried. Property sold by distant heirs to
a veteran of the Napoleonic wars, in 1818

Gardens at Bartons End 1556–1817

Date	The Garden	
1556–1599	1556	A small bed of medicinal herbs outside front door started.
	1557	Bed edged with flowers, alexanders, violets, etc.
	1558	Tree stumps removed and garden extended.
	1559	Quite a bit of land cleared; vegetables, fruit and a new-fangled plant from Flanders—the hop—planted.
	1580	Pigeon loft made and pigeons installed. Long-walk for archery made.
1599–1629	1600	Plank edging to beds. Orchard developed. New plants from Holland.
	1605	Rhubarb planted.
	1620	Pot herbs encouraged.
1629–1631	1625	Flowers amidst the grass.
1631–1660	1632	Raspberries and gooseberries grown.
	1650	Skilled gardeners employed.
	1658	Nightingales welcomed.
1660–1665	1660	Orchard in prime condition.
1665–1705	1665	Talking to the trees tried.
	1670	New flowers introduced.
	1680	Cousin Barton in New England sends some seed, scarlet runners.
	1685	Potatoes tried.
	1698	Many imported plants introduced.
	1700	The Munroyds cherish their gardener.
1705–1752	1720	Junipers planted.
	1725	Sweetpeas grown.
	1748	Topiary tried.
	1750	Great development of garden. Many flowers, vegetables and new fruits introduced.
1752–1764	1754	Magnolia planted.
	1758	Greenhouse built.
1764–1808	1764	Various animals in the garden. Capability Brown refuses to plan the garden.
	1766	Grandiose garden plans abandoned.
1808–1817	1768	New peaches grown.

The People

John Hackshaw m.1797 Caroline Harris
b.1770 d.1833

William Hackshaw m.1819 Emily Hempstead   3 sons   2 daughters
b.1798 d.1852

Alfred Hackshaw   David Hackshaw m.1844 Victoria Kristen
b.1822 d.1898   b.1823
Disliked farming,
settled in Venice: Oscar Hackshaw
on death of his father   b.1845
let the farm to:

Emmanuel Burrows m.Marjory Rummer

and subsequently to another:

William Daker

In 1899 the farm was sold away from the house by Oscar Hackshaw, nephew and heir of Alfred Hackshaw. The house left unoccupied for 10 years.

Property bought very cheaply by an artist (1909):

Robert Dunchester m.1903 Myfanwy Evans
b.1870 d.1949   b.1884 d.1956

Robert F. Dunchester   Sloane Dunchester m.1935 Thomas Frazer
b.1910 d.1958   b.1912 d.1958   b.1914
m.1935 Louise Cavanagh (1)
     who m. (2) James Endicott
     no issue

Phillip Frazer m.1962 Desirée Barton   Caroline   Myfanwy II
b.1937   of Duxbury, Mass.   b.1939   b.1942
     b.1939   no issue   m.1967 Giles Thompson
     no issue

Phillip Thompson   Caroline   Sloane Myfanwy III
b.1969   b.1971   b.1974

Gardens at Bartons End

Date	The Garden	
1818–1833	1830	Mowing machine for lawns.
1833–1852	1840	Modern strawberries planted.
1853–1869	1853	Garden neglected, except vegetable plot. Giant potatoes White Elephant grown.
1869–1899	1870	Extensive nettle beds left by William Daker, as, he emphasized, they produced such beautiful butterflies.
1899–1909		The garden returning to the wild, except for a small patch.
1909–1949	1910	An old-fashioned sphairistikè court made (forerunner of lawn tennis). The garden gradually restored.
	1915	Vegetables replace flowers in many beds.
	1920–25	Garden restored.
	1940–45	Lawns dug up, vegetables and potatoes planted.
1949–1958	1950	Garden now restored.
1958–1984	1960	Garden divided into two.
	1965	Considerable embellishments of the garden as property becomes an old people's home. Some raised beds provided to make gardening by the patients easy. Herbicides used.
	1979	A water garden and a nature garden made out of old bomb crater.

NOTE

The superior letters in the text refer to the notes,
pp. 229–32, and the superior numbers to the
bibliography, pp. 251–4.

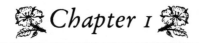

Chapter 1

Starting the Garden,
1556–99

THE WEALD of Kent where Richard Barton farmed in the sixteenth century was once a richly wooded valley, lying between the high ridges of the North Downs and the Ashdown Forest. The river Medway, joined by the Beult and numerous tributaries, drains the area to the north and flows into the mouth of the Thames. The Rother flows south, discharging itself into the English Channel below Rye, at that time a coastal town and a port. Westward from the high white cliffs of Dover the land gradually gives way to the low, rich sheep pastures of Romney Marsh before it rises again to make the South Downs.

In later times Kent became known as the Garden of England for the pink and white glory of its fruit blossom and the bines of its hop gardens. Dickens in *The Pickwick Papers* has Mr Jingle epitomise Kent to Mr Pickwick with the words, 'Kent, sir—everybody knows Kent —apples, cherries, hops and women.' But when the garden of the present book was begun in the heart of that favoured county the countryside looked somewhat different. The orchards were only starting, and as the use of hops in beer was illegal they were not grown.

The rivers were important because they not only provided drainage but also cheap transport, for the roads were bad and thus expensive to use. For instance, a packhorse would carry about 280 lbs., a one-horse wagon on a bad road some 1½ tons, but a barge, pulled by one horse from the tow path, transported 20 or 30 tons.[1] Primitive locks, called staunces, were used on the rivers enabling small boats to move from one stretch to another.

The Weald had originally been densely wooded; it was but little used by primitive man who confined his activities to the higher ground. As the population grew and agriculture developed, more and more clearings were made in the forest and productive farms established in its place. By the time Bartons End was built in 1555 only patches of the indigenous forest remained. The process of destruction was accelerated by the demands of the iron and glass industries for charcoal, those of shipbuilders for timber, of farmers for houses and land, and of all classes for fuel for their homes. Bartons End was, in fact, built on a patch of old forest which was specially cleared for the purpose. Progress in the Tudor age eventually cut all the Wealden woods, except small patches here and there.

Cleared forest became valuable agricultural land and at first was used on the communal, open field system. By this method each farmer had a number of strips of land in each one of his village's three fields, strips that were cultivated in common, a system retarding progress, as no one individual could improve his land when it was in so many separate bits. When the open fields were enclosed, mostly by mutual agreement, and each man's strips consolidated into enclosed fields, improvements in farming became possible and the modern style of farm evolved. The Barton family were among the pioneers and by 1555 there were no open fields left in their district, though there were a few areas of common grazing. In general the Kentish farmers were richer, more enterprising and more independent than the majority of Englishmen.

Richard Barton was a progressive farmer and a good father. He tried to make provision for all his offspring; there were dowries and marriages for the girls — usually arranged by the respective parents without much consultation with the parties directly concerned — Bartons Farm for his eldest son and some career or provision of land for his remaining boys.

Richard Barton was proud of his fine farm and of being a 'Man of Kent', that is, one born east of the Medway as distinct from the 'Kentish Men' born on the other side of the river. The Men of Kent maintained that they had never been conquered by the Normans. After the Battle of

Hastings their ancestors, carrying green boughs, marched to meet William and in return for ceasing to attack the invader made an agreement with him under which they retained all their ancient customs and privileges, among which was gavelkind. Gavelkind was a system of inheritance by which a man's estate at his death was divided equally among his sons, a custom which broke up farms into ever smaller units. To prevent his splendid holding being fractioned at his death, Richard spent considerable sums on lawyers' fees, making an elaborate will by which his farm, Bartons, passed undivided to his eldest son, Richard Pearce.

Richard's second son, John Barton, aged eighteen, returned home in the spring of 1555, not having lived at the farm for eight years nor having seen his parents for five. He had spent the previous eight years with an uncle near Guildford. It was the custom in those days for the children of the more prosperous families to be sent away from home to be brought up by strangers or relatives, and the uncle, Barnaby Barton, and his wife gave the boy much love and a good education. John could read and write, developed a love of books and, very important in his subsequent life, he could figure, although his knowledge of Latin was weak.

Richard Barton proposed to make John a farmer. He said that John must make his farm from any land he could wrest from the waste and the woods, a considerable task and one that the young man took very seriously. Making his farm became his main interest; he could hardly bear to indulge in any activity that did not lend itself to that end. Naturally his father helped him and John got new ideas from the textbooks of the time. As it happened the garden that eventually grew up almost by accident proved to be a source of wealth as well as pleasure.

Richard Barton also arranged a marriage for his son with a neighbour's daughter, Mary Halstead, and built a house for them, which was known as Bartons End because it stood on the edge of the family's lands. The young couple had known each other as children and agreed to their parents' proposals. In 1556, when the house Richard had built for them was completed, they were married amidst great rejoicing, feasting and the bucolic humour of that age.

The building itself was a typical Kentish farmhouse, built of a stout oak frame with filling walls of wattle and daub. It had a thatched roof and was near a minor road. There was a large, central, brick-built chimney stack with two fireplaces, back to back. The larger, with a bread oven by its side, was in the main hall; the smaller fireplace served the parlour.

The fields, as they were wrested from the wilds, grew the usual crops, wheat, barley and oats, and beans. Young John, like his father, was progressive and experimented with new plants, such as the Dutch grass or wild white clover, St Lucerne, turnips and field cabbage, all of which proved very rewarding. Another advantageous step was the use of horses, rather than oxen, for ploughing. Milk was produced, but yields were not high. It did not keep well, and was largely made into butter and cheese. Nevertheless, the milkmaids knew that if pans and buckets were well scoured and put in the sun, the milk kept for longer. The light was sterilising the vessels.

When John Barton started to make his farm England was entering her golden age. She had a forward-looking, progressive people and no burden of a distant empire to support. The country was very empty. There were only four million people in England, though Kent tended to be more densely populated than many other parts. Eighty per cent of the population lived in the country and, as far as the Bartons were concerned, the Kentish soil was productive. Kent even exported corn. In 1558, two years after Bartons End was constructed, the very able Princess Elizabeth was crowned queen and during her reign England became increasingly prosperous.

The class system prevailed, but was not resented; consequently it was accepted by nearly all. The gentleman, knowing that his social inferiors knew their place, consulted freely with them on current affairs or on the best way of doing a job. His son and the farmer's son went to the local grammar school if both showed ability enough, and both were equally beaten for making a false concordance.

The Bartons were Protestants and at the time John Barton's house was built they were a family that kept very quiet in local affairs and politics. The Bartons had every reason to lie low during the reign of the Catholic Mary Tudor, who came to the throne in 1553, for she did not like Protestants. When she was succeeded by her sister Elizabeth, England again had a Protestant ruler.

The East Anglian branch of the Barton family were Puritans and some of them felt so oppressed by even the reformed Church of England that they emigrated to the Netherlands. There they were welcomed and allowed to worship as they wished. They led a useful life but were not very happy, because they found their children becoming Dutch men and women, knowing nothing of England. Later on this led some of them to join the emigrants, sailing in the *Mayflower* or subsequent vessels to America, where they founded colonies in New England. The Kentish Bartons' contacts on the Continent and in America in time played a part in shaping their garden, as we shall see.

Both the Bartons and the Halsteads were forward-looking people, ready to try the new ideas of the Elizabethan age. The Halsteads had educated their daughters as well as their sons, in the belief that knowledge was the key to success in any walk of life. If the Queen could speak Latin and Greek, why should not their girls at least have some little skill in writing and figuring? Let the world see they were the children of freeholders and not ignorant peasants.

Both John and Mary Barton were absorbing the new thought and believed a great future awaited them provided that modern ideas could be adopted. Baconism, the learning from experiment and investigation of first causes, was in the air.

They read what were the textbooks of that age on farming and gardening. John's standby was Fitzherbert's *Boke of Husbandrie*, the fifth edition (1552),[31] and Mary had William Turner's *New Herball* (1551).[69] Turner's book was well illustrated, clearly written and gave the names of plants in 'Greke, Latine, Dutch, French and in the Apothecaries Latine and sometimes in Italian'. Mary could not aspire to grow the 500 or so plants mentioned, nor was she in sympathy with the constant references to the views of the classical authors, arguing that what a man found to be good more than a thousand years ago and more than a thousand miles away was not necessarily for the best in the new enlightened age in which she lived. But she was drawn to Turner's book by the hard knock delivered to the received ideas of those times in the title itself: '. . . *with the virtues of some herbes with diverse confutations of no small errours that men of no small learning have committed in the intreating of herbes of late years*'.

Herbals were popular works: just before John Barton died, Mary read John Gerard's *Herball*[35] which appeared in 1597.[a] Gerard's book dealt with more than 3,000 products, and was filched mostly from the work of a Belgian author called Dodoens; it was illustrated with a job-lot of plates found in the Netherlands, so that wrong names were assigned to some of the pictures. The main objections of John, Mary and their son Thomas to the *Herball* were that it had very little to say on the growing of the plants and advised the use of substances expensive and difficult to obtain. One ought to be able to grow one's own medicines, Mary thought, and she claimed to have done just that over the last forty years. The book's pretensions to scholarship and its ostentatious display of classical knowledge were most irritating. Moreover, Mary had spotted at least two errors in the naming of the pictures.

A book Mary found to be of greater use than Gerard's *Herball* was the first book on gardening published in English, Thomas Hyll's[b]*A Most Briefe and Pleasante Treatyse of teachinge howe to dress, sowe and set a Garden* (1563).[43] Described as a 'booke for the simple and unlettered' (how the unlettered were to read it is not mentioned) it appealed to Mary because, though some information was drawn from Pliny and similar authors, there were also many sound and original observations, which greatly helped her in the garden she was making. It became a popular book and ran to nine editions by 1608. In 1566 she was delighted to find that Hyll was attacking the implicit faith in astrology, as it affected the growing of plants, with a book called *Anti-prognosticon contra inutiles astrologorum praedictiones Nostradami*.[45] Hyll's main attack was against the astrologer Nostradamus, but he had a number of observations the Bartons found very sound too. For example, they agreed that when sowing seeds, the condition of the soil was more important than the position of the stars, as other authors had suggested.

Another book that Mary found useful and attractive appeared in 1573, Thomas Tusser's *Five Hundreth good Pointes of Husbandry, united to as many of good Housewifery*.[70] Its appeal was in the rhymed couplets that gave sound, practical advice. The Bartons owed a fine strawberry bed to that book: they had carefully searched the woods for outstanding plants.

> Wife, into the garden, and set me a plot
> Of strawberry roots, of the best to be got:
> Such growing abroad, among thorns in the wood,
> Well chosen and picked, proove excellent good.

The vast amount of study needed to master all the 'government and virtues' of the plants in the herbals was beyond the powers of the average person and served to keep the professions of doctor and apothecary as closed shops. There was also too much reliance amongst them on the classical authors, on astrology and on the doctrine of signatures, this last a survival from medieval times. The doctrine held that if a plant looked like some organ of the human body then that plant must be a cure for diseases of that organ. For instance, the eyebright, with two dark spots like eyes on the upper of its four petals, must obviously be good for defects of sight. This is not to say that all the herbal remedies were ineffective. Many were efficient, particularly those with diuretic and laxative qualities. Mary's first essay into gardening was in this field: her herbal medicines were based on the general beliefs of the day and, as she got older, on her own experience of dosing family, friends, servants and neighbours.

For her first herb bed Mary collected plants and seeds from her parents, friends, travelling packmen, the common lands and woods. After a year's work she had established borage, chervil, chives, coriander, cowslip or paigle, cumin, dill, eyebright, fennel, foxglove, furze, marjoram, mints of various kinds including pennyroyal, parsley, poppies, 'purcelaine' (purslane, an early arrival from America), rue, sage, savory, 'time' (thyme) and violets.

Establishing this varied collection had taken considerable effort and to draw attention to it she decided to edge her bed with the violets, which also had a medicinal use. This led her to cultivate other simple flowers which were mostly decorative, such as alexanders, camomile, marigolds and primroses, though only camomile and primroses were suitable for edging. She and her maids made many visits to the woods searching out plants, mostly violets, with larger flowers, deeper colours and stronger scent. In the wild every now and then a white-flowered violet would be found and these she always dug up, establishing a pretty edging of white violets to her herb bed. She was thus selecting white flowers and helping in the preservation of this recessive character. In the wild a plant with larger flowers or differently coloured blossoms might well not have any survival value over smaller flowered ones and thus would not necessarily survive in the struggle among violets for space, light and nourishment. But near Bartons End, plants with the character-

Marjoram

Garden-sage

Eyebright

Wilde-rue

Fennel

Parsley

istics of larger size, deeper colour and scent had what one might call a hidden advantage. They appealed to Mary Barton, who collected them, planted them out and propagated from them. Quite a demand for Barton Whites arose in time among her friends, and these aberrant violet plants survived because of their appeal to gardeners.

At first John Barton thought Mary's flower borders a waste of effort. He was a second son and would inherit none of his father's farm: it was up to him to establish a new farm on the land reclaimed from the waste and the woods his father allowed him to adopt. Everybody should help towards this main objective, he felt, and not waste time on growing plants just because they looked pretty. Mary changed this attitude when she pointed out the value of the pomanders she would make, which were then believed to be sure specifics against the spread of disease. The pomander was a light wicker ball or empty orange skin filled with aromatic herbs and flowers and often stuffed with cloves, an exotic and expensive import. In Mary's pomanders dried scented violets and pinks played an important part; they replaced the too-dear cloves.

Not content with the white violet borders, she established a special bed of them, each year weeding out any purple-flowering plants. She grew marigolds and primroses and also planted camomile, an attractive sweet-smelling herb and a useful one, which was used in the form of infusions for curing indigestion and cramps in the limbs and which was eventually used to make an extensive lawn. The powdered camomile flowers were also used in the form of compresses and applied to wounds, burns and swellings.

Others of the flowers had medical properties, too. The alexanders, according to the mid-nineteenth-century gardener, G. W. Johnson, were 'the helper of man' and served to cure many ills. The blanched stems were also used in salads and tasted something like celery.

The medicinal herbs proper, which included a number of decorative flowers, had a vast diversity of applications in professional hands. Mary's diuretics were chervil, fennel, furze flowers, parsley, rue and savory, and all except rue and furze were also used in the kitchen. With regard to furze, there was an old saying, 'When the furze is out of bloom kissing time is done'. The furze flowers the year round. From its yellow colour it was held to be good against jaundice, another example of the signature theory. Fennel was particularly valuable when cooked with fish, for it 'consumed the flegmatic humour that fish have', a humour that was known to plague the body. To Mary, unfenneled fish was almost as doubtful a food as raw fruit: great care had to be taken, for example, when eating fresh strawberries. The dangers of eating fresh fruit, based on the best classical authority, were probably given publicity in order to deter the picking and consuming of fruit by children, servants and strangers passing through an orchard.

Mary's herb garden had some laxatives, such as black dogwood, violets and flax. Violets were also used in perfume and in pomanders.

Many preparations were employed to promote beauty. For instance, cowslips, the herb of Venus, aided beauty and restored it if once lost. An ointment made from the flowers removed wrinkles and the objectionable tanning of the skin from sunburn. Sage blackened the hair. Mints stirred up appetite, lust (as did also the heartsease or pansy) and anger, and were not to be given to choleric people. Rue, on the other hand, prevented lewd thoughts. Rue was a most useful herb, almost a panacea; it was said to promote urine and menses, it was an antidote for poisons and the bite of a mad dog or snake, as was also mint. It was never to be given to pregnant women and was used by witches as an abortifacient.

Remedies leading to the healing of wounds, ulcers and bruises were often wanted and Mary prescribed dill and pennyroyal, which also eased childbirth. Mint was to be avoided as it kept a wound open. Expectant and nursing mothers were advised to take savory and fennel, while would-be mothers could be helped to conceive by a course of sage. The brain and thinking were improved by marjoram and sage, which also warmed the stomach, promoted sneezing, eased earache and made a perfumed toilet water.

The herb bed, with its edging of pretty flowers, was carefully tended and extended. It aroused considerable admiration among the neighbours and farm hands and was likened to the 'knottes', or raised flower beds, in the gardens of the nobility. By 1558, when she had lost her first baby some months after his birth and was again pregnant, Mary determined to enlarge her garden, enlisting the help of two of her maids, Nell and Dorothy, who had become as enthusiastic as their mistress. Their aim was to grow 'strewing-herbs' for the house floors and roses from which to make rosewater.

It is a mistake to think that our ancestors did not mind the many unpleasant smells of those days. These came not only from the farm, but also from the earth privies, the scantily washed humans and the domestic animals. To combat these annoyances the privies were usually put outside the house; soap was made by boiling fat with potash and used to some extent, but the main method of overcoming odours was to use counter-smells, that is, to carry a pomander and sniff it when some objectionable odour was filling the air, or to grow sweet-smelling plants and scatter them around the house. Strewing herbs on the floors of rooms took the place of our carpets.

To get these herbs Mary needed more land. The understanding with her husband, who secretly was proud of her efforts with the medicinal herbs, was that she and her girls could reclaim as much land as they liked, so long as they did not call on the men or horses for help in the process.

Bartons End had been constructed on two acres of land reclaimed from coppiced forest, a good source of poles, fence rails and hurdles. The coppiced sets were hazel, ash and sweet chestnut, the standing timber oaks and ash, with an occasional elm. The trees on this area had been felled to provide the main timbers for the house, and the coppiced poles cut, but the stumps had been removed only on the actual house site, for a few yards around it and on a site for some outbuildings. Mary could only expand her garden on to land containing these substantial tree stumps. Removing tree stumps in those days was very hard work: in fact it still is, though today we get machines to do most of the grubbing out.

In the spring of 1558, Mary made a start on some of the nearest stumps. Every Monday she visited them and rubbed off or cut out all sucker growth that they had made. She argued that, if she persisted, such treatment would kill them in the end, as in fact proved to be the case. But a dead stump was as much an obstacle as a living one, for it would take a very long time to rot away, and so she hit on another idea. This was to burn out the stumps. It is a difficult thing to do, as usually they are green and have big fire-resistant roots running through the earth, so that the flames need some help.

One of the important products of those days, provided mostly by the horse, was nitre, potassium nitrate. Nitre crystallised out from the animals' urine and was found in the earth beneath stables and cattle byres. It was much in demand for making gunpowder; the Queen's nitre men could enter any premises, dig up the earth in stables, extract the nitre and carry it away, and nobody could say them nay. The earth was washed with water, then strained, the solution boiled and concentrated and allowed to cool, when the precious nitre crystallised out.

The production of nitrate, an essential plant food, in the soil is an example of how various life forms in an environment are linked to each other, for it is produced by the action of bacteria. Nitrogenous organic compounds, such as proteins and urea, when they get into the soil are fed upon by many kinds of bacteria, and the nitrogen they contain is converted to ammonia (NLH_3). Another genus of bacteria (*Nitrososomas*) then converts the ammonia to nitrite (NO_2) ready for yet another genus (*Nitrobacter*) to add an additional oxygen atom and produce nitrate (NO_3). The nitrate in its turn combines with potassium salts in the soil and with other elements as well to produce the potassium nitrate, desired as much by the plants as by the nitre men. The potassium in the soil was mostly derived from wood ash. The Bartons knew that ashes sprinkled in the stables kept them sweet and helped the nitre develop.

Potassium nitrate is a great promoter of growth in plants. The compound is absorbed into the plant, and its three elements (KNO_3), potassium, nitrogen and oxygen, combine with carbon obtained from the gas carbon dioxide (CO_2) in the air and other elements to form plant tissues. Nitrates are used in explosives, such as gunpowder, because they readily give up their oxygen (potassium nitrate is 48 per cent oxygen by weight), which makes the reaction so quick that an explosion takes place. Nitrates also assist any burning process.

Mary had seen slow matches prepared by soaking string in nitre solution and then drying it. She decided to collect some nitre, illegal though it might be, from the earth beneath the stabling of her own two horses. This obtained, she got holes bored in some stumps by Nell's father, Thomas Claridge, using a brace and bit, an expensive and valuable tool in those days. The man lent his help because he was interested in the idea and half thought the stumps might explode and set the house alight. He would keep an eye on his daughter's safety and be in at the excitement if any fireworks developed. In dry weather the nitre solution was poured into the holes and topped up from time to time over the next few days.

At last the great moment came. On a dry afternoon Mary had a number of buckets of water assembled as a precaution and the ever-present long-handled rakes kept handy. They were used to pull off burning thatch from roofs and were one of the foremost fire precautions of that age. A small fire was lit over a treated stump; the wood beneath spluttered a little and the fire gradually burnt down the stump and along the main roots in a few hours. The nitrate fed oxygen to the wood, thus keeping the fire going, and the ground was left crumbled, porous and full of health-giving mineral fertilisers.

John Barton came back in the middle of all this and was astounded to see what was happening. His first instinct was to berate 'old' Thomas (he was at least forty-five) for countenancing such a thing, but finally, seeing what a success the operation had been, he began to think that the women were not so stupid after all. He was gratified to think that his nitre had been used to extend his garden by the skill and enterprise of his wife.

The stumps on a good half-rood of land had been cleared in early July and the next thing to be done was to plant it up. It was intended for strewing-herbs, mostly camomile, but not enough plantlets of this could be found to cover any considerable area, so the three women concentrated on collecting thyme as well. Scarcely a thyme plant could be found within two hundred yards of the house that summer; Mary and her maids had collected them all for their new lawn.

In those days lawns would sometimes be made of plants other than grass; camomile and thyme were often used.[c] Today camomile lawns are again coming back into use: though shorter lived than turf, they need no mowing and are aromatic underfoot.

Stripping the area around Bartons End of thyme plants had quite an effect on the ecology of the area. For instance, at least six species of caterpillar of Lepidoptera (butterflies and moths) fed on the thyme. Two of them fed only on this plant and another only on thyme and its near relation, marjoram. They were respectively the large blue, the wild thyme bug and the lace border. The other three species had a wider range of food plants. The large blue used to be found in Kent but was lost to that area in the early seventeenth century. Until quite recently it was found in the south-west of England, but now, alas! it is extinct all over the country. Both man's activities and its complicated life history played a part in these events.

The large blue had a strange relationship with certain kinds of ants. The female butterfly laid eggs singly on thyme flowers in early summer. After a week the eggs hatched and the larvae fed for three weeks on the flowers. The young caterpillars were aggressive; if two happened to meet they would fight, the vanquished being eaten by the victor, the race thus preserving precious protein food collected with such effort from the thyme. By mid-August, after the second moult, the larvae were 0·12 of an inch long and then, to entomologists, they seemed to vanish. No fourth instar larvae or pupae were ever found, yet the large blue adult butterflies appeared again the following year. The distinguished entomolgist, F. W. Frohawk, discovered in about 1912 what happened. The adult butterfly laid eggs on the thyme growing near the nest of one or other of two species of fairly savage red ants, *Myrmica scabrinodis* and *M. laevinodis*. By the end of the third instar the caterpillars developed a special honey gland, the secretion from which was much liked by ants. When a wandering ant found a fourth instar caterpillar the latter exuded honey which the ant licked up and it usually ended by carrying the larva back to its nest. The larva facilitated the process by assuming a hunched-up position making its transport easy. Once within the nest the caterpillar fed on ant larvae, the guardian and nurse ants raising no objections, seduced from their duty as they were by the offer of the delicious honey secretion. This was a remarkable reversal of behaviour. Normally the larvae were the ants' greatest treasure and they fought fiercely to defend them. Such behaviour presents a curious analogy to drug addiction in man: the entrancing substance was worth any sacrifice.

The caterpillars slept the winter in the nest and started feeding on their hosts' young again in the spring, eventually obtaining full growth. Then the caterpillar pupated, hanging from the roof of a gallery in the nest, never in any way molested by the ants. After about three weeks (it would now be mid-May) the butterfly emerged; it crawled—a somewhat wet and bedraggled creature—through the nest passages where it had passed some ten months. The adult was covered with loose, waxy scales which came off and gummed up ant jaws should any guard seek to investigate the strange being in their nest. The butterfly eventually reached a nest entrance and emerged into daylight, climbed a stalk,

Large blue butterfly on thyme and attendant ant with butterfly larva

expanded and dried its wings in the usual way and resumed its normal life cycle.

The ladies' action in stripping the area around Bartons End of thyme plants was a step in the sequence of events leading to the extinction of the large blue in Kent. Concentrating a species of plant in any one area, as in farming and gardening, usually makes life easier for the animals feeding on that plant, because their young do not have to search far and wide for their particular host but find it just next door; things were different in the case of Mary's thyme plants, however. This was because, though the thyme plants were moved and throve, the red ants were not touched. The life cycle of the butterfly was interrupted.

The many eggs were laid on the abundant thyme flowers in Mary's new lawn. The resulting caterpillars throve and, full of good food, reached the third instar, when they fell to the ground with their honey glands secreting the ant bait. But the ants' nests were mostly far away. Only very few ants passed through the thyme. Most of the expectant caterpillars withered and died or were eaten by birds and other predators. A few caterpillars were taken back to nests by other kinds of ants but only the red ants mentioned suited the large blues and if a few caterpillars did manage to survive in a 'strange' nest they turned into dwarf adults with scant reproductive powers.

It is the red ants that were the key to the existence of the large blue butterfly. If there were no red ants there could be no large blues and modern conditions do not suit the ants. Beautiful though the butterfly was, yet it was a parasite and suffered the fate of many a parasite, human or animal, of being too successful. If the host is overburdened it may die, taking the parasite with it.

Though the large blues lost by the collecting activities of the Bartons' women, the red ants gained. With most of the thyme plants removed from the area they were no longer exposed to the temptation of the honey secretion. The ant larvae that would have been eaten by the caterpillars lived, and the nest numbers grew. Daughter nests were formed nearby, but by the time they had spread to the area of the garden's thyme lawn there were very few large blues about. It was too late: male and female butterflies in any area must be present in a certain number if the sexes are to meet, mate and continue the species: how dense populations need to be in order to secure mating is a skilled exercise in applied ecology. Even when butterflies are numerous in an area it sometimes seems strange that the sexes ever manage to mate. A male and female large white, for example, will flutter around each other, in and out of foliage for minutes at a time in the courtship dance; and more often than not these mating manoeuvres result in the two aspirants losing each other.

Ants are peculiarly susceptible to drug addiction. There was a big wood ants' nest in the woods adjoining Bartons End which was establishing colony nests on the edges of the Barton lands. The nest, a cone of broken twigs and pine needles, was gradually growing as the ants throve. This success attracted the attention of a Staphylinid beetle (*Lomechusa cava*), a creature parasitic on wood ants. One day a young female adult of this species of beetle followed a foraging wood ant back into the nest. She was immediately challenged by a nest guard. The beetle was ready for this challenge, and promptly discharged a repellant spray at the ant, which at once stopped its attack. The small, broad ($\frac{1}{4}$-in. long) beetle then moved quickly forward into the nest, stopped in a wide part and remained very quiet for an hour or so, which enabled it to absorb something of the nest smell, a signal the ants respect. *Lomechusa* then started to advertise its presence by giving off a special fluid, sweet, narcotic and most attractive to the wood ants, which liquid spread out over some bunches of hairs, known as trichomes, on its back. *Lomechusa* first offered this to an ant with a comparatively empty crop; it was soon eagerly feeding on the beetle's exudation. Passing ants were attracted to the beetle, stroking its head to encourage the fascinating secretion. The only dangerous moments for the beetle were after it had been left alone for a while. As it had not fully acquired the nest smell, the creature, by itself, might be challenged by an aggressive passer-by. Safety lay in the beetle's being accompanied by a few attendant addicts. After two days the *Lomechusa* was never challenged: it had now got the required background scent and was welcomed everywhere. The beetle followed a nurse ant back to the brood chamber and there, just like the large blue caterpillars, fed on the nest's precious treasure, the young ant larvae. The guards and nurses, intoxicated by the secretions on the beetle's trichomes, made no objection at all. The beetle now started to lay eggs on a pile of ant eggs and the nurses cleaned and tended them in the same way as they had cared for their own ova.

On hatching, the *Lomechusa* larvae fed on ant eggs[d] and, as the beetle multiplied, so the ants became more and more slaves to the secretion. They increasingly neglected the young, gave up foraging for food, sorting the material brought into the nest or cleaning the nest. The queen, unfed, died, then the whole nest and, with it, the *Lomechusa*'s source of food. The nest died because the secretion had deprived the worker ants of the will to put into action the emergency procedures for obtaining a new queen. Normally, if a nest's queen dies, the ants will turn a worker into a queen by means of special feeding, or raid another nest and capture a princess. The death of the nest did not seem to worry the beetles, now adult and descendants of the original intruder. They just walked out of it and looked for another colony on which to play their confidence trick.

However, there was a factor which prevented the *Lomechusa* beetle multiplying to such an extent as to destroy the wood ant, and thus itself, for ever. This is the fact that the nurse ants became so obsessed by the *Lomechusa* that they treated the beetle's eggs, larvae and pupae in exactly the same way as they did their own. That is fine for the eggs and larvae, but it did not suit the pupae. Ant pupae, when ready to hatch, are carried around the nest to favourable spots, there to be carefully tended and cleaned, and when opening time arrives the ants help the adults emerge, often cutting open the pupal case. But the *Lomechusa* pupae did not like this treatment. They needed to be left severely alone, to emerge from the cases unaided and to work their own way out of the soil. The ants' care of their parasites unwittingly killed many of them and preserved the ants themselves from extinction. In fact, a considerable proportion of the *Lomechusa* were killed by kindness.

Having spent so much effort in 1558 in clearing the stumps, Mary and her team were resolved to plant the new land. Not enough camomile plants or seed could be found to cover it all and the area round the house had been stripped of thyme plants. It seemed silly just to put the remaining space down to grass, using seed from the stackyard, so the next beds they set out were of mint. They collected plants from the banks of a nearby stream, from friends' and relatives' gardens and from damp places in the waste. They soon found they had at least two kinds of mint, the wild and the round-leaved. They made separate beds of each, thinking they could have separate uses and in any case were attractive plants. They cut the roots into short lengths of three or four inches, planting them in the prepared soil. Soon they had a very encouraging stretch, and a third kind was then planted, peppermint, which in time provided material for the house's new stillroom. The peppermint oil was much prized as a valuable medicine. The oil acts as a local anaesthetic and relieved many a toothache until a barber could be found to remove the source of the pain. It was also used to help digestion and relieve cramps.

But still the cleared land was not filled and, in view of Mary's enthusiasm for her new stillroom, the next beds were of roses, to be used for making rosewater. At that date roses were popular, and understanding and growing them was comparatively easy, unlike today when we have at least 250 species, endless hybrids, thousands of cultivars and but little agreement among *aficionados* on scientific and trivial names.

To begin with Mary collected wild rose plants from the woods and hedges. Even so they contained some hybrids and garden escapes. Her first roses were mostly the pink dog rose and the French rose, remarkable at that time for having a double flower and also known as the Apothecary's rose. It is interesting to note that *R. alba*, the white rose of York, was a hybrid between the red *gallica* and the white and pink dog rose (*R. canina*) and that the white colour dominated in the offspring.

The young women dug up plants from the hedges and woods and took, and successfully struck, a large number of cuttings. The plants were trained into hedges, on stakes and wires about five feet high and in rows the same distance apart. Shortly after getting the first three rose hedges established Mary obtained a prize from her mother-in-law's garden, a well-grown plant of the damask rose. This species had been brought back from the Near East by the Crusaders during the Middle Ages. Mary thought it a great treasure because it was very fragrant, the flowers were double and the petals incurved, with a green eye or centre.

Rosewater was much in demand and large quantities of petals were needed to make it: six pounds of them would impregnate a gallon of water. The infusion was used to flavour food, sweeten the hands and mouth, and as a restorative in medicine. We now know, of course, that rose hips from the dog rose are rich in vitamins, and it is very likely that rosewater helped the winter diet of the Bartons by supplying some of those elements. Rosewater was even used to help in the germination of seeds—Thomas Hyll maintained that these should be steeped in scented water before sowing. It seems likely that it was the water aiding the growth rather than the traces of aromatic oils.

Gerard in his *Herball* summarised the 'virtues' of distilled rosewater. It strengthened the heart, refreshed the spirit, was good for all conditions that needed a gentle cooling, it cured eye pains and induced sleep. In addition it gave a good taste to junkets and cakes. Another advantage, too—hidden from the users at that time—was that, being distilled, it was a source of sterile water, very suitable for washing a cut or wound.

Mary's extensive rose beds enabled her to make considerable quantities of rosewater and she sold it to local apothecaries and neighbours. John Barton began to see commercial possibilities in gardening, particularly after the visit in 1562 of a relative from The Hague. This cousin not only brought with him a pin of the new-fangled drink 'biere' but also specimens of that forbidden plant, the hop, used to make the confection. Henry VIII had passed a law prohibiting the use of hops in ale, but it was not much observed in practice. The Bartons and their workers considered biere a considerable improvement on ale, whatever the old king might have said. The adherents of 'good old English ale' accused the brewers of adding hops to ale in order to disguise how very small was the amount of malt they had used. One would like to know how today's 'real ale' enthusiasts would react to the drinking of hopless ale!

The taking of both ale and beer in the sixteenth century was an important aid to the preservation of good health, particularly in towns and villages, because the local wells might so often be contaminated with sewage. Ale, having been boiled during its manufacture, was safe to drink. Even though it might be starting to turn, owing to the activities of acetic bacteria, it was unlikely to contain dangerous protozoa or pathogenic bacteria.

John's father, Richard Barton, made ale for the whole family and started adding hops to it in 1565, mostly from Mary Barton's growing. She had put out the two plants brought from the Netherlands and in the first season was surprised to find how different they were. One produced hops and the other only a bunch of tiny flowers. However, having set them out, each on a little hill into which three long poles had

Hops

been set, she decided to keep both the useless and useful plant. In fact the hop is dioecious: male and female flowers are produced on separate plants. If no male plants are put into a hop garden, hops are still produced, but they are seedless and lighter in weight. If an occasional male plant is in the garden, then the hops become seeded, heavier and, some maintain, make better beer. The Dutch were great gardeners at that time, as they are to this day, and the Bartons' Dutch cousin, aware of this difference, had brought a male and female plant. Mary, noting the interest the hops aroused among the Bartons, carefully transplanted some of the shoots that came up in the spring and by the summer of 1568 had a dozen hop hills well established, all but one being females.

Richard Barton liked the hopped beer: he not only preferred its bitter taste to the rather sweet, mawkish ale, but he found that the hopped brew kept much better than ale and that he did not have to brew so often. It is a fact that the yellow hop resin, found on the flower 'petals' (botanically, they are not petals, but bracts) does have preservative powers. He was very pleased with his clever daughter-in-law and said he would provide her with a gardener so that she might go on with her interesting work. Soon a separate hop garden was established: it became a source of considerable wealth to the family in due course and exists to this day, but is no longer a part of the garden. In the late sixteenth century hops became so popular that a book was published about the growing of them—*A Perfite Platforme of a Hoppe Garden* by Reynolds Scot.[65] It was a thoroughly practical work; it described the best way of growing hops and avoided the astrology and the classical allusions most authors of that day found so irresistible. There were later editions in 1576 and 1578, though Henry VIII's law was still unrepealed.

Practical gardeners of Mary's day were getting suspicious of signatures and the zodiac as guides to their art; for one thing it was very complicated remembering all the different planets and constellations that governed a big collection of plants. However, many growers would have hesitated to break some fairly simple rules, such as not sowing seed during the waning of the moon: that would be asking for trouble, because, as the moon grew, so, they were sure, would the seedling. Strangely enough, it may indeed be better to sow when the moon is waxing. Lunar rhythms affect the earth's magnetic field, which in turn affects growth. Moroever, the pull of the moon not only causes tides in the sea but affects water everywhere. The moon also influences the atmosphere 'so that statistically it is more likely to rain heavily immediately after a full or new moon'.[8]

Another piece of old folklore which possibly has some scientific basis is concerned with the time of day at which medicinal herbs should be picked. The old apothecaries obviously would see the desired ingredient in their plant as increasing with the growing moon or rising sun, and it has now been noted that this is sometimes the case with the sun. For instance, the alkaloid content of the opium poppy is greater during the morning than in the rest of the day. However, it does seem a little extreme to postulate how certain plants should be picked, such as naked, facing the mid-day sun, as has been advocated, even today, by magically-minded herbalists. But there may be something in this dictum as regards sowing seeds. Seed should not be sown if the soil is too cold for it and, in cold weather, sowing is less likely to take place if the sower is obliged to be naked for the task![8]

Mary Barton soon acquired the reputation of being a skilled gardener and a woman able to supply herbs of her own growing to cure any ill. She found there was a constant demand for eye medicines. Those who came to her complaining of 'weak eyes' often were just long- or short-sighted and really needed spectacles, but these, though known, were not at all common, and so the supposed eye-strengthening plants were pressed into service. One of the best known was eyebright. At first Mary found this plant, which she believed to be a valuable eye-salve, very difficult to grow, because, anxious to bring it forward as quickly as possible, she kept her bed of it very clear of weeds, particularly of grass seedlings, abundant in those parts on account of the seed blowing from the farm's haystacks. The eyebright, however, is a plant semi-parasitic on grass. It can make its own carbohydrates, having chlorophyll-containing green leaves for the task, but it takes its minerals and water from its hosts. Although it can grow on its own, it only flourishes where grass grows as well, from which it sucks a certain amount of nutrient. As it grew best on the edges of her herb bed, which had a grass surround, Mary realised that the grass somehow helped her herb. She eventually gave up trying to grow it in the garden and collected the eyebright she needed from the meadows. The juice of the plant was mixed with white wine and dropped into the eyes, or distilled eyebright water was made in the same way as rosewater.

Agrimony was another eye medicine. Its bruised leaves were mixed with white of egg and white wine. Applied to the eyelids it was said to cure styes and to strengthen the sight.

Mary's gardener, working full time from 1568, was Thomas Claridge, her maid Nell's father. The garden now rapidly developed: more flowers were brought in and planted in beds, which were called knottes, in front of the house, though they were but poor imitations of the knottes then so fashionable in the gardens of the wealthy, such as those at nearby Lullingstone Castle and Penshurst Place.

A knotte was an elaborate design of raised beds, usually divided one from the other by low hedges bordering the paths. The paths separating the beds might be of coloured stones or gravel and the beds, which were raised six inches or so above the surface of the path, were of flowers or aromatic herbs. The hedges would be of box or other low-growing plants. There was an element of ostentation, in keeping with the spirit of the Elizabethan age, in having an elaborate knotte, because it was obvious that an immense amount of labour went into making and maintaining it. How satisfactory to be able to demonstrate that 'My knotte is bigger and better than your knotte because I can afford to pay more men than you can.'

Knottes were sometimes made rectangular in design, frequently in the form of a low, hedged maze. The Bartons' specimens were perforce rectangular because they used stout, painted planking as borders for the beds, often supporting them with sheep bones driven into the ground. Made in 1570, they were very simple; in no sense were they mazes, but the beds gave the Bartons great satisfaction. It showed the world that they were rapidly becoming more prosperous. About this time they gave up the pretence that flowers were only grown for medicinal purposes: they now grew them, and admired them, for their beauty, fragrance and novelty.

Aristocratic houses in the second half of the sixteenth century were giving much attention to their gardens and they set the fashion for the

Kentish farmers. Fashionable and attractive novelties, such as new roses from France, lilies from Turkey and new trees and fruits, were appearing in the grounds of the big houses. These new plants had a tendency to leak from such places. Some of the escapes were due to natural dispersion by birds, wind or mice, but most of the evasions had a human source. A large garden, especially if it had plenty of knottes, needed a large staff of gardeners, who all had relatives—to whom seeds, plants and cuttings would be smuggled from time to time.

By 1570 the Bartons had two knottes, one on each side of a wide path leading in a gentle curve from the lane to the front door, which path eventually became the drive to the house. They had a number of novelties growing in their new beds; some came from relations working at Lullingstone and Penshurst and some from their Dutch cousins.

The Barton flower novelties were blue primroses, marguerites from the Canary Islands, marigolds from the Mediterranean, phlox from America and a new scabious from southern Europe. These were scattered amongst a considerable collection of indigenous flowers, constantly being selected to produce bigger blooms or unusual colours, such as the blue primrose already mentioned. The other local flowers put into the knottes were the anemone or windflower and the Pasque flower, bachelor's buttons, columbine, daisy, foxglove and forget-me-nots.

Other native flowers put into the beds were an improved globe flower, which was probably a hybrid between the native plant and the Russian *Trollius ledebourii* which had somehow reached Kent. It was like a large buttercup. The list continues with mulleins, verbascums, usually called gillyflowers at that time, though the latter name is sometimes applied to wallflowers because of a similarity of smell. The latter only reached Bartons End in the 1580s and flourished exceedingly. There were also some native scabious, the devil's bit and the field scabious. Early flowers were represented by snowdrops and primroses, followed by forget-me-nots.

Dorothy Snell, the second of Mary's maids who helped in the garden, became very interested in these latter flowers and established a number of beds of different kinds. Today some fifty species are known, most of them nineteenth-century discoveries. From Linnaeus, the great Swedish naturalist (1707–78), onwards all have been given scientific names, but in those days the naming of living forms was very vague. First of all Dorothy found there were both perennial and annual kinds of forget-me-nots. She made four beds of perennial ones, all different. Three were collected from damp areas and one from the meadows. The water-lovers were: the water forget-me-not, which has shiny leaves and a broad flat flower; *Myosotis repens* Don, the creeping forget-me-not, with the leaves more hairy and a calyx with narrower lobes than the former species; and *M. caespitosa* Schultz, the tufted forget-me-not, with a small flower. The fourth perennial was *M. sylvatica* Hoffm., the wood forget-me-not with a rather larger flower. The annuals were: the field forget-me-not (*M. arvensis* Hill), the commonest in Kent; the early forget-me-not (*M. collina* Hoffm.) with a very small flower; and the yellow and blue forget-me-not (*M. versicolor* Sm.), which was greatly prized, although the most difficult to grow was the creeping one (*repens*). She also maintained small beds of these annuals.

Of course, neither these scientific names nor the common ones were given by Dorothy, but her keen eye and interest in plants had seen the differences between the many forget-me-nots growing about the place and she separated them out, telling anyone who would listen how they differed one from the other. She had a naturalist's mind and, though she could not read or write, she knew her forget-me-nots and gave them pet names, derived as time went on from the names of her mistress's children.

By 1570 Mary had had nine children, five of them still alive, a good number for those days. The youngest, a year old, was called John in memory of her first child, who had died shortly after birth. Baby John Barton II, Mary's last child, in due course became the father of a Barton family, one son of which emigrated to New England and set up a Barton clan there.

By 1580 the garden had become quite extensive and included a plot growing 'pot herbs', that is to say, kitchen vegetables, which made a welcome addition to the rather dull farmhouse diet of beef, mutton, beer and bread.[e] The main crops were beets, broad beans, cabbages, carrots, onions, leeks, parsnips, peas of two kinds—'raith' (that is, peas which were harvested three months after sowing) and 'rouncevall', the second much esteemed for their size and quality. Also grown were turnips and pumpkins, the latter being a rarity recently imported from France. The

Bartons got some seed, no questions asked, from one of the big houses.

The early successes in the Bartons' garden were almost entirely due to the amount of effort put into it. Work it was that made the garden, a fact which is as true today as then. However, knowledge is also important because knowledge can lighten work or prevent useless expenditure of energy. Mary, Thomas, Nell and Dorothy were not very well informed and wasted much effort. But on the other hand their usable range of plants was much smaller than today's, so they had much less to be knowledgeable about.

The Bartons had a number of failures among their successes. For instance, 'Portynggales' (Portuguese oranges) were being imported in considerable numbers in the latter half of the sixteenth century and their use was spreading down the social scale. They were not only delicious in themselves, and good for the health, but also the empty skins, sewn together again, made containers for the valuable pomanders. Mary found that orange seeds put into a pot of earth and placed on a windowsill soon germinated and sent up fine, dark green shoots. The seedlings, planted out in the open in May, throve throughout the summer, but the first winter killed them all. Had her knowledge been greater she would have known that the orange was not winter hardy.

It was common knowledge in the big houses. Sir Francis Carew had orange trees at his house at Beddington, Croydon, in 1562. He had them in wheelbarrows and trundled them indoors to a specially built house for the winter. Thus the 'orangery' was born, though it remained something only to be seen in aristocratic houses, and would not have been known to the Bartons.

The second year Thomas Claridge raised orange and lemon seedlings in pots and brought them indoors in the winter: but they took a long time to fruit, some five years, so great patience was needed. The first ripe orange was solemnly shared between Mary, Thomas, Nell and Dorothy, and pronounced much better than any Portuguese import.

Another difficulty for the Bartons' gardeners was the high cost of tools. When they started their garden a spade cost about 8*d*, a hatchet 6*d* and an iron rake 6*d*. For comparison, wages were about 4*d* a day, so to buy an iron spade a man would have to work for two days. To begin with, Mary and her two maids used a wooden spade shod with an iron tip. Their rake consisted of a horizontal bar of wood into which oak pegs were inserted attached to a wooden handle. The spade was awkward to use and made for slow working, but the rake was effective, though the pegs wore out fairly quickly: however, new pegs could soon be inserted. Technical advances in iron-founding towards the end of the century improved tools for both farm and garden.

By 1585 half an acre of land was under cultivation as a garden. Obviously the life there had greatly altered, though the actual weight of living tissue, the biomass, had hardly changed. In the garden there were some forty tons of vegetation in summer and a considerable number of resident animals, such as spiders, mice, moles and worms, but their total weight was only a few pounds, except on special occasions when human and animal visitors crowded in, as for a meet of the hunt or for a wedding party.

A new series of plants had replaced the woodland ones destroyed when the garden was made. Even so, some of the woodland life was able to adapt to the garden and thus persisted. For instance, some plants such as bluebells and primroses continued in the garden because they appealed to the Bartons, and some animals, such as the moles, persisted there too because they were clever enough to survive in spite of man's opposition to them.

What was the principal cause for the plant changes in the garden? Obviously, that the plants growing there appealed to man in one way or another and so man fostered them. That appeal could be either practical or psychological. For instance, certain garden plants produced useful food: broad beans, peas, cabbage, turnips, parsnips and so on. Others provided, or were thought to provide, remedies for disease. Those were the practical reasons for growing particular kinds of plants, though the reasons for growing some of the medicinal herbs verge on the psychological: the taking of a particular brew was thought by the patient to be doing him good and consequently did so.

The psychological appeal of some of the garden plants was of two kinds. Firstly there were the strewing-herbs, used to combat noxious smells in the house. Secondly there were the flowers, grown for their beauty. Thus, in the struggle for existence, a pretty face, gardenwise, could be as useful an asset as good food or curative value.

The animals on the site, in order to live and reproduce their kind, needed to eat, drink and breathe in much the same way as we do, and we are familiar with the process. Plants also must feed, 'drink' (that is, take up water) and breathe, but they do it in a manner completely opposite to that used by animals.

Animals feed on chemically complex substances which are part of another entity, be it plant or animal, that is, living or once-living material. They digest these complexes, turning them into relatively simple compounds which are absorbed by the blood, carried round the body and used to make new tissues or repair old ones. Plants, on the other hand, make complex substances from simple materials: they use the gases of the air, water, certain salts dissolved in the soil water, and light as sources of energy.

The new garden was the scene of a constant battle between the plants that wanted to grow there (the weeds) and the plants the gardeners wished to have there. This was just one facet of the great struggle for existence among plants and animals: it is particularly intense among individuals of the same species, and it is this struggle that has produced those species we know. This is the Darwinian theory of natural selection, sprung on the world in 1859.

Offspring produced by sexual intercourse in both plants and animals may differ a little from one or other of their parents because half the genes in any life-form are derived from the male parent and half from the female. It is the genes that determine the characteristics of any individual, and this dual source of genes means that there is considerable opportunity for their re-combinations when the method of reproduction is sexual. If the reproductive process is asexual, as with vegetative propagation by means of cuttings, buds or tubers, the offspring produced have exactly the same genetic make-up as the parent plant or animal. The gene contents of a Cox's Orange Pippin, or a King Edward potato, are exactly the same as that of the original Cox or Edward. Very occasionally a spontaneous change, a bud-sport, may be produced, but it is a rare event, unless it is deliberately induced by means of radiation or treatment with colchicine under laboratory conditions.

It can readily be seen that, using sexual methods, offspring differing from each other, often greatly, are produced. It is a common experience in any family. Brothers and sisters have a family resemblance but are not

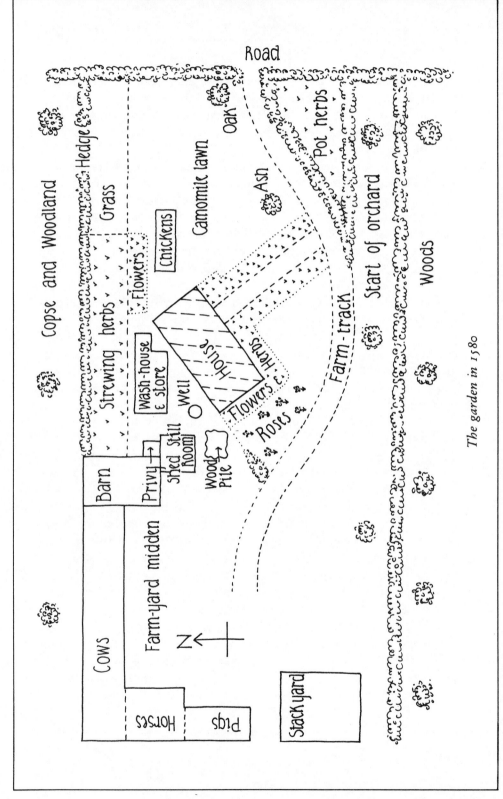

The garden in 1580

exactly alike, unless they are identical twins. In the wild, even in the Bartons' garden, offspring having advantageous and disadvantageous characteristics would arise, and in the struggle for existence, the disadvantaged would be crowded out, dying (or being eaten) before they reached the reproductive age.

If a particular difference gives a descendant an advantage over its siblings, such as resistance to a disease or an ability to use food to better effect, it is likely to survive, displace its rivals and itself produce in due course offspring, some of which will possess that advantage. In time the advantaged accumulate and a new species results.

By 1599 the Bartons' garden was well on its way to firm establishment and the fulfilment of the function foreseen for gardens by the great Renaissance humanist, Erasmus: 'This place is dedicated to the honourable pleasures of rejoicing the eye, refreshing the nose and renewing the spirit.'[27]

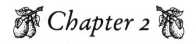

Chapter 2

Thomas Barton's Garden, 1599–1629

Flowers and Fruit

OHN BARTON died in 1599, aged sixty-two, and his son Thomas took over the farm, which he had, in effect, been running for the last four years. He, his wife and his mother, who lived until 1610, were devoted to the garden, and increasing prosperity allowed them to spend more time and money on it. They made some more small, rectangular knottes in front of the house and filled them with what we today think of as the old, sweet-smelling, traditional flowers such as promising roses, the native pinks and the imported sweet william, eglantine or sweetbriar, snapdragons, hollyhocks—very tropical sounding when called by the scientific name *Hibiscus syriacus* and actually coming from Syria at the start of the sixteenth century—wallflowers, bachelor's buttons, columbines, daffodils or Lent lily, lavender, valerian or allheal—a herb useful as a laxative and in nervous disorders—star of Bethlehem and paeonies.

Getting the seed, bulbs or plants of that collection was a considerable task. Several, such as valerian, star of Bethlehem and paeony, though today thought of as old English plants, were comparatively recent introductions from southern Europe and were somewhat rare. There were no real nurserymen, but the fraternity of gardeners interested in flowers was very active and growing in size all the time. They exchanged plants one with another and committed what today is considered a horticultural crime of the first order—they saved their own seed;

usually it was the only way to get any. With leaks from the big houses, gifts and exchanges, and the continuing collection of outstanding plants from the wild, the Bartons soon had a fine display of flowers.

The next major improvement was the planting of a more exotic flower, the tulip. Tulips exercised such an influence that a little later in the century they became a veritable madness, first in the Netherlands and then all over Europe. People impoverished themselves by paying enormous sums for rare bulbs. The tulip mania had something of a stock exchange gamble in it as well as a passion for the flower.[a] It is recorded that £250, an enormous sum for those days, was paid for a single bulb of a new variety called Viceroy, and even more for Semper Augustus. Neither of these expensive novelties is found today, unless perhaps they have been renamed.

Tulips came from the Near East. In 1554 Ghiselm de Busbecq, the Imperial Ambassador to Constantinople, saw, admired and collected some tulip bulbs and sent them to Messrs Fugger, the great bankers of Augsburg, who had magnificent gardens. The Fuggers planted them and distributed bulbs and seeds to selected friends and clients. Among the recipients was Clusius, the distinguished professor of botany at Leyden University. Clusius planted them in 1593 at the university, from where they were stolen, and the stolen bulbs became the parent stock of the great Dutch tulip industry. Eventually some reached the Dutch Bartons, who in turn made a gift of a few bulbs to Thomas Barton in 1608.

The Bartons were thus unique in their neighbourhood, and they carefully cultivated that attractive flower, placing it near their front door. What is more, by pure chance, one of the Bartons' tulips produced the 'break' so much admired by the Dutch. Breaking was the appearance of streaks of colour in the petals: usually the breaks were of red on a yellow or white background. They were mysterious in origin and not understood until about 1920. Plants grown from bulblets appearing around the base of a large bulb showing break also produced this pattern when they came to flower, but those grown from seed, the true seed formed in the flower, did not. It is now known that the break is caused by a virus disease. Viruses are usually transmitted by vegetative propagation but not by sexual reproduction. They seem unable to penetrate a membrane protecting the embryo in the seed. Thus the virus passes into the bulblet but not into the seed.

Tulip showing break disease

The Bartons End orchards started when Thomas planted apples, pears, quinces and cherries. It was quite common to have to wait ten or twenty years before one got a crop from a big standard apple or cherry tree in those days. Moreover, when the orchard was producing, the fruit might be stolen. Thomas Barton took the view that, even if the interval between planting and cropping were long, one was adding to the value of the farm and planting for one's children. In any case the orchard would be grassed, so there would be some grazing for sheep and cattle. As to theft, there were two remedies: one was to have a pair of mastiffs roaming the area and the other, possibly the more important recourse, was to be generous with one's fruit when it finally arrived.

There were two reasons for the slow cropping of the standard trees. One was the very grass itself and the other was the kind of root system the trees had. The first cause was not known to the Bartons and the second was only very vaguely appreciated at that time.

Grass, like all other plants, is engaged in the struggle for existence; anything grass can do to suppress competition from other plants or animals helps its future existence and extension. Grass seems to be able to produce a poison discouraging the growth of other plants trying to get food and water in the soil. It is continually producing fine fibrous roots, and as this occurs, the older roots stop taking in food and water, die and decompose. In rotting down they produce much CO_2 gas. This is not dispersed so readily in the soil as it is in the air and this gas checks the absorption of nutrients by young tree roots and thus the early growth of the trees. Fir trees are another example of this activity, though in reverse. Pine needles drop on to the ground and usually prevent the growth of any plants beneath the spread of the tree's foliage.

In 1600 thirty apple trees were set out in a portion of a meadow adjoining the house, a choice being made of trees growing in the wild (crabs) and those available in neighbouring gardens or from a rare nurseryman.

Getting reliable trees was difficult. Growers with good varieties of fruit were not anxious to part with trees or scions to strangers, and the Bartons decided to make most of the trees they wanted themselves. Young seedlings could be found in the woods, but could only be expected to produce very small apples. Friends and relatives had a few established apple trees, but no young trees to give away or sell, though they would willingly provide graft wood. This wood the Bartons could graft on to the crab seedlings, to small trees and on to other apple seedlings or stocks they came across. They could also sow the pips of good apples brought back from the market. All this meant that their choice of varieties to grow was limited.

From the start they decided to use grafted trees rather than plant seeds. They knew that seedlings would take a long time to reach maturity and they had an uneasy feeling that, for some obscure reason, seed did not always 'come true'. A pip grown into a tree from, say, a Queening, might be nothing like the apple from which it had arisen. The reason was obscure because no one really understood sexual reproduction, nor were they quite sure if sexual reproduction took place in plants. In accordance with the prevailing ideas of male dominance, the belief was that the male, human or animal, planted the seed in the female, who then nurtured the seed and produced offspring in the image of the father. The female was merely the soil in which the offspring grew. Today, of course, we know that half the characteristics (the blood or genes) of a sexually produced offspring are derived from the father and half from the mother.

Having decided to use mainly grafted trees to make their orchard, the next thing was to find suitable graft wood and the stocks to which that wood could be joined. The art was to make the joint so that the cambium layers—the living area—of both graft and stock would touch closely and thus grow together. Grafts always 'come true'. They are, in effect, part of the original tree though growing in another place. But the stock on to which the shoot is grafted does influence the kind of growth made by the tree: a dwarfing stock, such as Paradise, produces a small tree fruiting early in a comparatively short life, and a very vigorous stock like a crab makes a big tree only cropping after a long period of growth and living for a long time, some eighty years. The stock influences the structure of the tree but in no way alters its genetic make-up.

In the event, the graft wood Thomas and his mother found served to make a number of trees; although their naming was somewhat uncertain, they hoped that at least some would be of value. They had what were said to be Queening, Summer and Winter Pearmaines, Calvilles (which had white skins), Codlings or falling apples and some Russets. A neighbour gave them a tree of Baker's Ditch Apple, which amused them a little because, having relatives in the Netherlands, they knew this was a misnomer for 'Baker's Dutch Apple'. They also planted some crab apples selected from the woods and a rare variety from France, Court Pendu Plat, which is still extant and important as being one of the parents of the world's most flavoursome apple, Cox's Orange Pippin.[b]

The Paradise stocks were obtained from a Paradise apple tree being cut down to ground level, as were the chestnuts in the woods. The stool thus produced would send up shoots around its perimeter. These were earthed up, produced roots at their bases, were cut off below the roots against the stool and planted out in rows, ready for grafting. All the stocks from any one stool were thus genetically the same and when grafted with any desired variety would give the same kind of tree. The trouble was, as the Bartons found out in due course, there were many kinds of Paradise apple. Mr A's Paradise might be a very different kind of plant from Mr B's, one producing a dwarf and the other a giant. Moreover, the crab seedlings were just that, and while having a family resemblance, could differ greatly one from another.

In the early years of this century the confusion over naming of apple stocks was so great that the East Malling Research Station, near Maidstone, Kent, started investigations and, after some brilliant work, were able in the 1920s to supply Paradise stocks producing a range of plants running from very dwarfing (No. IX) to very vigorous (No. XXV).[c]

The young apple fruitlet, after the flower fades, will not grow into an edible apple unless the flower has been fertilised by the deposition on the stigma of suitable pollen. If conditions are right the pollen grain germinates, quickly grows down inside the stigma to the ovary, where the two sexes fuse to form the zygote, or embryo. Most varieties of apples are self-sterile, that is, pollen from another variety is needed to fertilise the ovaries and cause the fruit to grow. Moreover, certain conditions are needed to get good cross-pollination. One, obviously, is that the two varieties should flower at the same time, and another is that the pollen be compatible with the variety in question.

Today apples are classified into four main pollen groups and a variety in any group can best be pollinated by another variety in the same group. Thus, Cox's Orange Pippin, Group 2, should be pollinated by another

Group 2 apple, such as Worcester Pearmain, James Grieve or Bramley's Seedling.

The Bartons knew nothing of the need for pollination and had only the vaguest ideas on the existence of sex in plants. In spite of their ignorance, and perhaps as the result of close observation, the Bartons felt that a few crab-apple trees in the orchard helped fruiting. Somehow or other, it was thought, the vigour of the wild trees transferred to the domesticated ones. The crabs did, in fact, help the orchard to bear fruit, but not in the way the Bartons supposed. Crab apples are good pollinators for all groups and thus the crabs at Bartons End led to a good set of fruit in the new orchard. In today's apple plantations crabs are often planted here and there just because they are such a good source of viable pollen.

The apple orchard grew and cropped very well and was the start of a fruit and cider industry which in later years stood the Bartons and the Onways, who succeeded them at Bartons End, in good stead when Kentish fruit was becoming famous.

Thomas Barton in 1605 planted a few pear trees in the garden. At that time the pear situation was much the same as the apple one. The naming of varieties was confused as was also the matter of the stocks on to which they were grafted. Hardly any of the cultivars Thomas planted exist today, unless, as is quite possible, they have persisted under other names. As early fruiters he had Fairest Supreme and Queen's Pear; for the autumn there were Muscat Fleury, Green Sugar and White Beurrée; and for winter keeping Winter Beurrée, Dauphine and Colmar. Scions of these varieties were grafted on to seedling pear or quince stocks and produced a variety of different-sized trees. Four quinces and four standard cherry trees were also planted, these last in due course exposing the family to the supposed dangers of eating raw fruit. Such suspicions possibly were justified at that time. Hygiene was very primitive; dust from the dung heaps and privies blew around and fruit could carry pathogenic bacteria on its skin, causing illness in the eaters.

The human life at Bartons End and the garden life not only reacted on each other, but a complex web of interaction was constantly at work in the garden, all part of the vast turmoil which is the struggle for existence, with man the powerful arbiter deciding, within limits, what he will allow to survive and what not.

A plant might be so beautiful as to appeal greatly to the humans and be planted very extensively, thus replacing less appreciated or less fashionable species. The early dahlias, for instance, which came from Mexico in about 1740, were at first much liked by the aristocracy, and by the end of the century, having leaked from noble gardens through illicit sales by gardeners, by theft or by gifts, were spreading over the whole garden world. Thus dahlias by their charm had induced man to propagate them: without man's help the area they occupied would have been much smaller. Secondly, even plants harmful to man can exercise such a fascination for him that they become extensively cultivated: tobacco is an example. Though now known to be harmful, denigrated by King James I (1603–25) and most of today's doctors, the plant is nevertheless widely cultivated both in gardens and as a crop. On the other hand some plants, such as fruit and vegetables, influence humans by keeping them healthier. Others provide food for a wide range of animals, which are usually referred to as pests!

One can conceive of these successful garden plants as being somewhat sycophantic: their offspring, by adapting to man's desires, survive in the struggle for existence; but some resist—a blue rose for instance has not yet been bred in spite of great pressure. But plants in general are ready to produce, when suitably manipulated, such recessive genes as they can from their depths in order to satisfy their masters. The genes that will produce a novelty, or an improvement in the species, are mostly already in the germ plasm of that plant and, through the vagaries of sexual selection, natural or artificial, may one day emerge in the offspring, giving a yet more desirable plant. The statue, we are told by Aristotle, is already in the block of marble; it but needs the sculptor to release it.

Poets over the centuries have been fascinated by the peace and calm of a garden, the beauty of the flowers and trees. Wordsworth, for instance, contrasts the life of man and that of the flowers:[77]

> I heard a thousand blended notes
> While in a grove I sat reclined;
> In that sweet mood when pleasant thoughts
> Bring sad thoughts to the mind.

To her fair works did Nature link
The human soul that through me ran,
And much it grieved my heart to think
What man has made of man.

Through primrose tufts in that green bower
The periwinkle trailed its wreathes,
And 'tis my faith that every flower
Enjoys the air it breathes . . .

If this belief from heaven be sent,
If such be Nature's holy plan,
Have I not reason to lament
What man has made of man?

In fact, though, the garden is far from peaceful. It is the site of a constant struggle for survival. It is a struggle both between species but also within species. Wordsworth's periwinkle trailing over the primrose tuft was depriving the primrose of light, something essential to the primrose's continued success, and the pretty trails winding through the leaves and flowers were trying to throttle them. The invader was also seeking to send down roots from suitable joints and take in water and plant-food from the soil beneath the primrose tuft, further depriving the primrose of essential food. The primrose, on the other hand, was strongly resisting the attack of the periwinkle. Wordsworth's primrose expanded its leaves in its turn, to try and crowd out the periwinkle, and could even secrete mild toxins discouraging such bold advances. Even within the primrose tuft competition was rife. Successive leaves fought for existence, each seeking to get the available light and plant-food. The struggle was bitter, but moved too slowly to be seen by the poet.

Every plant enjoys the air it breathes, that is to say, it uses it to advantage, and does its best to get more of it than any of its neighbours. We may note, in passing, that although it needs a little oxygen it is mostly seeking the carbon dioxide in the air, so it prefers what we would describe as foul air. The exhaust air from the power station, provided it is free from sulphur, suits it much better than the fresh zephyr from the sea.

There is no quarter given in this battle between the plants. The weaker are squeezed out and die, or they may be attacked by parasitic plants or animals and cease to exist. No compassion is shown and the natural world is far more savage than the human one, for though man can be brutal he often shows care and compassion for his fellows—in wars the majority of prisoners are cared for and live. As a species, man is much nicer than the primrose.

As for the beauty of the flowers and trees, except where man has intervened with special and often spectacular breeding, the features we find beautiful in the natural world all have a utility value to the species displaying them. Flowering plants—the phanerogams—in order to secure their succession need to produce seed and to do so most of them need to be pollinated. Moreover, in order that advantageous changes in the species may be produced, it is better that cross-pollination takes place. This union of the sexes of different lines of descent may produce plants having advantageous or disadvantageous characteristics. The disadvantaged seedlings do not much matter, provided they are not too numerous. They will not survive. But the seedlings having a new advantageous item in their make-up will, and they in their turn will tend to pass on this advantageous item to their descendants.

The original reason for the existence of flowers is to attract insects and secure pollination. Insects are great pollinators, so plants produce flowers in order to advertise their presence to insects to whom they offer both pollen and nectar. In this way the plant husbands its resources. It pays to advertise because, if the advertising were not done, very much more pollen would have to be produced and pollen is protein-rich and thus expensive to manufacture: it makes big demands on the plant's resources of available food and light.

Some plants—the cereals, including grasses, for instance—do not need the services of insects to secure pollination. The wind is sufficient for them, but in order to be pollinated in the wild, vast quantities of pollen have to be produced and released under suitable conditions to drift over the countryside. In a field of wheat there are several million plants growing side by side and quite a small amount of pollen would effect pollination, but in the wild the pollen from a wheat plant might have to travel several metres before it found another receptive plant. This means that a vast cloud of pollen, containing precious protein, must be produced in order to secure fertilisation of most of the plants.

So important are insects to plants that they have produced many devices to tempt the insect Pandarus. Special colours and designs on petals are common, leading the visitor to the nectar glands, and covering it with pollen on the way. As insects can see ultra-violet light and we humans cannot, many such guide lines on flower petals are invisible to us, but will show in photographs taken using appropriate filters and film.

Special smells are also used to attract the right kind of insect, while trip devices exist in some orchids, in peas and in other plants to ensure that the visitor is dusted with pollen. The weight of an insect entering the flower pulls down an arm bearing pollen and deposits some on the intruder.

So important is cross-pollination to plants that they are prepared to give considerable resources to manufacture rewards for the performers of this task. The plants often produce an excess of pollen as payment to their pollinators, while nectar is produced solely for them. Bees are important crop pollinators and over its long history the Bartons' garden harboured many kinds of them.

The case of the bees is interesting because, in general, while there is savage competition between and within species to get the available resources in any area, yet some species appear to co-operate to mutual advantage. The bees at Bartons End are an example of this. The nectar in many flowers—beans, for instance—can be reached only by bees with long tongues. To overcome this disadvantage the short-tongued bees, such as certain bumblebees, *Bombus lucorum, B. mastrucatus* and *B. terrestris*, bite holes in the base of the flower (the corolla) and thus get at the nectar. Such bees are called 'primary robbers'[3] because they take the nectar but do not pollinate the flowers to any extent, though the general disturbance they cause might scatter some of the precious dust around and fertilise self-fertile plants. The hole having been made, other bees, known as 'secondary robbers', also use it to reach the nectar. At Bartons End the hive bees, which had long tongues and so were able to suck nectar from trumpet-shaped flowers, would use the holes made by the bumblebees as that was much easier for them, thus getting the honey and, ungratefully, performing no compensating activity in return. In seasons when the primary robbers were numerous, the hive bees were great users of the perforations, so that pollination, and thus the seed

Foxglove and bumble bees

setting, of many plants was not very good, though the honey yield might be good or better than usual.

It is obvious that it is to the advantage of any particular species of plant seeking to attract pollinators that an insect visiting it and collecting pollen and/or nectar, should fly off and next visit the same species of plant. It is no use to either plant if, say, a bee covers itself with bean pollen and then flies off to crawl into a foxglove flower. 'Flower constancy' is important, and the scent and taste of certain pollens and nectars may well 'fix' the insect on a particular species. In fact it is possible that the hallucinatory drug substances produced by certain plants, such as cocaine (though this is found mostly in the leaves), may be the plants' method of securing flower constancy. Is that bee working a foxglove from bottom to top, flower to flower, and then moving off to another foxglove nearby merely doing so because, after it happened to start on a foxglove, the next nearest flower is the blossom just above it, or has it been 'fixed' by the digitalis drug and is in for a splendid trip? Plants are ingenious mechanisms.

The co-operation existing between insects and flowers to secure pollination is remarkable. Some plants, such as delphiniums, aconites and *Epilobiums* have flowers arranged in a spiral around a spike. Delphiniums are co-adapted to existence with bumblebees. The flowers at the bottom of the delphinium spike have more nectar than those at the top, so a visiting bumblebee, anxious not to waste time and energy, starts at the bottom of the spike and works its way upwards; usually a bee leaves before it reaches the top. Having sucked nectar from a flower the bee moves vertically upwards to another flower, because this is the nearest one, though not the next blossom in the spiral. The bees are heavy, flying uses a lot of energy, and they are often carrying a dozen or so passengers—mites, such as *Parasitus fucorum*.[d] Conscious of the need to conserve energy, our bee rises one rung and is soon at work. The lower flowers are awaiting pollen but do not produce it and the upper flowers produce pollen but do not need it as their female organs are imperfect. The bumblebee thus flies off the top of the spike covered with pollen and drops to the bottom of another spike, where it deposits some of the pollen clinging to its furry body. This ensures cross-fertilisation, so important for the development of offspring adapting to new conditions or taking better advantage of existing ones. The two species have co-adapted to their mutual advantage; both have survived remarkably well in the Bartons End garden and many other domains.

When the copse and forest land were first cleared for the purpose of making the house and garden, many kinds of plants and animals were destroyed but some, among them the moles, were able to adapt quickly to new conditions, live in the garden and thus survive.[53] The mole is an ingenious and adaptable animal and soon found the Bartons End lawns and garden beds supplied as much, or even more, good food than its native forest. The Bartons, on the other hand, soon found the 'tumps' a nuisance and waged war against them.

They thought the moles were driving tunnels through their lawns in search of food, a view frequently held to this day, but it is not the case. The construction of that network of underground galleries is very hard work and though the moles eat any food they come across while tunnelling that is not the main purpose of the exercise; it would be far too laborious as a simple food-gathering activity. As well as being the site of their nests, the galleries are, however, traps into which burrowing worms and insects fall. The mole, regularly parading his network at the fair speed of about two and a half miles an hour, eats his catches before they have time to re-enter the soil. Once constructed, the tunnel system lasts a long time, though naturally a certain amount of maintenance work has to be done. That is why new molehills are pushed up from time to time.

A molehill is the spoil excavated from the tunnels in the soil; the galleries can be well underground, one and a half feet down being quite usual. Molehills are, of course, also the exits and entrances to the tunnels and they occur at irregular intervals. At the vertical shaft the expelled earth can well weigh 10lbs., which is a lot of earth for a 4 oz. animal to move in twenty minutes, the approximate time it takes to make a molehill. The earth moved is about fifty times the mole's weight. The coal miner at the coal face, with all kinds of mechanical aids, shifts about a ton of coal per hour, say five times his own weight in twenty minutes.[e] Two hundred yards of tunnels mean that a pair of moles have shifted about a ton of earth to establish their network.

The mole's main food is earthworms, so they tend to set their pitfalls in areas where those creatures abound, such as lawns and soils with a high humus content. They are admirably suited to burrowing, only the front legs being used for this purpose. The back legs serve to anchor the body against the walls of the tunnel, together with one of the forward legs—or hands. Anchored thus, the mole scoops earth with its free paw and sweeps it backwards. After working with one fore limb it then uses the other; it can also rotate its body in the tunnel and even work upside down. After a certain amount of spoil has accumulated behind it the animal turns round in the tunnel and pushes the earth towards a vertical shaft with its front legs, after which the soil is pushed up the shaft and expelled from the system. With all this digging to be done, the mole has very powerful shoulder muscles, and the front legs are well suited for digging, having in effect a sixth finger (the sesamoid bone of the wrist), making the 'excavator' broad and stiff.

The mole's tail is also an important organ. It is held upright most of the time, in contact with the roof of the tunnel, and thus supplies information to its owner on its relative position in a gallery.

Moles have a number of sense organs in their heads. They are not blind, as is sometimes thought, but have small eyes. As most of their life is spent underground, sight is not of the first importance. They also have ears, which are quite small, suggesting that the sense of hearing is not acute. On the other hand, sound must travel easily in the tunnel system, so that very sensitive hearing may not be needed.

The mole does have a very acute sense of touch, both in the snout and by means of stiff bristles on different parts of its body. These organs give the mole an appreciation of heat, cold, pain and vibration, the latter possibly of importance in mole control. The long bristles, like those of a cat, tell the mole a great deal about its environment. Running along its maze of passages in the dark, it must avoid bumping into the walls and junctions. The bristles respond to the slightest touch of a solid object and, in all probability, to air compression waves as well, so that the animal can detect an obstacle, and food too, before running into it.

Moles, like mice, have a keen kinaesthetic sense, that is to say they remember a sequence of actions leading to a certain result. For instance, the mole knows that by going so many paces this way or that and turning that way or this at a junction, it will reach its sleeping 'nest', or 'fortress'. This kinaesthetic sense is also possessed to a slight extent by humans. When we enter a familiar room in the dark a hand goes to the exact spot and switches on the light: normally we do not have to fumble for the switch. A mole's kinaesthesis is much more developed than ours and helps it to lead a successful life in its extensive 'underground'.

The nests are cavities excavated in the soil and filled with dried grass and leaves. The females give birth there and tend their young, and males may sleep in a nest out of their breeding season. The 'fortresses' are a little more mysterious. They are the big, above-ground molehills, sometimes a yard high, occasionally found in a gallery system. Fortresses usually contain several nests and may well be a retreat for the animals if heavy winter rains give rise to flooding in the tunnels.

Moles still exist today in the Bartons End gardens: from time to time a hill springs up in the orchard, copse or flower and vegetable beds, but they have not been seen for twenty years in the lawns: that is because the noise and vibration from two-stroke mechanical mowers drive out both moles and their main food, earthworms. Moles live for four or five years, so the present ones are something like the 190th generation of the original ones in John Barton's garden.

Over the years all sorts of measures have been taken against them. Mark Barton, for instance, set his gardener in the summer of 1625 to watch a molehill that had sprung up in the long-walk. As soon as the animal appeared the man would either catch it with his hand or kill it with a spade. Professional mole-catchers were encouraged to work in the Barton fields and gardens, their rewards being the skins, much in demand for making caps, waistcoats and ladies' coats. Isaac Munroyd even paid his mole-catcher £2 a year at Christmas, allowed him to keep the skins and did not enquire too closely as to whether the man occasionally took a rabbit or pheasant as well.

The mole-catchers used wooden traps set into the mole-run and activated by a springy bent twig, such as willow. They were baited with worms, or a bit of meat, and were heavy to carry about and laborious to set. And by no means did they always catch the animals. A mole, finding a strange object in its run, would frequently make a by-pass tunnel around it. Even if a mole was caught, it was not necessarily the end of mole activity in the system. A mole's network is its territory and as such is defended with great energy by the holder. Though the birthrate is not high, there are usually, at any rate in summer, a number of young adult

Mole and tunnels

moles looking for a territory, one undefended by an experienced occupant. When a mole is killed its galleries may quickly be occupied by a younger and more active animal, a state of affairs very satisfactory to the professional mole-catcher. The mole-man might take a rich harvest from a badly affected area and reduce damage to a crop, pasture or garden, but he made no significant reduction in the overall population of moles in his area.

One winter's day in 1794 Sophia Munroyd, well wrapped up, was taking a walk in the frozen garden at Bartons End when she was surprised to see a molehill of brown earth coming up through the dazzling snow, then four inches deep over the lawn; it was a remarkable sight. The molehill rising out of the snow made her think the little animals could bore through solid ice and earth frozen as hard as granite and that thus they could be compared with the 'hard rock men' of Bohemia and Cornwall, the miners who were famous for tunnelling in the most formidable rock. In point of fact, earth beneath snow seldom freezes more than a millimetre or two down, and the little miner Sophia saw at work was just digging normally. Moles sometimes dig tunnels between earth and snow, which look like surface runs when the snow has gone.

Averse to killing these remarkable animals, Sophia thought she would try to make them leave her lawns alone. She found that putting elder leaves and flowers into the galleries repelled the creatures, a method that still seems to work, provided that the leaves are renewed about once a week, but it is only effective if, as is always the case in pest control measures relying on repellance, there is somewhere for the repelled animals to go. In other words you eject the pest on to your neighbour's property, but if he is also using repellants the pest may decide to remain where it is, unpleasant though it may be, because there is nowhere better to go.

Modern methods of killing moles are either gassing with hydrocyanic acid gas—a fast-acting, deadly poison that gives a quick death—or by baiting with earthworms soaked in strychnine, also a very poisonous substance but one leading to a painful death.

Moles feed mostly on earthworms, but they also eat mice, dead birds, eggs and chicks, slugs and insects and small amounts of vegetable matter. They make stores of living earthworms, biting their heads off so that the worms stay alive but make no attempt to escape. Earthworms have an inborn fear of moles: they often know when a mole is approaching and may even hurry to the surface in order to escape. Lawns which are kept free of earthworms, through their acid nature or through being treated with de-worming compounds, are not likely to hold any moles.

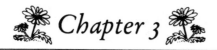

Chapter 3

Thomas Barton's Garden, 1599–1629

The Long-walk and Lawns

A T T H E time of his mother's death in 1610 Thomas Barton, helped by his son Mark, now aged twenty-five, was making a long-walk. It was intended for archery practice, a government-encouraged sport, for gunpowder had not yet fully replaced the bowman in war. Mark wanted to make a bowling green, but his father would not allow it—bowls was so popular and led to such high gambling and quarrels that it was officially discouraged. An Act of 1541, still extant in 1610, required anyone who had property of a value of £100 per annum to obtain a licence to make a bowling green. Bowls was thought to be a dangerous pastime for the young. Mark accepted his father's ruling, took up archery and became a very good shot.

The long-walk ran from east to west in front of the southernmost corner of the house. Father and son decided to make the walk of grass, but to have an edging of camomile and thyme, backed by dwarf box on the south side and a yew hedge on the north, which latter took a long time to grow. The stretch was 115 yards long and exists to this day.

The heavy land was carefully prepared. At the end of August 1610 it was ploughed, by a two-horse team, and several loads of farmyard manure were incorporated. It was an earnest of Thomas's keen interest in the garden that he diverted some of this valued commodity from his fields to such a frivolous purpose. In September the long-walk was ploughed again, then harrowed and rolled. The next step was to remove stones, break any remaining clods and then hand-rake the area until a fine tilth had been obtained. It was decided to collect as many turves as possible from close sheep-cropped pastures on the North Downs, but transport was difficult, so no more than a few yards at the firing end of the walk were turfed. Thomas's method was to place the turves grass-side down and hammer them into place with a large wooden beetle. They were kept moist and soon grass started to come through and form a close sward. The rest of the long-walk had to be seeded. During the summer hay seed had been carefully collected in the hay barn and from around the haystacks, and broadcast fairly thickly over the seed bed. Naturally the seed was a mixture of grasses, most of them fairly coarse in nature. The area was again lightly raked and rolled.

The hay seed mixture was by no means the most suitable one for establishing a lawn; the desirable kinds of grasses for producing good and plentiful hay, or rich fattening pasture, are not those giving a close, neat lawn. The Kentish pastures, particularly those in the Romney Marsh, were famed for fattening sheep and had a considerable percentage of perennial ryegrass and a good quantity of wild white clover, in those days a fairly recent introduction from the Netherlands, as well as other indigenous clovers. Other grasses also present in the hay seed were the bents, fescues, dogs' tails and smooth- and rough-stalked meadow grass, and these poorer grasses, from the farming point of view, were just those most suitable for making a lawn.

The hay of those days also contained a number of flowers, which in the nineteenth century and until fairly recently farmers regarded as weeds, but some people now think may be of value to the animals eating the produce: possibly some weeds, such as dandelions, supply various substances needed in the diet. The Bartons' hayfields were often adorned with attractive flowers, such as buttercups, the ox-eye daisy, the yellow rattle—rather damaging to pasture, as it is poisonous, but the cattle avoided it—self-heal, knapweed, spotted orchid, yellow-purple vetches and bindweeds crawling up the stems of grasses. Docks were also found in pasture and were damaging: a special scoop-like tool on a long handle was used to get them out.

The hay seed naturally contained seeds of these flowers and weeds as well as the grasses but the gardeners of those days liked to have flowers in their lawns, so that close-growing plants, such as the daisy and clovers, and even a few dandelions, were welcomed. A patch of taller flowers, such as the ox-eye daisies, would be allowed to appear here and there, the mowers carefully avoiding them as they worked. Naturally all sorts of weeds would germinate together with the grass seed.

The lawn seed having been sown, the next task was to keep the birds off it. The birds acted as though they had suddenly and unaccountably been provided with a big supply of small grain food especially to fortify them against the coming winter, an impression birds give to the sower of grass to this day. The children of the farm-hands were recruited for the task of disabusing the birds of this idea. The young people rather enjoyed it, although at least some of them had to be on the site from dawn to dusk. Their enjoyment was in making a great deal of noise unreprimanded and in practising sling shots with small stones against the raiders. It was as good as a holiday and there would be rewards, maybe a piece of cake or some bread and honey.

Soon after the first autumn rains in October the grass was starting to show green and the weeds were coming up as well. The coarse grasses and the unwanted couch grass established themselves more readily than the fine ones, the bents and fescues, and another hay sward would have established itself had not steps been taken to stop it.

The first step was to remove the worst weeds. In fine weather in November and December the older children were called in to go over the incipient lawn, foot by foot, along lines marked out by cords, to remove unwanted broad-leaved seedlings, such as docks, plantains and most of the dandelions, with a broken knife or similar blade. They were told to leave the daisies and the newly-arrived wild white clover. An old saying was, 'When you can put your foot on seven daisies at once you know that summer is here.'

The lawn was now rolled with a light wooden roller a day or two before the next step, which was mowing. Constant mowing encourages the fine grasses and sets back the coarse ones. The mowing was mostly done with a small lawn scythe, though sheep shears might be used on difficult patches. It was a laborious operation and, except for bowling greens, was not done as frequently as it would be today. A well-kept lawn was a sign of prosperity: so much work had to be put into it. The art of mowing a lawn, it was said, was to do it when the grass was wet with dew, though there were cynics who maintained that this adage had only been put out for the purpose of getting the men to work early in the morning. The scything of a lawn was a difficult task and the workers took great pride in it. A skilled man would leave no mark on the surface, unlike the long line pattern of today's roller mowers. Some of Thomas's mowers took great delight in the unnecessary sharpening of their scythe blades with a whetstone early in the morning near the house. It made a great deal of noise but it was no good the master complaining: had he not insisted that the grass be cut with the dew on it?

As the lawn established itself there was a regular sequence of poling, rolling—a heavier stone roller being used—and mowing, followed by the sweeping up of the grass. Poling was done by passing a tapering, pliable ash pole, fifteen to eighteen feet long, over the surface, which knocked down and spread the worm casts. Rolling was not done if the land was wet.

By 1615 Thomas Barton had established a nice sward to his own satisfaction, though the many flowers in it would have been frowned on by today's gardeners. In the autumn he would give it a dressing of well-rotted farmyard manure, which did much to maintain it in good condition.

In 1616 a number of hollows and bumps were beginning to occur in the lawn: they in no way affected the use of the walk for archery, but Thomas Barton thought them unsightly and set about eliminating them. Hollows were more serious than bumps, because water collected in them and drowned the grass. The cure for both conditions was simple. The turf was cut, folded back, and soil either added or taken away, then the turf replaced, beaten into position and watered.

The next trouble was considerable wear at the firing points, at 100, 80 and 60 yards from the targets, where the turf was worn. This was overcome by moving the line of targets a few yards east or west and re-seeding the damaged areas. The moving of the targets naturally meant that the firing lines also moved. Thomas was anxious to have a fine lawn and realised he did not want coarse grasses or tall flowers in his sward, that is to say, he had to avoid using hay seed for re-sowing worn patches or making new lawns, and he and his family set about collecting grass seed from hedges and meadows, keeping each kind separate. They found creeping bent and meadow grasses had good spreading powers and soon restored the worn patches. His wife Elizabeth Barton began to cultivate these grasses, sowing short lines of the different kinds she had collected in her vegetable plot. It was another horticultural activity which brought money into the family: in time there was quite a demand for her lawn seed.

By 1625 the long-walk was getting very patchy. There were a lot of weeds coming up and, pretty as the daisies were, they were too numerous. It was largely due to impoverishment. That spring and summer Thomas devised a daisy cutter, an old broadsword sharpened, fixed to a long pole and swung backwards and forwards over the turf.[a] The sword, being two-edged, cut the flowers off as it swung both ways. It was not an ideal solution to the daisy problem, for though it removed the offending flowers it probably strengthened the daisy plants by diverting the plant food which would have gone into the seed towards making vegetative growth and yet stronger patches of daisies.

In the spring and summer of 1626 the farm children were again called in to remove daisies, dandelions, cat's ear, plantains, creeping thistle, coltsfoot, buttercups and any other strong-growing, broad-leaved plants that were pushing out the grass. The struggle for existence in the lawn was as fierce as anywhere else; it was waged between plants and animals all the time and was much influenced by man's activities. From time to time he intervened to restore the conditions he wanted, as, for instance, when Thomas Barton acted against the weeds threatening to take over his long-walk.

Many of these weeds are tap-rooted and contain considerable reserves of plant food, enabling the plant to send out new shoots every time top growth is cut off, but if the tap root is injured the plant usually dies. Grass on the other hand is fibrous-rooted, and is constantly making new roots. It has great powers of recovery after injury, the commonest injuries being either grazing by animals or mowing which, superficially, is much the same thing as far as the grass is concerned.

In fact, however, different animals graze in different ways. Horses open their lips and bite off the grass between the upper and lower incisors. Thus they can cut the grass close to the ground and a short, thick growth suits them. As they are not ruminants they have to masticate the food as they go and so feed much more slowly than cattle or sheep, which take in the grass as fast as they can, swallow it at once and later regurgitate it for proper mastication.[68] Cows spend about eight hours per day feeding, and seven chewing the cud. A cow curls its long tongue round the grass and tears it off, pulling it into its mouth by holding the herbage between the teeth of the lower jaw and the upper dental pad. Sheep and rabbits feed very close to the ground and like a dense 'lawn-like' sward. Sheep can eat ragwort in moderate amounts, though it is poisonous to cattle. Thomas Barton sometimes penned sheep on the long-walk to rid it of ragwort, which had invaded the lawn due to the activities of a few rabbits and lack of attention to feeding the grass. Ragwort is poisonous to rabbits, so they leave it alone and just eat the grass away; meanwhile the ragwort seeds profusely and spreads over the impoverished land. The sheep-grazing plan was only partially successful because sheep can only consume a certain amount of the weed; they will be poisoned if they eat much of it. Other advantages of using sheep, however, were that they ate down the grass more closely than a mower could and thus discouraged the coarse ryegrass. They also returned some of the plant food to the turf in their dung and urine. But hand weeding had to be resorted to as well in order to get the long-walk back into good condition. The lawn also needed proper feeding.

When animals graze a pasture or lawn some of the plant food is returned to the land, but when a lawn is mown and the cut grass collected and taken away, much fertility is being removed from the site. If the food is not returned in the shape of compost or chemical fertiliser the lawn is impoverished and the grass is unable to repel the invasion of weeds, particularly of the tap-rooted ones, which can send a root deep into the soil to gather food not available to the fibrous grass roots.

When Thomas Barton realised that sweeping up the mowings and carrying them away was taking food out of the land, he only swept up at every other mowing, unless the grass was very long. Leaving the mowings *in situ* returned some food to the soil but it also increased the organic matter near the surface and encouraged worm activity and the growth of fungi. Worms made the lawns unsightly with their casts, and some fungi made nasty bare patches. A not very damaging fungus which the mowings encouraged, and which delighted Thomas's youngest daughter, Penelope, was *Marasmius oreades*, the fairy ring. The fungus lives only on certain kinds of organic matter in the soil and if a growth is established it soon uses up its food material in the immediate neighbourhood: it can only acquire more food by its hyphae—the root-like

Fairy ring fungus

strands making up the fungus—moving outwards in the soil, which they do, usually releasing a certain amount of nitrogen in the process. The nitrogen turns the grass greener and a 'fairy ring' is formed, expanding ever outwards, because there is no food for the fungus inside the ring.

Little yellowish-white toadstools grew up from time to time in the ring. Penelope usually picked these magic growths and took them to the kitchen, where they were put into the soup. She assured everyone that the fairies' toadstools were benevolent and would bring good luck to all who drank the pottage.

Different species of grass behave in different ways and it is these differences that man exploits in order to get the kind of grass he wants. The farmer needs a big weight of nourishing grass for his beasts. The gardener desires a close sward of a beautiful green, with or without a scattering of flowers to relieve the monotony, according to historical date, fashion or personal preference.

The aim of all the grasses—as of most other forms of life—is to secure their succession in the greatest possible number. One might say that the aim of the perennial ryegrass is a world in which perennial ryegrass is the only life, a world which might very well come about if we indulge in a large-scale nuclear war.[b]

To secure their succession, grasses propagate themselves both by means of sexually-produced seed and by vegetative means. The seed provides opportunities of producing cultivars better adapted to particular conditions, and vegetative reproduction enables the grass to recover from grazing and mowing. Naturally, grazing and mowing prevent the production of seed, but cutting off the leaves has the effect of causing more shoots to emerge from the core of the plant, a process known as tillering. This is the main reason why constant mowing produces a thick sward. Other vegetative means used by grasses are the continual production of fibrous roots and of rhizomes and stolons. The new roots push into adjacent areas and send up green shoots which struggle with any other occupying plant, or take over bare patches unless conditions there are very adverse. As the new roots arise, the old roots die, decay and produce CO_2 gas, a substance helping the grass to overcome other plants occupying the site.

Rhizomes are modified stems which push through the soil just beneath the surface. The stems are hollow but are solid at the joints where adventitious roots may form, going down into the soil; leaves and stems may then push upwards into the air. An example of a grass with rhizomes is red fescue. Stolons are similar stems running over the surface of the soil. In the usual course of events rhizomes and stolons are low down and out of the way of grazing animals and mowers, unless the animals are very hard-pressed for food; the growths thus provide for the continued presence of the grass on the site. In some grasses, such as bulbous meadow grass, the lower internodes swell up with a store of plant food and become bulbous.

The soil at Bartons End, particularly those bits of it under the lawns, teemed with life: it contained enormous numbers of animals, protozoa, bacteria and fungi as well as the extensive root vegetation. Soils are not a solid mass of particles and humus pressed together like a piece of rock, there is plenty of space between the particles, though the spaces may be very minute. Collectively they are known as the pore space and under the Bartons' lawns it amounted to fifty per cent of the volume. The pore space is occupied by water or air and is an ideal medium for the growth of bacteria, protozoa, vegetation including fungi, and comparatively large animals such as earthworms, slugs and even moles. Without its minute inhabitants the soil would not support any vegetation and there would be no animal life in the world.

The bacteria ran at something like 4,000 million per gramme (112,000 million per ounce) and the protozoa, feeding largely on the bacteria, were there in similar numbers. By the time the long-walk was established—it was about a third of an acre in size—it carried about 1,800 lbs. of bacteria and some 50 lbs. of protozoa in the top nine inches of soil.

The fungi were also very numerous; one of them—the fairy ring—has already been mentioned. Fungi can be divided into two kinds, the saprophytic, living on dead organic materials, and the parasitic, which attack living plants. Some of these growths use both ways of life; having killed a plant by parasitic attack they then live on the dead material saprophytically.

The care given to the long-walk at Bartons End—the dressings with compost and manure, for instance, and the mowings—had made the soil beneath it very fertile, so it carried a considerable amount of fungal growth. A fungus starts its life as a spore which, on germination, produces a white or colourless tube-like growth, known as the hypha; usually it is very thin, less than the thread of a spider's web, and not visible unless it is white. This growth continues, becoming the mass of mycelium, and it can be very extensive. As the mycelium increases it produces another kind of growth—the fruiting body or sporangium, such as the mushroom. This body produces spores in vast numbers which are then blown about by the wind or carried in raindrops, some of them reaching favourable spots, germinating and thus continuing the life of the species.

The quantity of fungus beneath the long-walk in summer was considerable and can be presented in startling terms. For instance, the length of mycelium in an ounce of fertile soil is about 1·77 miles per ounce,[63] that is, say, 21 million miles under the long-walk. This mycelium plays an important part in making soil humus. As the mycelium grows it competes with plant roots for food in the soil; this food is converted to proteins and carbohydrates both in the fungus and in plants, the difference being that the fungi have no chlorophyll so cannot manufacture complex sugars and proteins for themselves, as plants do. Fungi absorb them more or less readymade from the organic matter on which they are living, mostly plant residues. The fungi thus collect nitrogen, as proteins, in their tissues. As the fungi live they therefore also die; the dead mycelium is then attacked by bacteria and the nitrogren of the protein released as nitrate. It is this nitrate that makes the dark green band, about a foot wide, of the fairy ring.

Nitrates, that important plant food, reach the soil in a number of ways: by the decomposition of organic matter, such as decaying roots and compost, either present in the soil naturally or added deliberately; by the action of nitrifying bacteria, particularly *Azobacter* in the nodules of leguminous plants' roots, in fixing atmospheric nitrogen; from rainwater, particularly during thunderstorms; and by the application of chemical manures, some of which actually are nitrates.

Nitrates are lost from the soil by being used by plants to form their tissues; by being washed out of the soil by rain; or by being converted to gaseous nitrogen by denitrifying bacteria.

The mycorrhizal fungi found in soils are also important, but not greatly so to lawns. They are fungi living in a symbiotic state with certain plants, particularly trees. Competition between all living forms in any given environment is not necessarily fierce. Some kinds of life have found that mutual co-operation pays: that is symbiosis. Some of the mycorrhizal fungi surround the rootlets of a tree with a mass of mycelium from which hyphae push their way into the plant itself and into the surrounding soil. The fungus extracts plant food from the organic matter it is breaking up in the soil and passes it on to the plant. The plant, in its turn, supplies carbohydrates, such as sugars and proteins, to the fungus. It is a mutually beneficial system.

Fungi, together with bacteria, flagellates and amoebae, play an important part in making and maintaining soil fertility and structure. The top six inches of soil under the long-walk had a considerable quantity of them, about 800 lbs. of bacteria, 500 lbs. of mycelium and 50 lbs. of protozoa (flagellates and amoebae), in all about 3 per cent of the organic matter in its soil.

The biggest weight of resident animals in Mark Barton's long-walk was made up of earthworms. They were important in establishing the lawn and maintaining it. The fact that some species spoiled lawns by making casts was not of much importance in the long-walk as, to begin with, it was only used for archery. Later on, when a bowling green and lawn-tennis courts were made, steps were taken against these creatures, a poor return for their efforts in promoting the establishment of the lawn in the first place. The earthworms under the long-walk were mostly of the two cast-forming species, *Allobophora longa* and *A. nocturna*, the former, in spite of its name, being shorter than the latter.

It was Charles Darwin who, in 1881, first drew scientific attention to the importance of earthworms with his book *The Formation of Vegetable Mould through the Action of Worms with Observations of their Habits*.[21] He showed the great effect they had in creating soils of good structure and fertility; however, earlier naturalists, such as Gilbert White, had already commented on the subject.

Earthworms are more numerous in grassland than in cultivated areas: two or three years after the long-walk had been established there were about 100,000 earthworms in it, weighing in all about 32 lbs., which is quite a considerable biomass. This is understandable when we find that the weight of vegetable growth in the above- and below-ground habitats of a piece of land tend to be equal. For instance, the weight and spread of a tree's roots tend to equal the weight and spread of its branches. The weight of earthworms in a pasture is usually equal to, or a little more, than the weight of cattle or sheep feeding on that pasture.

Darwin calculated that the casts on an average piece of grassland amounted to 10 tons of earth per acre per annum and that they added one fifth of an inch of soil to the surface each year. Modern research confirms the weight figure,[63] though 11 tons may be nearer the average, but not the increase in depth of soil, which is now thought to be 6–8 inches per century, the rate at which Stonehenge is sinking into the countryside. The pushing up of such large amounts of earth is one of the reasons why old ruins and artifacts get buried. Stones and other solid objects on lawns and pasture gradually sink into the soil as worm-casts accumulate above them. A halfpenny that Mark Barton dropped while inspecting the lawn in 1610 is now some 26 inches below the surface.

Worms improve soils in many ways through their way of life and their feeding. They often burrow to great depths, four and five feet, and improve drainage by means of the passages left behind them. The channels also improve aeration and help the escape of excessive CO_2 gas from the soil. Worms feed on organic matter in and on the soil, such as non-aromatic leaves, meat, fat, and cattle, horse and sheep droppings. Leaves are drawn into their burrows in a particular way, showing that worms have some intelligent appreciation of circumstances. Darwin, using leaves of different kinds, including some he made himself of coloured paper, found that earthworms always seized a leaf by its pointed end, thus making it much easier to get it into a burrow than if it were taken by the broad end or by the side. This was in marked contrast to ants, reputedly so intelligent, which drag objects along the surface haphazardly with no concept of doing it in the easiest way. The leaves are taken in at night to be used as food during the day, so that it really is the early birds that get the worms as their night's work is ending.

Worms have no eyes, but nevertheless are sensitive to light by means of receptive cells, called eye pits, scattered over the body. Nor do they have ears. Darwin found that they did not react to sound but were sensitive to vibrations. He had earthworms in pots and found that when they were on the surface of the soil there was no response to a bass C or treble G played on the piano, but if the pot was put on the piano itself the vibration from any note sent them back to their burrows at once.

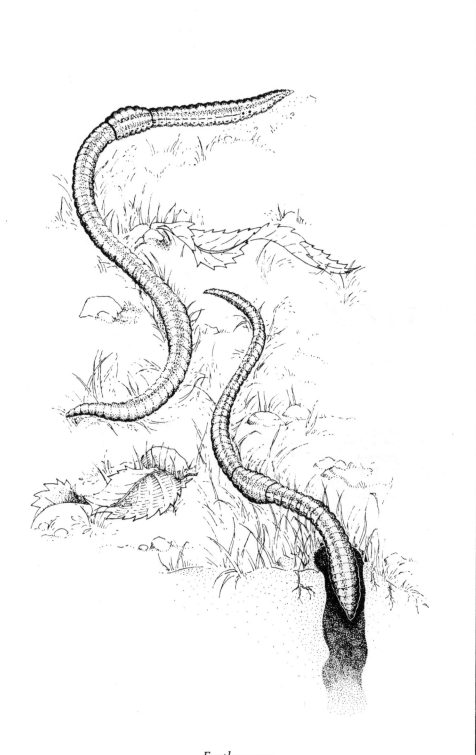

Earthworms

Worms sometimes emerge for no apparent reason and move over the surface; the Bartons thought this showed that they were being chased by moles, but moles are more trappers than hunters, so that was not very likely.

Worms make their burrows in two ways, firstly by forcing a passage through the soil and secondly by eating it. As there is considerable pore space in any soil the earthworms can squeeze the particles closer together and construct a tunnel, though, like all tunnelling, it takes a lot of effort. The second method is to eat the soil, absorb the organic matter or worm food in it, and eject the rest, as worm-casts on the surface in the cast-forming species, or tucked into empty pockets in the soil in the case of other species.

Earthworms are made up of a number of segments separated each from the other by a partition. The worm moves by expanding and contracting these segments, which can be made long and thin or short and fat, both states retaining the same volume. If a worm wants to move forward it makes some hind sections short and fat and thus anchors its rear in the burrow; at the same time it makes its forward sections long and thin and thus moves them forward. A wave of muscle action passes along the body. The contracted and thus fat region is assisted in its anchoring action by a number of bristles (chaetae) which project backwards from each section and help to prevent its moving towards the rear. This anchoring effect is noticeable when we watch a comparatively large bird—say a thrush—trying to pull an earthworm from its burrow. The bird usually finds it very difficult and has to exert itself fully, although the worm is only relying on its expanded segments, as the backward sloping chaetae are no help in resisting the tugging action of a bird, unless, as may sometimes be the case, the bird is pulling on the rear end of the worm.

Earthworms have a brain of sorts which enables them to co-ordinate movement. A nerve chord runs from two forward ganglia, one just above and the other just below the pharynx, right through the body to the tail end, with a ganglion in each section. This nervous system allows them to profit from experience, that is, to learn things, such as which way to turn in a maze of tunnels in order to obtain food. Worms need damp conditions, and if weather is dry earthworms go deep in the soil and curl up in a hollow they either find or make. This is known as aestivation— the opposite of hibernation.

As a worm's mouth is very small it cannot eat any particle larger than 0.08 inch in diameter. This means that a soil selection process is going on where worms abound, the finer particles continually being brought to the surface. They thus promote a good soil structure from the point of view of plant growth. The empty passages may make it easier for thick-rooted plants, such as the tap-rooted docks and dandelions, to establish themselves.

Large quantities of earth pass through the bodies of earthworms, but it is difficult to estimate the exact amount. A. C. Evans[29] calculated that 4–36 tons of earth per acre per year go through the various kinds of earthworm beneath grass, of which 1–25 tons are expelled as worm-casts. Where the cast-formers are abundant the surface soil is rich in silt and clay, has a better structure and more plant food, and if the grass is ancient, the stones and coarse particles will have sunk to considerable depths.

Earthworms mix soil far more than digging and ploughing. The worms also remove dead plant remains from the surface of soils. If the soil is too acid (less than pH 4·5) the earthworms cannot thrive and the dead vegetation builds up, year by year, on the surface, making a dense mass through which only strong-growing plants can grow. This accumulation eventually becomes strongly acid peat.

The making of the good soil at Bartons End owed a great deal to the activities of earthworms and it is ironic that the Bartons, Onways and Munroyds regarded them with such suspicion over the years. As farmers they thought the worms ate their green corn and as gardeners most of them thought the worm-casts a nuisance on their lawns. It was the naturalist Gilbert White who, in 1777, first appreciated what the worms were doing for the land.

> . . . earth without worms would soon become cold, hard-bound and void of fermentation: and consequently sterile . . . Worms seem to be the great promoters of vegetation, which would proceed but lamely without them, by boring, perforating, and loosening the soil, and rendering it pervious to rains and the fibres of plants, by drawing straws and stalks of leaves and twigs into it; and, most of all, by throwing up such infinite numbers of lumps of

earth, called worm-casts, which, being their excrement, is a fine manure for grain and grass.[74]

Many seeds, particularly those of wild plants, are able to remain dormant in the soil for a long time. It is the plants' means of surviving bad weather and adverse conditions. Worm-casts on lawns are not only a nuisance to players of ball games, and unsightly, but may also encourage the growth of lawn weeds. Small dormant seeds may be brought up by worms, especially if such seeds have been able to develop a resistance to the substance in the worm's gut, and germinate in a worm-cast when brought to the surface. Also a worm-cast, flattened by being trodden upon, makes a nice little spot of bare soil suitable for the germination of a seed alighting on it, such as a dandelion or thistle. Once such a seed has got a start it is likely to persist, owing to its habit of growing close to the ground and suppressing the grasses round it.

Although on the whole earthworms greatly benefited the garden, there were also some adverse activities. For instance, they not only pulled fallen leaves into their burrows but they also pulled in leaves of growing plants if such leaves happened to bend over and touch the soil. From time to time at Bartons End rows of lettuces were damaged in this way. The tunnels the worms made damaged the roots of delicate plants, and they spread the spores of fungal diseases. Some earthworms were the essential intermediate hosts of certain tapeworms, such as *Amoebotania cuneatus* (Linstow) in *Lombricus terrestris*, and others sheltered the worms causing 'the gapes' in chickens.

There were a number of other worms in the long-walk as well. There were the small eelworms or nematodes and the minute Enchytraeids.

The nematodes are not segmented, like earthworms, and are from 0·02 to 0·06 inch long. Some are free-living in the soil while others are parasitic on plants, certain species being serious pests.

Nematodes need a lot of moisture but when soils are drying these tiny worms pass into an inert, or spore-like state, in which they can survive for some time. In this dust-like condition they can be blown about by wind and carried on the feet of birds and insects.

The nematodes were the most numerous of the kinds of animals in the garden at Bartons End. In the summers beneath the long-walk there were some 14,000 million of them and they weighed about 70 lbs., between a quarter and a fifth of the weight of the earthworms. They feed on bacteria and plant tissues and consume considerable amounts of oxygen as well;[54] those under the long-walk used some 320 litres (70 gallons) a day at normal temperature and pressure.

A number of plants including some grasses and clovers in the lawn became hosts to parasitic nematodes, such as the meadow nematode (*Pratylenchus pratensis*), but they did not do much damage to the sward.

Eelworms, being so numerous under the grass, naturally were attacked by predators. Some of the large nematodes attack and consume the smaller ones, but a most interesting predator is a number of specialised fungi. A common species is *Arthrobotrys oligospora*. This fungus grows in the soil and every now and then its hyphae form a ring composed of three sensitive cells. Eelworms move around in the soil and if one starts, just by chance, to pass through such a ring a mechanism is triggered. The cells suddenly expand and trap the eelworm. The fungus then sends hyphae into the creature and feeds on it. This fungus is still active at Bartons End.

The Enchytraeid worms in the soil beneath the long-walk were not so numerous as the nematodes: there were only about 38 million of them, weighing some 6 lbs. They were mostly in the top inch or so of soil.

The garden soil also contained considerable numbers of jointed-limbed, cold-blooded arthropods, such as mites, spiders and insects, and molluscs—slugs and snails. Of course, the smaller the animal the more numerous is its population, as has already been seen with the worms. The mites were the most numerous creatures: the long-walk had about 317 millions of them in the top foot of soil. Next came the very small Collembola or springtails, which are primitive insects: there were some 93 millions of them. They were followed by a miscellaneous collection of other insects, such as the larvae of flies and beetles, and some spiders. This mixed lot can be put at 57 millions, giving a total of 467 million arthropods all struggling away beneath the grass, seeking their own particular way of life, and out of sight of the humans. But not always out of mind. At times conditions under the grass may become so favourable for a particular species that it thrives enormously and can become a pest, from man's point of view. For instance, in the summer of 1625 Mark Barton found several bare patches on his magnificent lawn. Close inspection showed them to contain leather-jackets which, unknown to

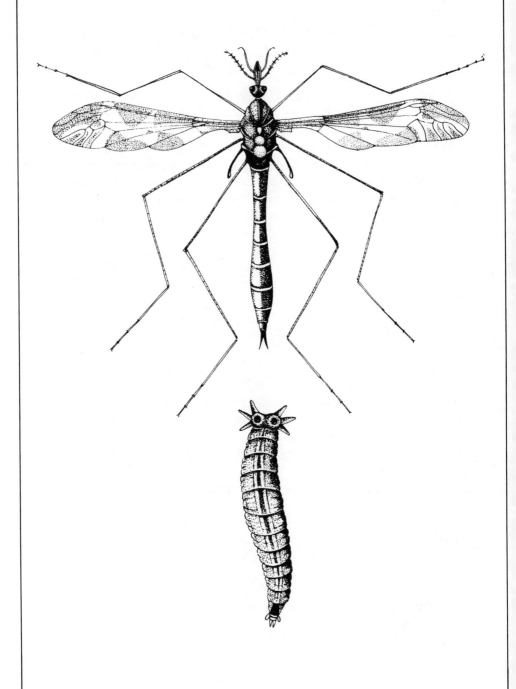

Daddy-long-legs and larva (leather jacket)

Mark at the time, were the larvae of the crane fly, or daddy-long-legs (*Tipula*), apparently feeding on the roots and stolons of the grass. The crane fly was also called father-long-legs and Harry-long-legs, and a long-legged spider went by the same names. As the tough crane-fly grubs only feed at night they were not observed eating the grass, though that would not have been very obvious in any case as usually they were just below the surface. Poking around with a piece of stick or a knife soon showed these 'worms' to be present, evident culprits.

Mark Barton did not realise that the troublesome grubs were the larvae of the daddy-long-legs. The long, tough, legless maggots were held to arise from 'corruption' in the soil in the same way that maggots were thought to arise in meat. The belief in the spontaneous generation of life persisted for a long time, and it was only finally extinguished by Pasteur's experiments in the late nineteenth century.

There is a wide variety of crane flies in Britain: some three hundred different species are now known. Most of their larvae feed on decaying wood, leaf litter and plant remains in the soil, but some of them—the daddy-long-legs, for instance—will also eat roots. Some of the species live in water and feed on the debris at the bottom of ponds. The adult flies do no direct harm as they can only suck up liquids with their prominent, hollow beaks. They have no sting, though some of them look as if they have one.

The leather-jackets damaging Mark's garden were the common grey kind (*Tipula paludosa*) and to this very day an outbreak may occur from time to time. Mark overcame them by going out at night with a lantern and picking them up, raking the bare patches and destroying the larvae and pupae. He also fed chickens on the site so that they picked up the leather-jackets along with their food. Today this is considered too laborious, and insecticides such as bromophos and benzene hexachloride are used.

Related Tipulidae are some of the masses of tiny flies found swarming over grass on a warm summer evening and rising up and down as they hover over it, hence one of their names, bobbing gnats. The Tipulidae come in a wide range of sizes. The bobbing gnats have a wing span of 0·06 inch and the big one, *Tipula maxima*—the daddy daddy-long-legs, so to speak—is about 2½ inches across the wings. *T. maxima* is the biggest fly in Britain, but not as damaging as *paludosa*.

Among the other insects were the very numerous springtails, unusual insects in that they have no 'complete metamorphosis'. Most insects start life as an egg (as, of course, does all animal life, ourselves included) and then successively become larvae, chrysalids and adults, all very different conditions.

Collembola have no such metamorphosis. They hatch as tiny springtails from the eggs and grow and grow by successive moultings; theoretically there is no limit to the size they could become, though in practice they do not have more than five or six moults.

An insect has no skeleton: instead it has a comparatively tough yet elastic skin to which the muscles are attached: it increases in size by growing a new softish skin beneath the hardened old one, splitting off this outer shell and expanding the new skin beneath it, which then hardens. The process is complex. For instance, the muscles have to be detached from the old skin and then attached to the new one. Moreover, it takes time and the creature is very vulnerable to attack during moulting. Pupation is a complicated process, too. The larva, or caterpillar, forms a hard case, the pupa, then inside it seems to turn itself into a thick paste which slowly becomes a bedraggled, squashed-up adult. Splitting the case open at the right moment, the creature emerges to pump its wings full of blood, dry out and become a handsome butterfly, or other kind of insect, according to species. Each stage between moults is known as an instar, and wings only develop inside the pupa or during the last but one instar.

Springtails, or Collembola (the word comes from the Greek: *kolla* = glue and *embolos* = peg, a reference to the ventral tube on the first abdominal segment, which secretes a gum) have no truck with a complete metamorphosis. They came into existence a very long time ago—before the common insect metamorphosis had evolved. Collembola find the incomplete system suits them, so they persist in their primitive way. They escape danger by springing away from it, by means of the furcula, a prong formed by the final abdominal segments and hinged at the rear. Normally the furcula is held against the abdomen by means of a sort of hook on the third abdominal segment, the hamula. The furcula can be released suddenly to jerk the animal into the air. Springtails can spring distances several times their own length, giving them the advantages of flight without the complications of growing and using wings. Being so small the wind often catches them up and carries them to new areas.

The creatures feed mostly on leaf litter and decaying vegetation on and in the soil, but two families, the Neelidae and the Sminthuridae, have developed a taste for living vegetation and sometimes damage crops. In 1651 a yellow species (*Sminthurus viridis*—yes, yellow, in spite of the name, *viridis* = green) took a liking to Elizabeth Onway's purple medick or La Lucerne, as they called the new 'grass' from the Netherlands. The springtails caused considerable damge to the lucerne and the Onways named it the Lucerne flea. It also developed an appetite for peas and beans. There was not much the Onways could do to oppose the pest, though they found that hoeing between the plants made a lot of dust which the insects did not like, and their numbers then fell.

Mulching plants with leaf litter and compost can help their growth by supplying plant food and helping to conserve water in dry weather, but it can also favour the development of certain animals which will damage that growth. Leather-jackets, some springtails, cutworms (the caterpillars of the yellow underwing moth), and certain others, as well as slugs and snails, are examples of potential garden pests encouraged by mulching.

The lawn grasses attracted a number of butterflies and moths, the caterpillars of which fed on those plants. The adult Lepidoptera laying their eggs on the long-walk and, over the centuries, the other lawns, had not chosen a very good site because, just as the young caterpillars were developing nicely on the tender grass, along would come a scythe or mowing machine and their food would then be cut off, to wither or to be collected and composted. In spite of this hazard some caterpillars did reach the adult stage, and there were other places round the garden and in the orchard and copse where grass grew undisturbed, so quite a number of attractive grass-feeding butterflies could be seen around the garden.

Nests of the garden ant were found in the lawn from time to time, sometimes being dug out and given to the chickens as food and sometimes being left, if they did not cause too much of an obstruction, because they were always 'attacking' the greenfly, such pests on roses and broad beans. This view was completely wrong. The garden ant encourages the greenfly and protects it from its enemies. In return the greenfly sucks up an excess of sugary sap from the tender shoots of growing plants and excretes some of it, on which the ants greedily feed. These activities will be discussed more fully in a later chapter, as will also those of the slugs and snails.

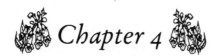

Chapter 4

The Garden of Mark Barton, his Daughter Elizabeth, his Grandson Mark Onway and his Great-grandson, James Onway, 1629–1689

T HOMAS BARTON died in 1629. By that time the garden was very decorative and many new flowers and vegetables had been introduced into it. Dorothy Snell's collection of forget-me-nots—she had died in 1610—had been carefully tended by Thomas Barton in remembrance of his old nurse, and by Thomas's son Mark too. Dorothy had played the same game with John and Mary Barton's grandchildren as she had with their children: each in turn was the curator of a bed of forget-me-nots. The flowers were well named, for they all loved and remembered their 'old Dorothy' in spite of her strictness.

Mark Barton was forty-four when his father died and he inherited the property, but he only lived for two more years himself, dying in 1631. He had three children, only one of whom, Elizabeth, survived infancy. In 1626 Elizabeth married Robert Onway, who took over the farm and garden when his father-in-law died so comparatively young. Robert himself did not live to a great age; he died in 1660 aged fifty-five and his son Mark, named after his maternal grandfather, did much to develop the farm and garden. In fact, it was this interest in the garden which, indirectly, was the cause of Mark's early death, aged thirty-eight, in 1665. In that year he went to London to discuss the sale of that increasingly popular, though still illegal, plant—the hop—the cultivation of which had been started by Mary Barton. In London Mark

Onway was bitten by a rat-flea infected with the plague, caught the disease, was hurried home in great pain and died, fortunately without infecting any more of his family. He and his wife Prudence (née Sefton) had had two children, James and Prudence, and the young James inherited Bartons End.

By the time Mark Onway died in 1665 considerable effort and money had been put into the garden. There were new flowers, herbs and vegetables mingled with the older established varieties. In 1665 the main 'florist's flowers'—that is, species grown because of their attractiveness—were: anemones, both the native wood anemone and the recently introduced star anemone from Italy; auriculas from the Alps; campanulas—Canterbury bells or bellflowers, the rampion and the clustered campanula; carnations—pinks and gillyflowers, the sweet william, the German Carthusian and the clove carnation, so called because of its perfume (clove carnations were used as a substitute for the expensive African cloves); columbines, both the granny's bonnet and the New England columbine; comfrey; cyclamens —the round-leaved and the common; the double daffodil; the elacampane, the flower Helen of Troy was said to have been holding in her hand when she was abducted; foxgloves; mallows—the round-leaved, the curled, recently introduced from Syria, and the musk; the hellebores,[a] or Christmas roses from Austria—the native hellebore and the stinking hellebore or bear's foot; hollyhocks—the common indigenous marsh mallow and the fig-leaved or Antwerp hollyhock, a recent introduction at that time from the East; honesty, so called because of its transparent seed pods; honeywort or wax-plant, and hedge honeywort or bastard stone parsley; lavender; wild lovage adapted to the garden; marigolds, both the French and the 'African', strangely named since it came from Mexico in 1596; lilies—the native lily-of-the-valley, the white lily from the Levant and the Turk's cap which preceded it, having been brought to Britain by the returning Crusaders; pansies, or heartsease; and poppies, such as selections of the wild poppy and the garden or opium poppy.

Considerable attention had been given to rose cultivation in the developing garden. By 1665 Bartons End no longer produced rosewater for sale and consequently the area devoted to the flower was considerably reduced, although the kinds of roses grown had increased. New seedlings were planted from time to time and at least four new species of

Anemone, sweet william, auricula, carnation and poppy

Rosa had been introduced. There was a new sport of the damask rose, the Provence or cabbage rose, the evergreen rose and a recent arrival from Germany, the Frankfurt rose.

Introductions from North America were the spiderwort and the Michaelmas daisy. Tulips have already been mentioned, and in the garden at that date were the wild tulip or common tulip from the Levant, the narrow-waved and the Lady's or Clusius's tulip. Finally, wallflowers were very common.

A number of flowering shrubs had also been added to the garden, among them two much-prized novelties, the lilac (*Syringa vulgaris*) and the mock orange (*Philadelphus coronarius*) from Asia Minor and Italy respectively. In due course considerable confusion grew up around the names of these two plants. The lilac's scientific name is often used as the common name for the mock orange, a quite different plant called after its flowers and scent, which are both somewhat like orange blossom. Both species were known in Turkey and to Gerard, who found the mock orange 'in very great plentie' in 1597. He classified them together under the name *syrinx*, a pan-pipe, because the wood of both plants is a hollow filled with pith which can easily be removed—both woods are used in Turkey to make pipes. Gerard called them the Blew Pipe (lilac) and the White Pipe (mock orange) and the botanist Bauhin gave the latter the name *Philadelphus*, though in Asia Minor the plant was a symbol of deceit, not of brotherly love, as *Philadelphus* suggests. Even so the popular name syringa persists to this day. The error was abetted by M. Lemoine, a French nurseryman, who raised a number of *Philadelphus* hybrids in the early years of this century, calling them syringas of various kinds.

There is a wide divergence of opinion on the quality of plant odours. Mark Onway liked the strong smell of the mock orange. His wife, Prudence, said it was far too strong; it stifled her and was never to be brought into the house, though she would allow it to be used in pomanders when pestilence was around. Many others besides Prudence disliked it as well. Gerard for one, and the famous gardener E. A. Bowles (1866–1954), in his great Hertfordshire garden, wanted *Philadelphus* in his collection of shrubs but so disliked the smell that each year he had all the blossom picked off, a quite considerable task.

It was during this period that the Bartons End garden first saw privet, another strongly-scented plant, which the early seventeenth-century gardeners were beginning to trim into shapes—topiary was being born. The common hawthorn or May tree lent itself to topiary as well, though great care had to be taken not to bring the blossom into the house for if one did, so it was said, bad luck would follow.

The herb garden still existed, but it was not used as extensively as it had been. Nevertheless some useful introductions had been made, such as the true rhubarb, valuable as a laxative; Adam and Eve in the bower, or the dead nettle, its biblical name being derived from the two stamens in the flower; the blessed thistle; saffron and the nasturtium, which had come from America.

The vegetable garden had increased in size and many new species had been added; among them were the cauliflower, French and runner beans, marrows, spinach and asparagus which, though a native plant in western England, had not been much grown in the Bartons' garden up to then.

The New England Bartons had a strong sense of family and had kept in touch with their Kentish relations through letters telling them of the wonders of the New World, the chief of which was religious freedom, starting to be marred, unfortunately, by the fear of witchcraft. The Kentish Bartons in return sent their colonial cousins political news of England, such as the execution of Charles I in 1649, the Commonwealth, and the restoration of the monarchy in 1660. They also arranged supplies of goods needed in America, such as nails, tools, glass quarrels (small diamond-shaped panes for windows) and seeds, such as wheat, rye and barley, seeds of herbs and flowers, and livestock.

John Barton in America sent back a selection of seeds which included a number of American flowers, such as nasturtiums, lobelia, sunflowers and the Michaelmas daisy. He also included some scarlet runner beans. All these novelties were carefully planted and cared for on germination, and it is thus not surprising that the beans were first admired for their flowers: it never occurred to Prudence Onway that those coarse green pods could be eaten. The few big seeds were collected and dried; most of them were given to friends and relatives as seed and the remainder used in soups. About 1680 it was discovered that the pods made a good vegetable, provided the stringy edges were cut away.

The Onways were even more confused over the potato, the true seed (the berry) of which had also been sent from their colonial cousins. There purported to be four kinds of potatoes—the Spanish, or sweet potato (*Ipomoea batata*); the Virginia potato (*Solanum tuberosum*) which had white flowers; the Irish potato, also *S. tuberosum*, but thought to be a different species because it had purple flowers; and the Canadian potato (*Helianthus tuberosus*), now known as the Jerusalem artichoke.[b] Peru is much more likely to have been the country of origin of *tuberosum* than Virginia, and even in Peru it was not a wild plant but an artifact bred and cultivated by the Incas for hundreds of years.

The *Solanum* seed when planted at Bartons End in 1660 sent up its shoots, and the flowers, appearing in July, were much admired. Elizabeth Onway used to read the family copy of Gerard's *Herball* and, noting that the author, as depicted in the frontispiece, was holding a flower of that plant, assumed that its main use was to produce these pretty flowers. The potatoes themselves were ignored: it was not at first realised that they could be used as seed for the next crop, seed which in fact would produce a bigger and earlier harvest of tubers. Nor were the Onways at first much inclined to eat the potatoes: one of the names given to them—the tuberous nightshade—made them sound dangerous.

The Onways took their second crop in 1661. Prudence Onway then experimented in cooking the potatoes according to a recipe she had received from a friend. This friend had been in the West Indies and there had eaten the sweet potato, so she tried to make the 'Virginia' potato taste like that. The potatoes were peeled, put in a dish with sugar and spices and slowly baked. Sugar was an expensive and scarce item and so Virginia potatoes were not much eaten by the Onways. It should be noted that they had received no instructions on how to cultivate the potato, and so grew them on flat ground, without any of the earthing-up done today, and by experienced growers even then. The Onways' crops thus had many of the tubers exposed to the sun; this causes them to go green, become bitter and a little poisonous to some people. They cannot have provided a very attractive diet.

In 1665 Prudence read John Foster's book *England's Happiness Increased* (1664),[33] in which the cultivation and use of the plant was described, but she and her family were still very suspicious of it as a food. Gradually potatoes came to be accepted as a useful nourishment

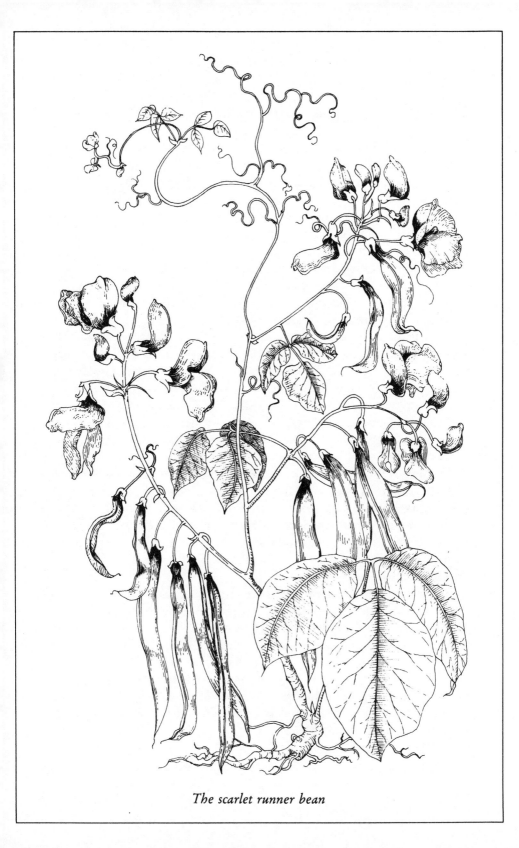

The scarlet runner bean

and were increasingly grown, but the farm-hands, on their cottage plots, resisted using them for a long time. Vegetables, as food, were despised, they were 'the food of poverty'. Perhaps the labourers knew instinctively that a food so easy to grow would lower their standard of living.

Towards the end of the seventeenth century a mysterious disease was noted by the Onways: the potato leaves became curled and crinkled and when the condition was bad the plants had a poor crop. In the eighteenth century this condition became more and more frequent. A number of theories were put forward to account for it, the favourite being that continued vegetative reproduction, that is planting tubers wrongly called 'seed potatoes' year after year, led to a loss of productivity. To maintain strength male vigour needed to be injected from time to time. The suggestion fitted nicely into the *machismo* of the age, and strangely enough growing potatoes from the true seed, the dark berries that formed after the flowers faded, gave plants free of curl. But they also produced plants different from the parent plant. The seed did not 'come true'. One never knew what sort of crop would arrive from true seed, nor would the tiny seedlings give yields as big as those obtained from the usual (tuber) potato seed. It was generally held that a good potato variety would not last more than fourteen years, that it had exhausted its vigour by then.

The reason for the success of the seedlings was not the supposed one. The curl condition, and several other similar conditions as well, such as mosaic, were due to virus diseases, transmitted from a diseased plant to a healthy one by greenflies. Such a virus infests all the tissues of a plant, except a few cells at the growing tips of a root or shoot, and the embryo in the seed. It cannot pass the layer protecting that embryo. Thus the true seed remains free of virus.

In the potato bed where aphids are numerous and where there are a few diseased plants, the virus will spread to many plants; the tubers become infected and so does the next crop if they are used as seed. But in wild and windy areas aphids do not thrive, hence the importance of Welsh, Irish and Scotch seed potatoes, grown in such aphid-free places. With no greenfly present—no vectors—most of the plants remain free of curl, even if a few of them are diseased. Moreover, a person who is growing potatoes for seed roots out and destroys any affected plant as soon as it is seen.

By the end of the eighteenth century the Munroyds, who had succeeded the Onways at Bartons End, and their neighbours, were getting poor crops of potatoes because of these diseases and found making new varieties from the true seed very difficult and time-consuming. Every now and then they would buy seed tubers of what was claimed to be a wonderful, new, fruitful and delicious cultivar, only to find it was as much diseased, or soon became so, as any of their own seed. Many people tried to unravel the mystery. In 1815—the year of Waterloo—a friend in Scotland, knowing Charlotte Munroyd's interest in the subject (she held the potato to be a useful food for the labouring classes), sent her a paper by a Mr Thomas Dickson of Edinburgh, on the disease.[23] This author was wrong as to the cause of the trouble—he held it to be due to the planting of over-ripened tubers—but he did touch on what eventually turned out to be the best way of overcoming the disease. Anxious to procure unripe tubers for seed he suggested among other things, that they be 'obtained from a part of the high country, where, from the climate and other circumstances, tubers are never over-ripened'.

Over-ripeness had nothing to do with the matter: the absence of aphids was the key to the cure. It is interesting to note how often an advantageous procedure is advocated for the wrong reason.

Of recent years, infestation of potatoes with these diseases has become very widespread. For instance, by the 1960s there was no virus-free seed of the popular variety King Edward. However, some scientists managed, with delicate instruments in a laboratory, to cut off a few cells from the tip of an infected shoot of this cultivar which, as mentioned above, would be virus-free but carry all the genetic make-up of the original King Edward plant. These cells were then transferred to a growth medium in a test tube, where they took root and grew into a tiny plant. In due course the plant was put out, grew big and produced tubers which were genetically pure, virus-free King Edwards. The variety had now been reconstituted. The seed was carefully multiplied for several years, and now King Edwards are as popular as ever and virus-free seed can once more be bought.

In the early eighteenth century the Munroyds accepted the potato as a valuable food, as did, slowly, the farm-hands. The competition to grow the biggest tuber for the local flower and vegetable show became intense. A variety named White Elephant could be made to produce vast potatoes—ones weighing $1\frac{1}{2}$ lbs. each were quite common. The cultivar was well named, because it was almost useless as a vegetable: it peeled badly and boiled away to a soggy pulp, but it provided a fine element of competition in village life.

Mark and Prudence had had a great affection for their orchard which, in the 1660s, was in prime condition. Most of the crab-apple trees had been grafted over to more promising cultivars, such as Pome Water, Juneating and Adam's Pearmain. Many new pears were also planted: there were Autumn Berg, Winter Bergamot and Cadillac among many others with but local names.

They believed, or perhaps only half believed, that they could benefit the trees by talking to them, a thing advocated for house plants to this very day. The idea was in the air. An acquaintance of theirs, called R. Austen, in 1676 even wrote a book about the subject.[7] Trees in general seemed to be so ancient that the question arose as to what language should be used, a point which does not seem to be considered by today's plant talkers. The Onways pondered on the use of Hebrew, Greek and Latin, which would have restricted their conversation very much, but they thought that trees were so old and clever that they could understand all languages and thus they might as well use English. There is no evidence that they ever got any answer from the trees, though the sighing and sawing of the branches and leaves in a summer breeze might have been considered a reply in some strange tongue. Nevertheless the Onways felt their talking had helped the trees grow so fine. Strangely enough, there is a scientific explanation for the fact that talking to plants might help them to grow, at least as far as house plants go. The human breath raises the CO_2 content of the atmosphere around them and thus increases carbon assimilation.

In fact, the idea was so much in the air that it caused Hannah Carpenter, an elderly maid of Prudence's, a certain amount of trouble. She, like her mistress, was fond of the orchard and joined in the talks with the trees. Hannah had a favourite cat, a black one, which was devoted to her; she had rescued it as a kitten and the creature would follow her around and ride on her shoulder. Hannah, in addition to talking to the trees, carried out a number of more practical measures, such as pruning, thinning the fruit, guarding it from theft and picking it.

One day in autumn she chased some boys who were stealing apples out of the orchard, and her cat at that moment jumped out of a tree on to her shoulder. The boys denounced her in the village as a witch, saying the cat was her familiar spirit and also that it was well known she conjured the trees with all sorts of strange words. Moreover, she grew all sorts of dangerous herbs, such as rue, foxglove, aconite and Devil's bit, from which she made simples and cast spells. As this last plant was said to cure plague and calm fevers, it was only its name that was sinister. It might have gone very badly with the poor woman had not her mistress roundly defended her, abusing the magistrate, the parson and the constable for stupidity and ignorance and saying that if an accusation of witchcraft were to be a defence for apple-stealing, there wouldn't be a tree, no, nor a sheep, safe in the whole county. And since when, she would like to know, was it wrong to make medicine from the Devil's bit, a plant that had cured many a fever and plague victim?[d]

Another factor in the success of the Onways' garden was through following the sound advice given in William Lawson's book *The New Orchard and Garden with the Country Housewifes Garden*, published originally in 1618, with many subsequent editions up to 1695.[e] The second part of the work particularly appealed to Prudence Onway as it was the first work addressed to women gardeners.[50]

She appreciated the skill of her gardener and saw to it that he had good wages, a comfortable cottage and a reasonable supply of flowers, fruit and vegetables from the garden he tended and loved so well and, as Lawson advised, allowed him good help to end his labours, which are endless, a formula for success as good today as then.

There was great pleasure to be derived from beholding and smelling an orchard and listening to the birds. The Onways, following Lawson, appreciated ' . . . a brood of nightingales, who with several notes and tunes with strong delightful voice out of a weak body, will bear you company night and day.'

In general, the kinds of plants and new varieties of existing species were first cultivated in the gardens of the big houses, from whence they moved down the social scale, as already indicated, but exceptions were the raspberry and gooseberry. To begin with these fruits were only grown by the cottagers, who found them in the woods. Mark Barton planted some improved raspberries obtained from the Netherlands in

Nightingale

1632, and some gooseberries from Lincolnshire the following year. Both fruits became very popular with the family, though pregnant women were cautioned against them, or any fresh fruit come to that. The gooseberries did so well and the fruit was so easily transported, that a half-acre plantation was made and the crop sent to market, becoming an appreciable source of income.

The period covered in this chapter saw, among the upper classes, the triumph of Baconism. Not only had Sir Francis introduced to them the concept of experiment, rather than acceptance of authority, in uncovering the secrets of nature, but they had also realised the satisfaction given to the soul by these activities. Of gardening, Francis Bacon wrote: 'It is the purest of pleasures . . . It is the greatest refreshment to the spirit of man: without which buildings and palaces are but handiworks.'

Similar sentiments were going down the social scale and the occupants of Bartons End, successful farmers, were among the first to adopt them. The English were prosperous. 'The Spaniard eats, the German drinks and the English exceed in both,' wrote Thomas Muffet in his book *Health's Improvement*, published in 1648.

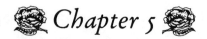 *Chapter 5*

The Garden of Joseph Munroyd, his son Isaac and his grandson Charles Munroyd, 1689–1764

I<small>N</small> 1689 Joseph Munroyd, then aged forty-nine, a London merchant though of farming stock, was planning to marry a youngish woman, Ruth Breadman, who was twenty-four years old and a Kentish farmer's daughter. He had accumulated his considerable wealth in the West Indies trade—the unholy trio of rum, sugar and slaves—and wanted to invest it in farming. It was his first marriage and he thought the peace and calm of a country life would suit him and his young wife very well. The newly-weds inspected a number of properties and became so enchanted with Bartons End that they offered James Onway a very good price for it. James, on the other hand, had heard such glowing accounts of the American 'plantations' and had seen so many strange plants from them, that he wanted to try his luck there. He accepted Mr Munroyd's offer, vacated Bartons End at Michaelmas 1689—the year after the accession of William and Mary to the throne—and went to America shortly afterwards. Joseph did not run the farm directly himself, but appointed a bailiff, the man who had been the Onways' foreman.

Three children were born to Joseph and Ruth, a boy Isaac, born in 1690, and two girls. Joseph died in 1705, aged sixty-five. It was the year of the success of Newcomen's steam engine, an occurrence that was eventually to change the world. Ruth Munroyd ran the farm with the assistance of the bailiff until Isaac married Anne Cobb in 1711, retired the bailiff who was now elderly, and took over the management of the farm himself.

Isaac and Anne also had three children, Charles, born in 1716, Ruth, and a girl who died shortly after birth. Isaac Munroyd worked very hard at both the farm and garden, leaving a flourishing property to his son Charles in 1752.

Socially ambitious, Charles repeatedly urged his father to raise the status of the family. Kentish farmers, he maintained, were as good as anybody. They were now property owners whose fortune had been started by Charles's grandfather, Joseph Munroyd.

Charles married comparatively late in life, in 1752 when he was thirty-six and just before his father's death. He led up to this marriage with the wealthy Susannah Aylesford, the only child of a rich sea-coal merchant, with a scheme for greatly improving the farm, house and garden. Perhaps he felt he would never get Susannah to accept a man living in a thatched house with old-fashioned beamed ceilings. He had to get the house into such a condition that, when his father died, it would be fit to receive so distinguished, that is to say rich, a person. Obviously the improvement of the farm would have to come first. Then the house could follow and Susannah—and he was as much in love with her charming self as with her money—would accept him. They would live in their tiny 'love-bower', the improved bailiff's house, until they inherited the farm, but the matter must be handled in the right way.

The main alteration to the farm that Charles pushed through, with his father's easy consent which surprised Charles a little, was the making of a new farmyard, with its attendant buildings, to the west of the stables, thus keeping the smells away from the house and, unknowingly, improving hygiene, because now the midden no longer contaminated the well. Another house was built for the new bailiff and a hop oast established for drying and storing what was, by this time, a most paying crop. Provision was also made for storing fruit and making both cider and beer. The old farmyard eventually became part of the garden.

Charles thought he had been fortunate in getting his father to set these changes in motion. Isaac, however, while he had no objection to Charles's desire for 'improved status', agreed to the changes because he thought they would be profitable. He particularly liked the idea of getting the smelly farmyard away from the house and the well. Insects and all sorts of creatures from the yard were constantly getting into the well, and surely that could not be good for one's health.

Charles's efforts to improve the house were also made easier because here his mother was his ally. The main changes carried out included the replacement of the thatch by tiles. It was an economy, said Charles, because tiles did not need constant renewal, as did thatch. The big barn was also tiled. Ceilings were added to most of the rooms, lath and plaster being used to cover the beams. A pump was installed in the kitchen, which made the water supply cleaner and more convenient. Another pump was put into the garden well, enabling plants to be watered more easily during the summer.

Charles's complicated, deep-laid scheme appeared to be successful, for he and Susannah were married in 1752 with great rejoicing; but in fact Susannah loved Charles well enough to have taken him unschemed, with unfashionable thatch, beams, farmyard smells and all.

During the Civil War and the Commonwealth (1642–60) people had had neither the desire nor the opportunity to add many new plants to their gardens, but by the time Joseph Munroyd purchased the property in 1689 the country had experienced nearly thirty years of garden development, which included the import of novelties from abroad and the continued selection of better, that is bigger or more strikingly-coloured varieties of native plants. An example of the last was the improved irises, obtained by searching for outstanding samples of the wild yellow flag. Such flags were one of the first additions the new owners made. Not many of these new plants had been used in the Bartons End garden before the change of ownership.

The imports James Onway saw on his neighbours' estates were quite a factor in making him decide to sell Bartons End and emigrate to the plantations. Persuaded by that killing solace, tobacco, and the new food, the potatoe (as it was then spelt), that America was the place for the modern man, he tended to regard any plant novelty, such as the auricula from Asia Minor, as American.

That left considerable leeway for the new owners of Bartons End to improve the garden. Among the introductions that Joseph Munroyd and his young wife, Ruth, first made were selected varieties of native plants—such as the flags—and the more decorative yet very poisonous aconites (*Aconitum hapellus*) came next. Witches were said to delight in it, and its presence in Hannah Carpenter's herb bed had been one of the items cited in the indictment against her as a witch.

Among the improved native plants Joseph Munroyd introduced were better periwinkles, which later got the strange name of 'the pleasures of memory',[a] and larkspur (*Delphinium ajacis*) whose scientific name is derived from marks at the base of the petals, like the letters A I A I. Other improved long-naturalised or native plants added around 1691 were hyacinths, cyclamens and the Jerusalem cross—the brilliant scarlet flower from East Russia, so called because it was in the shape of a Maltese cross.

The curiously-named melancholy gentleman appeared in the Barton flowerbeds in 1697, although it had first reached England from Austria some seventy years earlier. It had a number of other names too, such as dame's violet, night-smelling stock and Queen's gillyflower. The scientific name, *Hesperis tristis*, arose from the Greek for evening, the time of day when its flowers were most fragrant and, presumably, gentlemen most melancholy.

In 1698 two by then quite common trees, originally imported from Switzerland, were planted, the laburnums *L. anagyroides* and *L. vulgare*, the seeds of which were very poisonous. About the same time some newly improved natives, such as cornflowers, snapdragons, night-scented stock, field delphinium, feverfew, and St Patrick's cabbage or none-so-pretty (*Saxifraga spathularis*) were planted. The generic name of the none-so-pretty means 'stone-breaker'. Because it was often found growing in clefts in rocks, it was thought that saxifrage roots could split stone. Though roots of vigorous trees can in fact do so, the Saxifragaceae are not capable of it. As the plant was thought to subdue rocks, it was also supposed to be a cure for stones in the bladder.

Auriculas were already known in the garden, but around 1712 a craze for new and showy ones arose. It was not quite as intense as the tulip mania of the previous century but nevertheless had many of that malady's symptoms. In 1716 Isaac Munroyd paid £5, a considerable sum in those days, for an imported specimen, as part of the celebrations for the birth of his son Charles. It was something like today's variety, red dusty miller, and was much admired.

A few years later another burst of activity took place, leading to the appearance of both new native and imported varieties. In 1720 Anne

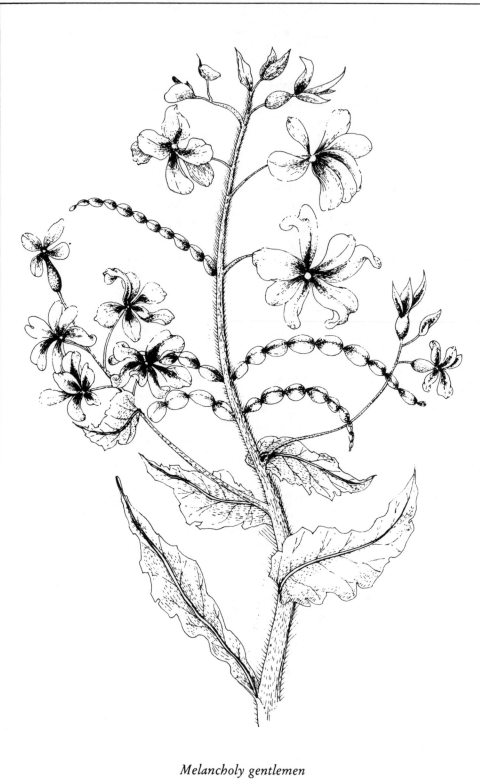

Melancholy gentlemen

planted a juniper tree. It throve and by 1725 Anne was using the berries in her stillroom to flavour her aqua vitae; she was in fact making a sort of gin, large quantities of which were imported from the Netherlands and called 'genever' from the Dutch word for juniper. Another use for juniper berries was as a substitute for pepper. That year also saw the introduction of a plant which became and has remained immensely popular—the sweet pea, which originated in Sicily.

By 1730 a number of by then comparatively common garden plants had been added to the beds. There was the evening primrose, which liked its new situation (it had come from America) and flourished like a weed. As the name suggests, the flowers open in the evening and attract night-flying insects. Others were Aaron's, or golden, rod from America, marguerites, and Virginia stock, misnamed as its origin is southern Europe.

By the time Charles Munroyd was twenty-five in 1741, he began to take a great interest in the garden. As part of his plan to raise the status of the family, he destroyed the old forget-me-not beds because he thought them dull and old-fashioned, and planted out garden chrysanthemums and shepherds club or mullein, which he mistook for a novelty, though it was but an improved form of a native plant.

Needless to say, Charles's activities in the garden were intensified when he started courting Susannah Aylesford. He tried to incorporate the latest plants and fashionable garden devices, such as a gentleman might be expected to have. For instance, he built a gazebo to the north of the house; it overlooked the public road and was quite the latest thing. He explained to his father that it was a place to which he might retire to enjoy peace and quiet and be 'safe from his friends'. Moreover, Susannah would have to visit such a fashionable novelty: he would then be alone with her, as there was hardly room for more than two people in it.

Charles's new plants were first of all magnolias. The comparatively small-flowered swamp magnolia or beaver tree was introduced in 1749, but after the marriage and the birth of their second and only surviving son, George Munroyd, in 1754, the elegant, big-flowered Carolina Bull Bay magnolia was planted by the sunny south-east wall of the house and is still there, though it is fast failing.

Two more novelties put in during the same period were both American plants, phlox or the wild sweet william, *P. maculata*, so named because of the spots on the stem, which was much admired, and the catalpa or Indian bean tree, which was not of much use in the win-Susannah campaign as it takes several years before it produces any of its attractive foxglove-like flowers.

Charles was rather attracted to what we might call 'stunts' in the garden, and he found one in the dittany, fraxinella or burning bush. It was not a particularly new introduction to England. It had come from Germany at the end of the sixteenth century, but it was an attractive novelty in Charles's eyes. He often used it to amaze visitors, for in dry, sunny weather the bush discharges a cloud of volatile, essential oil which can be ignited by putting a lighted taper to it. The resulting flash and puff of smoke do not seem to harm the plant, but always surprise spectators. During their courtship Charles would often invite Susannah to go with him to see the bush burn, which she would do, but accompanied at a discreet distance by a maid carrying a bucket of water, both as a safety measure and to comply with the proprieties. No dittany is found in the garden today: the trick was done once too often and the bush burnt down. However, the garden now has the American burning bushes, another genus, so called because they are covered with flame-coloured flowers.

Naturally, all these changes had to be paid for; not only did the plants have to be purchased but extra gardeners had to be employed. Isaac, who loved the garden, was content to let Charles have his head, provided the alterations and additions were not too outrageous. They had money to spare; the hops were a profitable crop and easy to transport, while any apples and pears not sold as fresh fruit could always be made into cider and perry. The cattle and farm crops were doing well. Nor did he object to the Aylesford money. He had the same idea as Lady Bracknell, of a much later era: she, it will be recalled, did not approve of mercenary marriages but never dreamed of allowing the fact that she had no fortune of her own to stand in the way of her marrying the rich Lord Bracknell.[73]

During his courtship of Susannah Charles began to wonder if his new garden was being built on the right lines and conceived the idea of visiting Lord Mountravers' grand country house, situated some twenty miles away, to see how the nobility arranged their gardens.

Today we tend to think the viewing of great houses and gardens by ordinary folk as a recent phenomenon, but this is by no means the case. If one was a gentleman, or looked like a gentleman, a tip to the housekeeper and head gardener would take one on a conducted tour, provided some entertainment was not taking place.

An introduction to the housekeeper obtained, Charles planned his visit with some excitement. He would ride over the previous day on his best horse and spend the night at a local inn, enabling him to be presentable the next day. He might, who knows, even meet his lordship or her ladyship in person and his well-built figure—adorned with his full-skirted green coat, a new gallooned tricorne on his head—make a favourable impression. They would then discuss gardening at length.

In the event, the plan was only partially successful. The garrulous housekeeper chatted interminably about the family when he was longing to get into the garden. The gardener on the other hand was taciturn and anxious to return to his work. Her ladyship was away. Lord Mountravers was in the gazebo and, as Charles approached, came out and extended a hand to the visitor, saying, 'I hope you like my little garden' (it covered some ten acres), adding almost before Charles could say anything, 'William, do not fail to show Mr Mumford [was this a deliberate insult?] the pine house and give him a pine if there is one ripe.' He then went back to the gazebo. Charles moved sadly away. However, the head gardener, seeing that his employer appeared to approve of the visitor, became more communicative. Charles saw and admired the orangery, the statues and fountains in the Italian garden, vistas, a lake, a maze, topiary, and wonderful bedding plants. He returned home that afternoon full of new ideas and feeling sure that he must have a 'stove', or greenhouse.

After his marriage Charles's introductions of new decorative plants slowed down. Caring for the novelties was task enough. After his father's death he developed his ambition to install a greenhouse and rather neglected the flower beds.

We now turn to some of the physical changes Charles made in the garden, and the alterations in the vegetable plots and orchard, which derived more from the gardeners employed than from the 'young master' himself.

Charles's first task was to improve the knottes; he removed the boards held up by sheep bones, which were starting to rot in any case, and replaced them by brick and stonework and hedges of box and lavender. He replaced the two sheepskulls on the top of the pillars at the entrance to the main garden by round balls of stone which, he had been informed, were just as effective in keeping lightning away, basically a true statement as neither was any use for that purpose.

Charles paid great attention to the hedges, of hawthorn, yew and privet, and joined in the fashionable practice of cutting them into shapes, such as neat cones, pyramids and animals. His father took the view that it was nonsense and absorbed an amount of labour far better used on the flowers, fruit, vegetables and lawns. Isaac regularly read *The Guardian* and had carefully kept the copy containing Alexander Pope's condemnation of topiary for showing to his clipping neighbours; later he dug it out to confound Charles when the latter took to the shears. Pope wrote:

> How contrary to this Simplicity is the modern Practice of Gardening; we seem to make it our Study to recede from Nature, not only in the various Tonsure of Greens into the most regular and formal Shapes, but even in the monstrous Attempts beyond the reach of the Art itself. We run into Sculpture, and are yet better pleased to have our Trees in the most awkward Figures of Men and Animals, than in the most regular of their own . . . And Ladies that please may have their own Effigies in Myrtle, or their Husbands in Hornbeam.
>
> 'The amiable simplicity of unadorned nature'—
> *The Garden of Alcinous* from Homer's *Odyssey*[60]

The satirist then added a catalogue of the trimmed trees available. One item was: '*Adam* and *Eve* in yew; *Adam* a little shattered by the fall of the Tree of Knowledge in the Great Storm. *Eve* and the Serpent very flourishing.'[b]

But Charles took no notice of such old-fashioned ideas and he himself and his gardeners produced a number of interesting shapes, his major triumph being a large S in yew, in honour of Susannah.

During the latter part of this period the Munroyds' gardeners made great progress in the vegetable section. Improved cultivars of cabbage, such as the Battersea and Sugar-Loaf varieties, were grown. They were known as Michaelmas cabbages, as they were ready for use then and

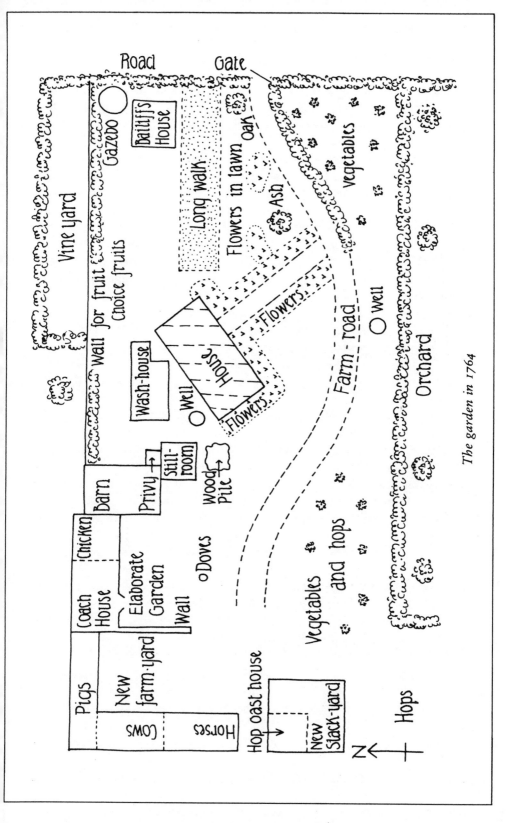

The garden in 1764

could be cut all through the winter. The Russian cabbage was falling out of favour and was being replaced by the rather flavourless Savoy, though that too would stand through the winter. Cauliflowers were much improved and there were two kinds of turnips, or rapes, for table use, the white and the purple-rooted. Various kinds of broccoli, known as the flat, red, white and long-sided, were also introduced. The purchase of seeds for the garden was comparatively rare: most gardeners saved their own. With Brassicas this meant that there was a great deal of cross-pollination among these crops and consequently a continual creation of new varieties, not necessarily showing any improvement over the old ones. As a result, for instance, of all this inter-pollination, the Munroyds' Battersea cabbage might be very unlike the original variety from that salubrious suburb.

In gardening books, such as James Wheeler's *The Botanist's and Gardener's New Dictionary*, 1763, which the Munroyds read, the author, in writing of asparagus, says the plants should be grown from seed 'and as much of the success depends on the goodness of the seed it is much better to save it than buy it at the shops'.[72] This is the direct opposite of today's advice.

The Munroyds had obtained some better asparagus crowns from their neighbour at Bartons Farm. They had a productive bed of this delicious lily from the 1690s onwards and extended and renewed the plot from their own seed. As is well known, it takes three or four years to establish an asparagus bed from seed, and during the early years of theirs the Munroyds planted onions, lettuce and French beans as catch crops between the rows of young asparagus. In the summer of 1696 Joseph sharpened a long thin knife and in the presence of Ruth, his wife, and the gardener, plunged the blade into the earth and cut the first stems. A feast was held that night and the gardener had his share.

Brassica crops, particularly the turnips, were sometimes badly attacked by the 'fly' or turnip leaf beetle and the Munroyds learnt to sow turnips between rows of spinach, as they found the turnips often escaped damage by those insects when so grown.

By 1750 the garden regularly bore a crop of potatoes; it even grew named varieties which kept constant, as the reproduction was vegetative, by tubers. Among the earlies were Smooth Yellows, Red Champions and Kidneys. Late, what we would now call maincrop potatoes were the coarse but heavy cropping Ox-noble and the Old Winter Red which, the Munroyds said, was never known to curl; but they were just lucky. In reality it was as susceptible to the virus as any other cultivar.

Other novelties were vegetable marrows and liquorice. This last was considered a valuable addition to the list of medicinal plants: it came from Italy in the form of rooted slips from the sides of stools. Two rows were planted in February 1723, but as no crop of roots could be expected for two or three years the land in the first year was planted with onions. In due course the black sticky resin was extracted from the liquorice roots by boiling them in water and it was used as a remedy for coughs. An additional important medicinal use for liquorice was for disguising the flavour and nature of many nasty items in the pharmacopoeia. The Munroyds even added a little of it to batches of beer that had not done well; it masked the off-taste.

For many years rhubarb had been a much esteemed, imported drug and a very expensive one: used as a laxative it sold at more than twice the price of opium and came from China via Russia.[c] The Munroyds tried to grow it, but without success, as they had the 'English rhubarb' (*Rheum rhaponticum*) and not *R. palmatum*, the Chinese kind, which the doctors required. The English rhubarb was the kind with edible stalks and poisonous leaves, as was discovered when the family became ill after using the leaves as a spinach substitute. They subsequently regarded the whole plant with suspicion.

The Munroyds continued to take an interest in fruit and planted several new kinds of apples, including the Ribstone Park pippin—a pippin was a fruit with flecks, or pips, on the skin—the Moil, Must and Golden pippin. The Ribstone pippin is found to this day. Similar improvements were made with the pears and it was soon seen that they throve better, and gave bigger crops, when grafted on to quince seedlings.

Isaac Munroyd was fond of black currants, or squinancy berries, and extended the area given to them, though Charles wanted to get rid of such a strong-smelling, unfashionable fruit. They were called currants because the fruit was like the dried, small, black grapes coming from Corinth. Anne found black currant syrup made a useful winter drink and helped relieve colds and winter sore throats, due, no doubt, to the

Vitamin C it contained. There were suspicions that she used black currants to adulterate coffee and thus lessen the expense of this fashionable drink that Charles called for so often. Tea was also an expensive luxury and dried black currant leaves were added to it.

All this time the strawberry beds were much the same as they had long been and consisted of strains of the wild strawberry, selected for larger size and taken from the woods. They were nothing like the modern strawberry, which arrived on the scene much later.

A great innovation had followed upon James Onway's reading of John Rose's book, *The English Vineyard Vindicated* (1666).[d62] In 1674, when he was twenty-two years old, he decided to plant a vineyard on a gently sloping piece of ground to the north of the house. It was successful and became one of the attractions that made Joseph Munroyd buy the property in 1689. The cider press also crushed the grapes and at times apples made up for any deficiency of grapes. James grew both black and white grapes and made the discovery that if black grapes were put straight into the press after picking the must from them ran white.[e]

For a long time Charles had wanted to add a 'stove' to the garden, that is a greenhouse, a thing becoming very fashionable in the early eighteenth century, but Isaac would not agree and Charles was only able to build his greenhouse in 1758, some years after his father's death. It was a lean-to construction on the south-west facing wall of the house and Charles introduced a novelty, three sky-lights in the roof. At that time 'stoves' were tall, glass-fronted structures with a solid roof and were at first mostly used to harbour lemon and orange trees during the winter.

The sky-lights had been installed because Charles had read John Evelyn's remark that 'light is half their [the plants] nourishment',[30] which was quite correct. At the same time he realised the house could get too hot and he arranged for the tops of every other light to open and for blinds of cane strips to be fitted inside the glass on the sunny side. The blinds were fastened at the top and rolled up from the bottom, being held and worked by a cord. The addition of the lights meant that a considerably bigger range of plants could be grown and seedlings could be brought forward in early spring for planting out in the garden as soon as the frosts were over. Moreover, Charles had the lights hinged so that they could be opened for ventilation and the prevention of overheating.

One of the difficulties of successfully using a stove was to know what the temperature was: it was comparatively easy to estimate its being too hot by just staying in the greenhouse a moment, but it was very difficult to know when it was too cold for most of the greenhouse plants. A rough test, used by Charles and Susannah at first, was to leave a saucer of water on one of the benches and watch for the moment when it started to freeze, but there were various objections to that. For instance, one might have to watch the saucer for a long time, say all night, and then again a lot of delicate 'stove' plants, when the temperature was falling, would be injured long before the freezing point of water was reached. Charles took a great interest in the glasshouse and eventually secured a scientific instrument for the purpose of controlling his greenhouse atmosphere, namely a thermometer. The first one he had contained strong brandy dyed with cochineal in the bulb but it was soon replaced with Dr Fahrenheit's instrument from the Netherlands, in which mercury was used. Both kinds of instruments are found to this day.

At first the greenhouse was heated in the winter with pans of burning charcoal. The trouble with charcoal is that not all of it burns, or rather, some of it burns only partially, resulting in the production of some poisonous monoxide (CO) instead of carbon dioxide (CO_2), which latter gas the plants like. Charles and Susannah gave up the use of charcoal after they had been made ill by the fumes, and used large candles instead. These did not give off much heat and finally, around 1760, they installed a coal- and wood-burning stove with a flue running along beneath the staging on the front of the house to the chimney at the far end. Doors were provided at both ends to enable the flue to be swept.

Charles and Susannah's enthusiasm for the stove led them into a number of errors at first, until they realised that not all 'stove plants' wanted the same conditions of temperature, light and humidity. On the back wall of the greenhouse they put a peach, an orange (the bitter orange, *Citrus aurantium*), a lemon and a coffee tree. Charles thought it would be interesting to grow his own coffee, little realising that one tree would not keep him supplied for more than a week or two, as even when fully grown it would not have produced more than one pound of coffee in a year, if as much, and Charles drank at least 12 lbs.

The conditions for both the peach and the coffee tree were good and they throve, but the next ambitious addition was a failure, a pawpaw tree, a new and fashionable import from the West Indies. There were two reasons for the lack of success; firstly, the pawpaw is dioecious—a word meaning 'two homes', male flowers being found on one kind of tree and female ones on another—and Bartons End had received a male plant. Male and female plants are indistinguishable until they flower, usually when they are some three years old, and even had they received a female one, no fruit would have resulted without pollination from a male. Secondly, the greenhouse was not kept warm enough in winter. The pawpaw died and was eventually replaced with a vine.

The failure of the pawpaw led Charles to seek some easier novelties with which to startle young George, his son, and the neighbours, and he lighted on the sensitive plant *Mimosa pudica*, which he grew in a number of pots. Charles, George and his friends got a great deal of amusement out of watching the leaflets fold together when touched: they maintained it was half plant and half animal. In warm, wet weather the leaflets not only folded but the stems drooped and even the pink balls of fluffy flowers somehow added to the general sadness. After such a display George Munroyd, at about seven years old, would often spend up to an hour watching the plant resume its normal bearing.

The action is indeed curious and one speculates as to the survival value of the output of so much energy. *Mimosa pudica* is not a rare plant; it is a troublesome weed in some tropical areas.Presumably the leaf-folding makes it less conspicuous to animals, mostly insects, that might eat it. It would also expose a lesser area to strong winds which, by shaking the plants, cause the leaves to fold and thus reduce water loss.

Charles's success with his half-animal, half-plant led him to look for similar curiosities, such as the insect-consuming sundews, native plants found in boggy land and hardly, in reality, needing to be raised in a greenhouse. He maintained that the sundews kept the stove free of insects because, if kept moist and when growing well, they consumed a lot of them. The sundews obtained most of their nitrogen by capturing and digesting insects. It is a curious life-form and a remarkable piece of development in the evolutionary struggle for survival. Insects are very abundant and are the food of vast numbers of animals. Many birds, for instance, rely on them as food for their young: that plants also should partake of this bounty is only just.

The sundew is found in bogs where plant food, particularly nitrogen, is usually lacking. Successive evolutionary developments of some ancestral plant led its successors to seek a non-soil source of this chemical. The sundew has sticky leaves bearing a number of stout hairs, or spines, all round their edges. At the tip of each spine is a red globule covered with a sticky, water-white, glue-like substance, containing nectar and insect attractant, particularly those compounds appealing to flies and ants. Hungry insects, prospecting for food, start to feed on the glue and get caught; very few, once caught, are able to escape, and an insect's struggles only further entangle it with neighbouring globules and hairs. The struggles exhaust a captured creature and soon the other leaf hairs bend over the insect and the leaf folds over as well. Before long the prey is dead. Even if an insect does escape from the first contact, the glue is so attractive that it usually comes back for another attempt and, being now a little weaker, is likely to get caught the second time. When the insect is dead the leaf secretes an enzyme which dissolves the soft parts and enables the leaf to absorb the badly-needed nitrogenous food and also potash and phosphate, which may take several days. Then the spines fold back and the leaf opens flat again, revealing the sucked-dry remains of the insect, which eventually fall away; more glue oozes over the globules and the trap is ready for its next victim.

A strange thing is that if a non-digestible object, such as a tiny pebble, falls on to a leaf, the spines may bend over it, but they soon realise their mistake and fold back to the trap-set position. That is very like animal behaviour, and one can see how it fascinated Charles Munroyd, leading him to postulate the existence of enormous, tropical, man-eating plants in distant lands.

Spectacular as these events were, they did not much affect insect numbers in the greenhouse, because the troublesome insect pests, such as aphids, have such great reproductive powers. Killing a hundred or so of greenfly left enough live ones around for the aphid population to build up again rapidly.

Charles even collected the common wild arum, or cuckoo-pint, wake-robin, wild william, crow flower, meadow lichynie or lords and ladies, to give it some of its names, because this plant also seemed to attract insects—as well as cognomens. It is a successful plant and found everywhere, which is perhaps why it has so many names. Charles, interested in natural history, had by the time the stove was built

Cuckoo-pint with trap for flies

accepted the existence of sex in plants and knew that, in most flowers, unless the 'farina' from the male flowers, or the male parts (the anthers) of bisexual (monoecious) flowers, reached the female parts (the pistils), no viable seed would be produced.

In the lords and ladies, as Charles noticed at that time, the brownish column, rising from the green spathe, produces a cluster of anthers at its base, not at the top as is more usual in flowers: just above the anthers the cluster is protected by a ring of downward pointing hairs. Below the anthers is a ring of pistils, the upper ones bearing a circle of stiff hairs.

The flower produces a strong smell of rotting meat, noticeable even to the human nose. The smell attracts certain flies and midges that habitually lay eggs in carrion. The insects move down the spathe, through the ring of hairs and are then trapped in the space around the anthers, as they can neither go upwards against the ring of downward-pointing hairs, nor descend because of the circle of bristles protecting the pistils. In that space the insects get covered with pollen, but many of them die in the trap. This gave Charles, who had carefully cut open a number of plants and studied them, the idea that the species was an insect-eater, like the sundew. Though it does not despise the bonus of a little high-protein food, the main object of the trapping of the midges is cross-pollination. After a while the rings of hairs and bristles shrivel and allow those insects still alive, and now well dusted with pollen, access to the pistils below and an escape to the open air, carrying pollen to the pistils of other lords and ladies plants. The device was usually successful, for the lords and ladies, with its band of ripe red berries was, and still is, a common sight. It did not take to the greenhouse life very well, but Charles was able to germinate a small number of the red seeds so as to have a few pots of the lords and ladies to put next to his display of sundews.

Those curiosity plants were really Charles's toys: the great success of the stove, however, was the bed of perpetual carnations or gillyflowers which Susannah delighted in, not least because of their delicious perfume which masked the disgusting smell of Charles's lords and ladies. Why have them in the stove when they could be seen in almost any hedge bottom?

In a short while Charles became interested in gillyflowers and soon was as much immersed in the subject as he had formerly been in his half-plant, half-animal creatures. By gillyflowers he meant *Dianthus* spp., the carnations, pinks, sops-in-wine, and cloves, not the wallflowers, white-stocks or soap-wort which were also called gillyflowers. He was rapidly becoming a 'florist'.

Various *Dianthus* species had been grown in the garden for some time but in 1762 Charles acquired some roots of an improved cultivar of the perpetual flowering carnation (*D. caryophillus*), and plunged deeply into the subject, then becoming fashionable. He found that they only throve in the greenhouse and that there were two main kinds, Bursters, or Broken flowers (with a split calyx) and Whole Blowers, with a whole calyx. The second class was divided again according to the design and colouring into Flakes, Flames, Bizarres, Piquettes and Painted Ladies. A carnation mania began to grip the countryside and Charles organised carnation shows, at which he often won prizes, not so much, possibly, because of the excellence of his exhibits but on account of his social position. One of Charles's wins was secured by his obtaining the services of Mr Kit Nun, a barber of Enfield and a famous 'carnation dresser', to prepare his exhibits. He regarded it as money well spent. Mr Nun's skill lay in selecting blooms and 'dressing' them, that is, pulling out disfiguring petals, nicely balancing the flowers and tying a thread round the calyx to prevent its splitting, a thing now done with an elastic band at our florists.

The carnations were a great success and were grown in a special bed at the end of the greenhouse. A number of other plants were also grown in pots on the benches; they included the amaranthus, Joseph's coat or flower-gentle, a native of India and grown for its decorative foliage; cactus or torch thistle, which did not enjoy the damp atmosphere and was usually taken into the house, for its strange growth appealed to Charles; mountain cineraria, which could be induced to flower in winter; dumb cane, a novelty from America; fustick or Venetian sumach, a bush which soon became too big for the greenhouse; gloriosa or superb lily, a climbing plant that needed considerable support; gloxinia, and goldilocks.

Charles resisted the temptation to grow pineapples, then very fashionable in the noble houses, because it would have meant taking out the carnations to make room for them. Trying to grow too much is one of the things that happens to this day among tyro greenhouse owners. Charles already had too many species on his back wall and soon had to remove some. The orange and coffee trees had to go. Two additional innovations he made to the greenhouse were a tank in the floor of the building to hold water and a pipe running from the tank to the kitchen sink, where it had a swivel joint ending in a funnel. The funnel could be moved under the pump spout and the greenhouse tank replenished from time to time, thus saving much labour in water carrying. The advantages of a tank were that the water gradually acquired the house temperature, so that when the plants were watered they got no shock; also the open-topped tank helped to keep the atmosphere moist.

During this period the trees at Bartons End were not neglected. In the small copse the native oaks, chestnuts, ashes and elms were tended, the very old ones felled and new seedlings encouraged. In 1764 Charles brought in the supposed tree-of-heaven (*Ailanthus altissima*). Its origin was China and it was so called because the branches reached towards heaven. But the European specimens are wrongly named, for the true Chinese tree-of-heaven is *A. moluccana*; nevertheless, the branches of Charles's trees grew nicely upwards, as if trying to emulate their cousin *altissima*. It is dioecious and fortunately Charles obtained both male and female plants, so the red-gold twisty seeds scattered nicely in the wind. Today the tree is popular in town because it resists damage from the polluted air.

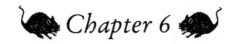

Chapter 6

The Garden of George Munroyd, Charlotte Munroyd and John and William Hackshaw, 1764–1852

Mammals

WHEN CHARLES Munroyd died in 1764, aged forty-eight, his widow, Susannah, was determined she would leave a magnificent garden for the coming of age of their son George, which would be in 1775. She toyed with the idea of sweeping the whole existing garden away and of getting a top man to design a new, modern, 'natural' garden for her. But several things discouraged her. 'Capability' Brown showed no interest in her approaches, for one thing; he had bigger fish to fry than Kentish farmers, rich though they might be. Then she was not the only trustee of the estate: she knew she would never get the family lawyers to agree to such a drastic change. Next, there were only eleven years to go to George's majority, hardly time enough to make the kind of garden she had in mind, and if she did make it, then the garden would demand a new house. Finally, it would be expensive: she was only thirty-five and might marry again. It would be as well to have some money in hand. No, she thought, she would improve the present place. She would have a *ferme ornée*, as Phillip Southcote had suggested in 1554: '35 acres adorned to the highest degree, planting trees and shrubs and flower borders . . . an ornamental walk all within a farm.'

One of the first things she did was to root out some of Charles's toys, such as the lords and ladies she had always detested. Next she built a new 'stove' and raised the fashionable pineapples. She abolished excessive displays of topiary, except the large S in yew that had formed such a feature of Charles's courtship; the yew, privet and hawthorn hedges were neatly trimmed to be straight sided, though a little narrower at the top than the bottom, thus assuring gaps did not occur. A third greenhouse, to the very latest design, appeared a little later and grew flowers and decorative foliage the year round.

Susannah cleared a bit more of the copse and built a south-facing wall, still there, on which to grow fruit. She had several of the latest kinds, such as the orange apricot, the scarlet Newington nectarine, three plums—White Mogull, Virginall and Queen Mother—and the Spanish Musk pear. Whether her 'Spanish Musk' had anything to do with Spain is difficult to say; it was, nevertheless, very good to eat. The creation of new pears and of pear names was enormous at that time and there was little consistency. Even Gerard had mentioned how numerous pears were in his day and of what varying quality. He commented:

> . . . myself knowe some one curious, who hath in one peece of ground, at the point of three score sundrie sorts of pears, and those exceeding good; not doubting but, if his minde had been to seek after multitudes, he might have gotten togither the like number of worse kindes.

Susannah was fortunate with the pears because her gardener grafted them onto quince stocks, very suitable for wall fruit, and planted several different kinds near to each other, which ensured pollination.

Susannah was particularly fond of peaches; she maintained that the open air ones were far better than those forced in the stove and she was not afraid of eating delicious, fresh, raw peaches, in spite of what the doctors said. She had a collection of six different varieties, two with names, Rosanne and Yellow Alberge, and four good trees raised from seedlings. She was determined to create some new, splendid varieties by sowing peach-stones, and insisted on doing this in a provocative manner. Several of the best fruits, marked with a bit of white cord, were left untouched on the tree. They ripened and were a temptation to pick, but woe betide anyone who did so; even young George dared not go near them. There they stayed until they fell to the ground from their own weight. The stones were then fully ripe and were sown at once in a bed of light, rich earth. They were protected during the winter with a straw covering and sent up strong seedlings in the spring. Making new

Keen's strawberry seedling

trees from stones was a long and tedious task, for it took from three to five years before a stone produced a fruit and that fruit, when at last it came, might be no better, or even worse, than its parent. However, starting with a fully ripe seed did shorten the period between sowing and fruiting. By the end of the century Susannah had produced a delicious, large and hardy fruit, which she named Charlotte, after her fourteen-year-old grandchild.

Another triumph during this period, although Susannah did not live to see it, was the new strawberry, a fruit that became of great commercial importance in Kent. Woodland, native strawberries were pleasant enough, but were very small and time-consuming to pick. The French 'hautbois' had more flavour but was hardly bigger. America was a great source of new plants, but the American strawberry was a disappointment. Although better flavoured it was the same size as the European varieties. In the early eighteenth century a French scientist, M. Frézier—with such a name, obviously a man born to study strawberries—brought back a large, white-fruited strawberry from South America. It was much cultivated around Brest. By 1762 a hybrid with the North American plant, the pine or ananas strawberry, was being grown at Cherbourg. But the real modern strawberry only burst on the world in 1821 when Michael Keen, a nurseryman of Isleworth, put out a number of hybrids culminating in the famous 'Keen's seedling'. It had 'enormous' ($1\frac{5}{8}$ in. diameter) fruits and a fine flavour. Everyone planted it, and everyone propagated it too.

In those days an innovator might not reap much reward from years of study and effort, for his new variety, once acquired by a rival nurseryman or any gardener, could be propagated by one and all; the innovator got nothing from such production. Today, in theory at any rate, an innovator can claim a royalty on the sale by others of a novelty. One of the reasons for the continual production of new cultivars was to secure the profits of the first year or two of success. After that everyone would be offering them.

Novel plants were profitable, and as the science and practice of botany spread, plant explorers proliferated and a quite simple invention helped their activity. It was the Ward Case.[71] Nathaniel B. Ward was a doctor: he discovered that many plants would grow well in a closed case; they took in enough CO_2 during the day and put out enough oxygen at night to make satisfactory growth, and required no outside air. The water they started with condensed and was sufficient. This enabled plants in such cases to be brought from abroad much more successfully than if carried in the open as deck cargo exposed to wind and salt spray. Today's fashionable sealed carboy growing strange plants, apparently for ever, is but a Ward Case.

When Susannah pushed back the copse and built the fruit wall, running eastwards from the dower house, she decided to plant rhododendrons in the first few yards of the copse. It was an acid patch and had plenty of peaty organic matter in the soil. The first plants put in were the Spanish rhododendron, a species recently introduced from Lusitania and Armenia (the ancient Pontus), having funnel-shaped, purple flowers. It throve in the Bartons End copse and started to squeeze out the hazels and cob nuts. The rhododendrons appealed to Susannah and her daughter-in-law Sophia and they added new species from time to time, such as a white *ponticum*, the yellow Siberian, the Daurian (*R. dauricum*) and a burst of species in the early nineteenth century from the Himalayas, *R. anthopogon*, *arboreum* and *campanulatum*. Bartons End became quite famous for its rhododendrons.

When Charles's son George succeeded him, at first under the guardianship of his mother, he was only ten years old. George cultivated his garden from an early age until his death in 1808; his heir was his wife Sophia. She died a year later and left the property to their only child, Charlotte.

Charlotte Munroyd loved the garden and did much to 'return it to nature' as was the late-Georgian fashion. She was sickly, however, and died unmarried, even though she was beautiful and an heiress with steel shares, at the age of thirty-one in 1817, leaving no will. The property, after its value had been considerably reduced by the complicated legal niceties involved, was sold so that it could be distributed, pro rata, to the heirs, descendants of Isaac Munroyd's daughter and a daughter of Charles Munroyd. The purchaser of the property was a Major Hack-shaw, a 'veteran' of the Napoleonic wars. The major had six children; he died in 1833 and the property descended to his son William. William married Emily Hempstead in 1819 and by her had two children, Alfred and David. William, who had become reasonably wealthy, died in 1852 and left the property to his son Alfred, then aged thirty. Alfred had become an aesthete. He disliked the idea of farming, industry and the professions, in fact work of any kind, and his father's money enabled him to live a dilettante life in Venice. To get rid of the responsibility, Alfred let the farm in 1853 to a tenant, Emmanuel Burrows. He did not sell it because his nephew, Oscar Hackshaw, son of his brother David, adored the place. He proposed to leave the property to young Oscar unless he himself married and had children of his own, which seemed to him to be unlikely. Marriage did not attract him. Venice did. The possibility of being both married *and* resident in Venice somehow did not occur to him.

During William Hackshaw's residence at Bartons End roses received considerable attention and the Bartons End garden acquired a selection of new cultivars from Rivers, the nurseryman at Sawbridgeworth, Hertfordshire. That firm's 1836 catalogue listed 524 rose cultivars, at prices from 1s to 3s for bushes and up to 10s 6d for standards. The great boost to rose growing had started in 1792, when George III sent Lord Macartney to China with valuable presents for the Emperor. The embassy had hoped to establish important trading posts, but at that time the Chinese regarded the rest of the world as barbarians subservient to the Empire, and the Emperor accepted the presents as long overdue tribute. The King was congratulated on running his province well and all Lord Macartney received was the Chinese rose (*Rosa chinensis* also called *R. indica*). The expedition seemed to be a total failure, but the China rose made all the difference to rose cultivation. Quite unconsciously the ambassador had done well for his country. *Chinensis* led to the tea and perpetual flowering roses and an enormous boost to the nurseryman's trade. Among the roses Sophia and Charlotte had were a new moss rose Rouge de Luxembourg, the huge Provence, or cabbage rose, a patriotic George IV hybrid China rose, a number of damask roses (which made good stocks for grafting), six sorts of China roses and some dwarf Chinas, a L'Isle de Bourbon obtained from France and hardly known in England, and Princesse Hélène, a hybrid perpetual, the first of a race of roses to triumph throughout the world.

An important garden discovery during this period concerned the sensitivity of plants to cold. The great frost of the winter of 1837–38 showed that many plants thought to be sensitive to it were not. To his

The dog rose and China rose

great surprise William Hackshaw found that the big-flowered magnolia survived, as did a fine, recently introduced *Leptosporium*, a strawberry tree (*Arbutus uredo*) and many other 'delicate' plants. Gardeners' ideas on plant tenderness underwent considerable change after that winter.

America had produced the potato, in everybody's garden by the time William Hackshaw inherited the place. However, William was undecided about the tomato, another arrival from America. He was somewhat put off by its names, such as love-apple, stinking golden apple and wolf's peach (*Lycopersicum*). One day in 1842 he heard his wife, Emily, enquiring of a packman if he had any love-apple seed. 'No, ma'am, I have none of that nasty, smelly stuff; you have nothing to do with them, ma'am. 'Tis only the lords and ladies and such like that go in for such stuff and they call them tomaties.' Mr Hackshaw was so annoyed by the down-grading of his social status that he immediately decided to grow them.

The family liked the tomatoes well enough. The first crop was planted quite near the house, but Emily maintained that their smell was so strong that they must never again be planted adjacent to a window.

So far the story of the garden at Bartons End has dealt mostly with the plant life there. But many animals lived in it as well, and whilst the mole and the earthworm have been described, it is time to consider the arrival, rise and fall of some others.

Like most animals in the garden, the mammals can be divided into residents and visitors. However, over the long period of the garden's existence the length of mammalian residence varied considerably. Moles, for example, were there from the start to the present day. Field mice, domestic mice and voles came and went according to circumstances, but were present for most of the garden's history. Stoats and weasels, preying on the mice and voles, resided in the garden from time to time, particularly when the rodent population was high. The humans deliberately placed certain animals in the garden. Little Prudence Onway, who was born in 1654, successfully tamed a bat and had hedgehogs, hediocs or urchins as pets for a few years from 1661 onwards. Three centuries later the Frazer children also kept hedgehogs as pets.

The long-tailed field mouse was often very abundant at Bartons End, but it did not reach plague proportions as once did the domestic mouse. The long-tailed field mouse is a fairly omnivorous feeder and thus it is attracted to gardens such as Bartons End with plenty of cover. It also finds it can get quite a lot of food from household rubbish, particularly today. These mice tend to work at night and in daylight retire to their nests. The nest is a chamber of about six inches in diameter, half filled with shredded grass, at the end of a tunnel several feet long.

Even though field mice attack and eat bumblebee comb and grubs, old mouse burrows are much used as nest sites by bumblebees, a fact which gave Charles Darwin an opportunity to illustrate in a homely way the interdependence of life. A good crop of clover seed, he maintained, depended to quite an extent on the number of maiden ladies living in the area. The clover could only be pollinated by certain bumblebees. The bees would be numerous if there were plenty of nest sites, due to the presence of many field mice making and abandoning burrows. But cats prey on and destroy mice. Many maiden ladies kept cats and the cats destroyed the mice, resulting in fewer sites for the bees' nests, leading to fewer bees, less clover pollination and a smaller yield of seed.[a]

The mouse's nest chamber usually has a side 'room' which they fill with seeds, berries and roots as food for the winter. They breed from March to October and their life span is twelve months or a little less. They fall victim to many predators—stoats, the furrier's ermine, weasels, foxes, kestrels and sparrow hawks, adders and even large toads.

Over the years the field mice only occasionally damaged the farm crops when they issued from their garden refuge and ate away the young corn. They often caused considerable loss to the garden crops, however, particularly to the seed beds of peas, beans, sweet peas and flower bulbs. The seed was mixed with all sorts of nauseous substances, such as tar and, later, paraffin oil, believed to deter the mice.

The short-tailed vole, sometimes called the short-tailed field mouse, was also found in the garden and there are still some in the copse today. It likes undisturbed grassland, so the vole population would grow in the copse for a few years after the periodical cutting of the trees, and in the garden at times when it was neglected and grass sprang up everywhere.

This vole's main food is the hard stems and leaves of grasses. The hardness is important to rodents because their teeth are growing all the time and have constantly to be worn away. If the incisor teeth get too long the animal cannot feed and dies of starvation. The same thing happens to rabbits and hares: they have two pairs of incisor teeth, distinguishing them from the rodents, which have one pair. The second pair is immediately behind the first and the teeth are smaller. The dentine, forming the inner bulk of the teeth, is softer than the enamel and so wears away more quickly, leaving a sharp cutting edge of enamel. The teeth grow continuously, in the same way as our finger nails. If one tooth is broken by some mischance the opposite one in the opposing jaw does not get worn away. It continues to grow, often curling back on itself, preventing the animal from feeding and leading to starvation and death.

The vole makes shallow burrows in the soil and also has surface runs below a mat of grass. Voles are not very adventurous and like to stay near their homes. They breed from February to September, and animals born early in the year may start breeding in the autumn. The life-span is about a year, and the population seems to rise and fall on a cycle of four or five years from, say, less than fifty per acre to more than five hundred,[52] but this last figure is as nothing compared to the numbers found during a vole or mouse plague.

Plagues of voles happen at times for no very clear reason, mostly in Scotland and wild areas with plenty of rough grassland, but plagues of domestic mice were known in the Bartons End garden, for races of the house mouse live in a number of different habitats. Mice, and John and Mary Barton, were the first mammals to live in the house. In a country area, such as Bartons End, there were, and are, three communities of the house mouse. They are the domestic and urban commensal (a commensal being a creature sharing the same food and habitat as another animal), now only rarely found in the house; secondly, the rural community, found in farms and gardens, now the most numerous kind; and thirdly, the feral community, found in fields and hedges. Note that they are all the same species, physiologically exactly the same: there is thus something in the folklore concept of the town and country mouse.

These different communities tend to keep separate. They do not precisely have territories, as do many animals, but each has a 'home range', that is 'an intimately known area in which it fulfils its life cycle and which it may share with a number of its species'.[68]

The house mouse is a very adaptable or 'plastic' animal and can live in diverse and contrasting habitats, such as cold stores and grain warehouses. A mouse can spend its whole life (a year to eighteen months) inside a sack of grain, never leaving it. Until fairly recently a favourite habitat for the rural community was the corn stack, a very comfortable abode which they seldom had to leave until the final catastrophe. Water was obtained from rain and dew on the thatch and the food supply was almost endless.

In a corn rick the mouse population can be from 50 to 2,000 mice and at the greater figure the mice eat fourteen pounds of grain a day. Mice nibble the corn, producing a lot of tail, that is damaged grain. The population doubles every two months and not only eats a lot of grain but fouls almost as much as it eats. At threshing time mice in hundreds poured out of the stacks into the Bartons End garden and countryside.

The arrival of the combine harvester did more to reduce the number of mice than any amount of poisoning or hunting by dogs and cats. Corn stacks are no longer built. Today the grain, threshed as it is reaped, is then taken to mouse-proof driers and stores. But the house mouse has by no means lost the struggle for existence. The corn stack may have gone, but the compost heap and rubbish bin replace it as a source of food, as do titbits from *al fresco* meals and picnics. The little rodents often find tasty bits in kitchen rubbish put into compost, while the main road lay-by is now the mouse's friend.

Mice are fast breeders. A female can become pregnant again one day after giving birth and, in a corn rick, the females can have ten litters a year: the theoretical maximum per year is thirteen to fourteen. Let us just see what this means if all the mice survive. Starting with the lowest figure in our rick, 50, it means we have 25 females. Let us suppose they have 4 mice per litter, two males and two females and 8 litters per season. In the first litter the 25 females produce 50 females and 50 males, 100 mice in all. In the second litter there will be 100 females and 100 males and so on; in the eighth litter 128,000 mice are produced, which at 1 oz per mouse is over 3½ tons. A stack weighing some 10 tons would collapse before 3½ tons of mice took it over. But, obviously, not all the mice survive. When numbers are impinging on food or living space predators step in and feed, and a system of mouse birth control starts to operate when females often bite off the heads of their young. Also a number of

Long-tailed field mouse

young mice leave the stacks and seek a living in the fields or, as in the case of Bartons End, gardens.

After some years of good harvests—as there were between 1680–90—when conditions are favourable for mice, though not necessarily for farmers, a population can rapidly build up to plague proportions and after a year just as suddenly fall again.

In the year 1684, when the house was occupied by James Onway, there was a plague of mice. Traps were set, cats encouraged, holes blocked, owls invoked, poisons (aconite, arsenic and others) put out. The population declined. But neither the rise nor fall of numbers, particularly the fall, have much to do with any dramatic change in the activities of predators or man, or the absence or presence of disease, but are due to a relatively small increase or decrease in the rate of breeding.

In a fast-breeding animal, like a mouse, it is fairly obvious that if all the young survived to live a normal life span the world would soon be knee-deep in them. Even in a slow-breeding one the increase is phenomenal, as for instance, in Charles Darwin's elephants. According to Darwin, a pair of elephants producing six young in their lifetime of one hundred years each, would, if all survived, give rise to nineteen million in 750 years. If they continued at this rate for the next 750 years or so the world would have room for nothing but elephants.

Such unrestricted population growth does not occur, not even in man, though in some areas it approaches it. To keep a population stable in numbers a certain 'survival rate' is necessary: this rate is the percentage of young born that survive to adulthood and it can be arrived at mathematically. Let us take the case of the domestic mouse. Here the formula for the survival rate is:

$$\frac{1}{\left(r + \frac{r}{2}\right)n} \qquad \text{where } r = \text{number of mice per litter and} \\ n = \text{number of litters per three months}$$

If in a normal population of, say, fifty pairs of mice per acre (that is a population the habitat can support under the existing ecology), the number of litters per three months (n) is 2, and the number of young per litter is 3, then the survival rate must be 16 per cent, i.e.

$$\cfrac{1}{\left(1 + \frac{3}{2}\right)2} \qquad = 0{\cdot}16 = 16\%$$

Now, if, due to plentiful food, a change occurs to, say, four mice per litter and four litters per quarter, not a very big alteration, then the survival rate must be reduced to just over one per cent to maintain the stable population level, a considerable difference from the former rate of 16 per cent. The calculation is:

$$\cfrac{1}{\left(1 + \frac{4}{2}\right)4} \qquad = 0{\cdot}01234 \text{ or } 1{\cdot}2\%$$

When the change first occurs the survival rate is not likely to drop much, if at all, so the population numbers rush up and there is a plague of mice. A decline then sets in. Competition for food and living space increases and the young mice are under strain. Although predators and diseases also increase, they are not today seen as the main reason for the collapse in numbers of the mice. It is now thought that the exhaustion of the adrenopituitary system of the animals is a considerable factor in the population reduction.[52] When the pituitary system is affected breeding is reduced and the population decline is further helped by the considerable proportion of aged individuals in it. The reduction of the breeding rate is the main reason for the change.

Now we turn to mammals resident in the garden for short periods from time to time: hedgehogs, rabbits, bats and squirrels.

Young Prudence Onway (born 1654) had been very interested in animals and plants. She adopted a hedgehog, which she had first heard and then found rummaging around in the garden. Prudence's hedgehog was unusual as it was an albino, a kind occasionally found to this day.

At first Prudence kept her new pet in a small pen in one of the stable's looseboxes, from which it could not escape. She made a nest for it in a box, using hay and dried leaves, and fed the animal generously with bits of meat, mealworms, other insects, slugs, snails, earthworms, acorns, berries and milk. Soon she was able to let her 'hedioc'—she called him Snowball—go free. He was too well fed to wander far from such a fine source of food. Prudence was great friends with the stableman, who warned her not to make much display of the hedgehog. The cowman, he said, was a declared enemy of hedgehogs as he thought they took milk from the cows. It is, in fact, not very likely that a cow would allow a hedgehog, an animal with very sharp teeth, to suck milk; on the other hand, hedgehogs will lap up milk from a cow lying down in a summer pasture when milk is oozing from her teats from a very full udder.

The cowman's war against hedgehogs arose not so much from a desire to protect his employer's interests (the thoughtlessness and unreliability of employees is a very ancient theme)[b] but from the fact that they made a very tasty dish. ''Tis the best meat in England,' he declared. There was something of the gypsy in him, and like them, he would gut the animal, stuff it with sage, onion and breadcrumbs, sew it up and cover it all over with wet clay. It was then suspended over an open fire and kept turning. When the clay cracked the meal was ready. The spines came away with the clay.

After a while the cowman reached a concordat with Prudence and promised he would not hurt Snowball. He thought perhaps the beast would attract females and thus there could be more fine suppers for the taking.

Prudence's albino was not the only hedgehog to live in the garden over its long history. Not only were other pet hediocs kept from time to time but at least once there was a feral population as well. William Daker, the tenant of Bartons End, 1869–99, a good naturalist but a bad farmer, had a pair and when he gave up the farm he just let them go. They survived and bred. When Robert Dunchester bought the property in 1909 there were at least two pairs roaming about the ruined garden.

Hedgehogs make a good deal of noise when they are searching for food: grunts, snuffles and clicks with their teeth, and even a scream if they are in pain. Hedgehogs, shrews and the large edible dormouse are the cause of many of the mysterious noises heard in the dark of the countryside; frequently they are the 'things that go bump in the night'. The dormouse was deliberately released at Tring, Hertfordshire, in 1902 and it has spread only quite recently as far as Kent.

Hedgehogs have two defence mechanisms against predators. The main one is the well-known device of curling into a ball so that the spines, which are modified hairs, protect it. The soft underparts are covered by the skin muscles drawing the prickled edges together, and the animal then presents a ball of spines to the attacker. This, alas! is no defence against a newer peril, the motor car. When on a road at night, and alarmed by approaching lights, the hedgehog, instead of dashing for the hedge, rolls itself into a ball and is usually crushed to death.

The hedgehog's second line of defence is its sharp teeth and head spines, which it can project forward; it will hold its own against any animal of its own size but curls up when a bigger creature, such as a fox or badger, attacks. Even so, foxes and badgers seem to open a hedgehog ball fairly easily, eating the animal and leaving the skin and spines on the ground.

The spines are strong and firmly attached. A hedgehog can be held up by one spine without harm to animal or spine, although the creature weighs some $\frac{3}{4}$ to $2\frac{1}{2}$ lbs. A spine has a narrow neck near its base and below this it expands again. The narrow neck makes a flexible joint, having two advantages. If pulled out, the spine breaks off at this narrow point and a new one grows from the follicle, just as a hair does in other mammals. The second advantage of the flexible joint is that, if the spine receives a push, as it often may, it is not driven into the animal, but curves over. Hedgehogs are good climbers and often fall from a height, the spines acting as a shock absorber. In fact, hedgehogs frequently deliberately drop from above, or curl up and roll down a slope! It is the quickest way of covering that bit of ground.

A curious habit hedgehogs have is covering their spines with frothy saliva from their mouths. It may well be that this saliva is a repellant or insecticidal, because one of the disadvantages of spines, instead of hair, is that the usual grooming cannot take place. As a result hedgehogs become heavily infested with fleas and mites. The sticky saliva, if not actually insecticidal, must gum up and immobilise many of those troublesome parasites. Prudence used to dust Snowball with the powdered leaves of fleabane and wood ashes to rid him of fleas.

Snowball would hibernate for the winter but started this process much later than most of the hibernating garden animals—hibernation usually started in December. Nevertheless, like other hibernating animals, he prepared for it by accumulating a big reserve of fat and by making a cosy winter nest. He could withstand cold conditions but could not have survived being frozen. Hibernation is a sleep-like condition in which the temperature of the body is lowered and is, in a

Hedgehog or hedioc

warm-blooded animal, a much more serious process than in a cold-blooded one, such as an insect, snail or snake. The fat serves to keep the metabolism going, but since the temperature of the creature is lowered, the life-process goes on at a reduced rate. It is the accumulation of fat that starts the process rather than a lengthening night and falling temperature.

As the body temperature drops it does so at a different rate in different parts of the creature. The extremities are cold, but the blood within the heart is at a comparatively high temperature, one which normally would awaken the animal. During warm winter weather the hedgehog may come out of hibernation and set out in search of food: it hibernates again when the temperature drops.

Unfortunately, hedgehogs are carriers of the foot and mouth disease of cattle and other farm animals.

Though rabbits were mostly visitors to the garden, there were residents at times, of two sorts. The most numerous were the tame rabbits, kept in hutches, but some wild rabbits started to make a warren in the garden early this century when the house was empty.

A characteristic of rabbits feeding near a warren giving on to open grassland, the usual kind of site, is their alarm response. A rabbit sensing the approach of a predator by smell, sound or sight, may do one or both of two things, drum on the ground with a hind foot or bolt for a burrow, which flight makes its white tail visible to all, including the predator. Both of these reactions make the animal more conspicuous and more likely to be shot by man or caught by a fox. But either or both of these reactions are also a warning to the other rabbits, which then react by rushing for the burrows, the mass of white bobs confusing the aim of the gunman and the rush of the fox, and giving the rabbits a chance to take cover. The first rabbit is thus showing altruistic behaviour; it would be more likely to survive if it just froze as hares do, or simply bolted for its burrow without drumming. By drumming it warns the other members of the colony. The warned animals are likely to be relatives, and thus custodians of many of the first rabbit's genes. By drumming that first rabbit may draw attention to itself and die, its genes being lost, but by its warning it will have preserved the lives of most of the same genes in its relatives. The gene pool will have gained.[22]

The popular belief that rabbits are very fast breeders is true: they are.

Nevertheless they have an almost unique system of birth control. First, rabbits will copulate at almost any time of the year, though the main breeding season is January to June, being at its height in March and April; the female does not have to be in oestrus, and ovulation is induced by copulation. Litters of three to seven young quickly follow each other. The female can become pregnant again some twelve hours after the birth of her litter. Gestation is twenty-eight to thirty days, so a litter a month is common and the early-born females will be breeding themselves before they are fully adult. These facts do not suggest that there is any restraint on numbers in operation, but nevertheless there is.[11] About sixty per cent of the litters conceived are not born. The embryos are not aborted and expelled, but are reabsorbed by the mother. In spite of this loss the rate of increase is still very large. A female rabbit's production per year is ten or eleven young. To secure a stable population this implies a survival rate of some two per cent, instead of a minute one were anything like all the embryos conceived to go to full time and be born.

A recessive 'lethal gene' appears to be at work here and at first it seems strange that natural selection has not eliminated this gene in such a successful animal as the rabbit. But further reflection suggests that restriction of births may not be unfavourable to the survival and expansion of the species. Fewer young means less intra-specific com-petition and a better chance of survival for those that are born.

Lethal genes may not have reduced the rabbit population, but in 1953 the disease myxomytosis very certainly did so: indeed it nearly extinguished the species. By 1959 rabbits resistant to the disease were appearing, and today they sometimes visit the garden and damage crops such as peas and lettuce, although they are not resident, even as pets.

Another curious feature of rabbits is their ability to eat plants poisonous to other mammals, such as deadly nightshade and the death cap fungus. After such a meal the rabbit's flesh is poisonous to susceptible animals, such as fox and man.[32] A French treatment for human poisoning by the death cap is to give the patient minced rabbit stomach and brains, and the treatment is said to have saved many lives. On the other hand, ragwort is poisonous to rabbits, and not to sheep.

Squirrels, the red or native squirrel, were in the copse when the garden was started and persisted there, and in the garden trees when they grew tall, until about 1900, when they started to be outnumbered by the American grey squirrel, a species deliberately introduced to Britain in 1876. Today the grey is the only squirrel resident in the Bartons End garden and they are skilled in exploiting their attractiveness, for the humans now resident in the house feed and make pets of them.

The decline of the red squirrel and its apparent replacement by the slightly larger victorious grey is not thought by scientists to be due to antagonism between the species,[52] although circumstances strongly suggest that the grey has replaced the red. While skirmishes between reds and greys have been seen, this is just territorial defence—both reds and greys fight their own species too in order to retain their plots. Nor are the reds more susceptible to disease than the greys. Where their ranges overlap the two squirrels live together and make territories without any more than usual quarrelling. Nevertheless, after an area has had greys in it for about fifteen years, the reds start to decline. The 'no antagonism' theory says that populations of animals rise and fall on a varying cycle of years and a long-cycle red squirrel decline may just be coinciding with the arrival and spread of the grey squirrel.

Both squirrels make their nests—dreys—high in trees. The reds prefer conifers and the greys prefer beech, but both species will nest in any kind of tree of suitable height and position. Squirrels forage mostly on the ground, and one of their characteristics is the collection of fallen nuts for winter food. Squirrels need a large store as they do not hibernate. A squirrel will collect a nut, run quickly to what appears to be a chosen spot and there bury it. The curious thing is that these places are not pre-selected but just random choices. By the time winter arrives they have forgotten the whereabouts of many of these hides and the nuts are left untouched. As a result the kernels germinate and another young nut-bearing tree starts up. Thus what might at first sight appear a waste of effort on the squirrel's part tends to be advantageous in the longer term. A buried nut is more likely to germinate well and make a strong seedling than a nut merely resting on the surface, and the random nut-buriers may be ensuring supplies for future members of the species. It is another example of unconscious altruism: by accepting a loss of winter feed the race is helping future generations.

Squirrels can swim well and think nothing of crossing a lake half a mile wide. Although they can be forgetful about their nut stores, they also show an ability to learn. A young squirrel gnaws away at a nut until by chance it just breaks open, but later on he gnaws a long furrow down one side, gets a tooth into the crack and splits the nut open, using much less time and effort.[51]

Bats flew through the garden from its earliest days because gardens generate insects, the bats' main food. Prudence Onway's tame noctule, 'Mr Milton', was a regular visitor and bat tracks in the garden were established when noctule bats lived in the attics in 1845. In 1903, when the house was empty, the north end of the roof fell in and allowed a colony of pipistrelle bats to establish a roost there. They also used the garden.

Strange features of bat life are their skill in flight and their capture of prey, mostly spiders and insects. Ultrasonic sound is used to locate flying insects. A sound signal sent out by a bat is reflected back to its receptive ears and tells the creature just what sort of things are in the air ahead. The bat is then able to seize the morsel, if it appears to be desirable, or avoid it if not. So sensitive is this device that a bat can fly around a darkened room and avoid a wire stretched across it. The signals are ultrasonic and inaudible to most humans under forty and to all of them over that age. It is a remarkable feature of bat life and akin to radar, except that the bats are using sound, travelling at about 600 miles per hour; radar uses electricity moving at the speed of light, 186,000 miles per second, the latter consequently having a vastly bigger range. Bats can only operate their system over a few yards. An example of their great skill may be seen in the fact that a bat may dive at a fisherman's artificial fly as he makes an evening cast. The bat may be caught by the hook, but usually it is caught in the wing, not the mouth. This means that the signal the bat was getting back showed it, at the last moment, that the prey was not desirable: the pursuer turned away, but not quite fast enough to avoid being hooked in the wing.

Bats are an asset to a garden. Their evening flight is fascinating to watch and they consume large numbers of pest insects. Admittedly they also take beneficial insects and spiders, but on balance they help in the struggle against pests.

Horses frequently passed through the garden in the general day-to-day work of the farm, but they can hardly be considered as visitors. However, during the nineteenth century there were regular visits of a number of ponies from about 1827 to the time of the abandonment of the garden.

The first of these regular equine visitors was a Shetland pony which, from 1827 to about 1832, the Hackshaw boys, Alfred (born 1822) and David (born 1823) had. Shetlands were the latest thing in diminutives. The boys sometimes rode it and were allowed to drive themselves round the garden and farmyard in a fine little pony cart. They took great pride in their smart turn-out and always gave the already gleaming brasswork an extra polish before setting out.

From 1848 until the neglect and then abandonment of the lawns, a pony came in from the farmyard stables to draw the mowing machine. Special leather- and woollen-soled boots were made for it, so that its hoofs would not damage the turf—it took no little effort to train the animal to bear with that footwear. The great skill and time needed in cutting lawns with a scythe, and thus its great expense, had stimulated inventors to mechanise the process. By 1830 a Mr Edward Budding had patented the cylinder lawn-mower; rotating blades cut the grass against a fixed blade and it was substantially the same machine as today's cylinder mower. The machine worked best against dry grass, whereas the scythe man got the best results from a damp growth, the reason he made an early start to his mowing, while the dew was still about.

William Hackshaw took to mechanical mowing with reluctance, but was forced to adopt it if he were to keep his grass looking smart. Wages, he maintained, were too appallingly high. He particularly hated the dark and light lines the mowing machine left as it pressed the grass down, first one way and then the other, as the machine's roller moved to and fro: today this pattern is the sign of the well-kept lawn. Mr Hackshaw liked to show his skill with the scythe and, rising at dawn in summer, cut much of the grass visible from the house that way. 'Who wants a set of damned railway lines in his garden?' he would exclaim. His enthusiasm for scything, and his efforts to get his children to join him, which they stubbornly resisted, were, no doubt, one of the background reasons for Alfred Hackshaw's taking against Bartons End when his father died in 1852.

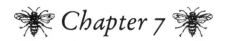

Chapter 7

The Gardens of Emmanuel Burrows and William Daker, 1852–1899

Insects

THERE WERE, and are, more species of insects in the garden of Bartons End than of all the other species of animals put together. To deal with them all would require several volumes, so that here we will only discuss them in general terms and give details of a few of them of particular interest to the property, such as some of the social Hymenoptera (bees, wasps and ants), the almost social Hemiptera, the aphids or greenfly, some butterflies and moths and certain garden pests.

One of the striking things about insects in any habitat is their utility in the general ecological scheme. They seem to exist for the purpose of being eaten by a wide range of animals, particularly by birds, spiders and some mammals, like moles, hedgehogs and foxes. Many birds, such as sparrows and tits, use their 'cuteness' to induce humans to feed them generously from food tables; their own nestlings they always feed on insects. Insects are a major factor in the transfer of plant proteins and carbohydrates to animals, and the amount of vegetation insects can eat when breeding is astounding, for, typically, the potential rate of increase in insects is very great.

The Insecta is a division of the Arthropods, the cold-blooded, jointed-limbed phylum of animals which also includes spiders, mites and crustacea. Insects usually have six legs at some stage of their life history and a body divided into three parts: head, thorax (carrying the legs and wings) and the abdomen. Most of them have a 'complete metamorphosis', that is, their life consists of four stages—egg, larva, pupa and adult. The capacity for enormous increase means that the resulting pressure on survival has led to the filling of every conceivable niche that can support insect life, and very varied life histories have developed. For instance, at Bartons End most Lepidoptera (butterflies and moths) over-winter as eggs or pupae, but the handsome brimstone butterfly finds it advantageous to pass the winter as an adult, usually hidden up among ivy leaves.

Insects are quick to take advantage of the introduction to their habitat of a new host plant or animal. When the much-abused hop was introduced, an aphid living on damsons and wild sloes found the hop to be much to its liking, adopting it as its summer host and causing a lot of damage to that profitable crop. In the autumn the hop aphids returned to the damsons and laid eggs. It would have been useless to the race to lay them on the hop bine, as that dies down and is lost during the winter.

Insect life is very different from that of man and it is difficult for us to appreciate it. It is a life in which the animal is quite unconscious of the reasons for its activities: the insect lives in the present and is unaware of what has happened in the past or what is likely to happen in the future. Nevertheless, many insects make elaborate provision for their offspring, most of which they will never see. Female butterflies take great care in selecting just the right leaves on which to lay eggs, so that the young caterpillars, on hatching, will have easy access to food and be protected from predators. One of two policies may be adopted. The butterfly may avoid leaves already carrying an egg, so that there may be no competition between the newly hatched young; an example is the red admiral whose eggs are laid singly on nettles. The other policy is to lay eggs in masses: for instance the small tortoiseshell lays a mass containing up to 1,000 eggs also on nettles. The tortoiseshell's eggs hatch in about ten days and split into groups of about 200; each group seeks a separate nettle, where the mass of young caterpillars makes a web and by concerted movements protects itself from predators.

It is instinct that directs the course of insect life, instinct being the pattern imposed on them by their genes. Insects can learn, but their powers of learning are very limited. Bees and wasps learn the way back to hive and nest: the queen wasp in the spring, on emerging from hibernation, starts to make a nest. Having found a suitable spot, such as a tunnel in the earth, she flies up and down outside the entrance several times, hovering and facing the entrance, in order to familiarise herself with the surroundings. It is called the 'orientation flight'.[25] If something, such as a stem of grass, falls over the passage, the wasp becomes confused and makes further orientation flights. The queen makes repeated trips to the selected spot carrying balls of the 'paper', or chewed-up wood, of which the nest is made. In the early return flights she lands near the nest and walks about to locate the entrance. Later on she has learnt exactly where it is and flies directly to it.

In the struggle for survival insects make up for their limited abilities of learning and intelligence by their enormous reproductive powers. A species of insect may solve a problem, not by using its intelligence, but by producing thousands of offspring, showing a range of differing characteristics, such as size, colour, food preference and so on. Among the many offspring there may well be some having features which solve the problem. This race will then have an advantage over its relatives and be propagated at their expense. The new characteristic then eventually becomes instinctive and part of the normal behaviour of that species. The hop-damson aphid illustrates one way of solving the problem of exploiting a new territory. Man, faced with a similar problem, spends a long time thinking about it and eventually despatches a Columbus, a Captain Cook, or an Aldrin and Armstrong with a mass of technical equipment. The insect just breeds and breeds until it solves the problem of exploiting a novel source of food, simply by producing some individuals which can use it.

Insects breed very quickly, for not only do they lay numerous eggs, but many kinds, aphids for instance, have several generations a year, so the rate of breeding helps them as well.

When Alfred Hackshaw inherited Bartons End he had no interest in farming it himself, or even of living there, so he sought a tenant for the place. Eventually, in 1853, a Mr Emmanuel Burrows took a lease on the farm, house and garden. Mr Burrows was by no means a poor man. He was another experienced Kentish farmer, but naturally took a tenant's view of the property. He and his wife Marjory liked the garden but were

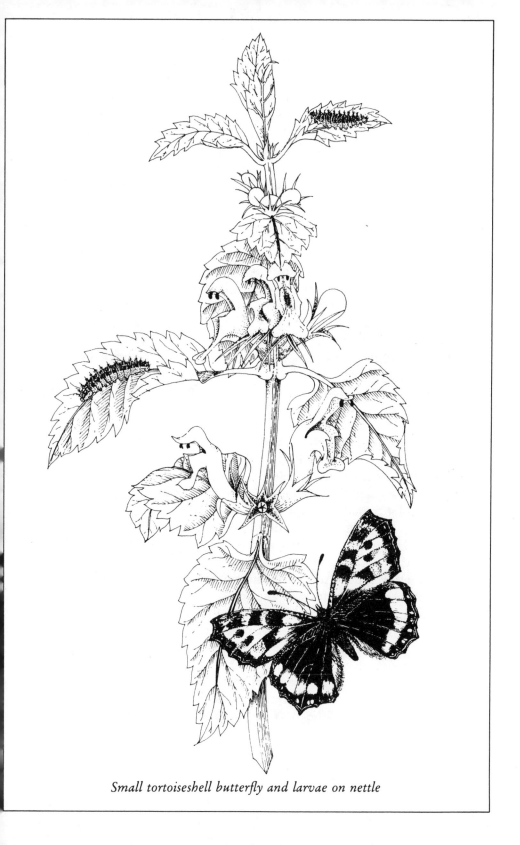

Small tortoiseshell butterfly and larvae on nettle

not going to spend a lot of money improving either it or the farm for the benefit of the landlord, who at that time would repay their efforts by increasing the rent at the end of the lease, as the property had now become more valuable. The late-Victorian legislation which eventually gave tenants compensation for improvements made during their tenancy, and for manurial residues left in the soil, were statesmanlike Acts which much advanced agriculture, but it came too late to affect the attitude of Emmanuel Burrows.

During this first tenancy, of sixteen years, the garden was mostly in the care of Marjory Burrows, an intelligent and very active woman. Her first economy was to reduce the time, and thus the money, spent on the lawns. She reintroduced the mowing machine and straightened many curving paths alongside the grass, which made trimming the edges easier, but an even better device, which has recently been rediscovered, was making a path edging of brick. The brick was at grass level and the mowing machine could have one wheel running on the brick and thus cut to the edge of the lawn, leaving only a little grass creeping over the brick. It was not as neat as the careful hand-cutting of lawn edges but it saved a lot of labour.

Marjory Burrows faced much the same problem that Mary Barton had had some three hundred years earlier, the getting of enough labour to run the place properly. Both husbands liked to see the garden neat, flowery and with a good vegetable plot, yet neither liked spending money on it, that is, diverting labour from the farm. Marjory would enquire of her husband, did he want them to be regarded as mere cottagers, surrounded by a wilderness of weeds? They could not afford to let the Hackshaws' fine garden go to ruin. 'Just think of our children's future, Mr Burrows. Do you want our girls to marry labourers?' Emmanuel eventually conceded defeat and gave Marjory a boy as a full-time gardener. But, he insisted, they must have just plain gardening and no nonsensical novelties from the ends of the earth.

The Burrowses had four children, the first three, at that time, being teenage girls. They all helped in the garden, so that with care the place throve, though on a lower level than when it had been under Hackshaw management. The exotics came out of the greenhouse, which was used mostly for raising seedlings, carnations and the suspect tomato. Marjory was so successful with the tomatoes that a demand for her seed arose, it being seen that, as the Burrows girls were models of propriety, the plants' supposed dire effects seemed to be unfounded. Very fine vegetables were also grown, particularly some new cabbages, such as the early Battersea and the later Sugar Loaf and Matchless.

In spite of the general neglect of the garden, compared with its condition in the days of the Hackshaws, a number of new plants, particularly ones that were easy to grow, were introduced in the late nineteenth century, so great was the pressure of the novelties being brought out by nurserymen.

Marjory Burrows adopted that great labour-saving device, the herbaceous border. She planted a number of species of achillea. She began with the common lawn weed, the yarrow (*A. millefolium*) or milfoil, and the sneezewort (*A. ptarmica*), which was a useful herb to promote sneezing and clearing of the head. Later she added some imports, such as the silver milfoil (*A. clavannae*) and the Caspian (*A. cupatorium*) with clusters of lovely yellow flowers. Next came the common cornflowers (*Centaurea cyanus*) and then the related species, such as the big-flowered centaureas from Armenia and the sweet sultan from Persia. Other plants in the border were the leopard's bane (*Doronicum pardalianches*), its related smaller-flowered *D. plantagineum*, various globe thistles, lupins, Michaelmas daisies from North America, phlox, also from America, and some sedums, particularly the gentian-leaved *S. gentianoides*.

Mrs Burrows, ever striving to keep down labour in the garden, also introduced ground-cover plants and found periwinkles and lilies-of-the-valley very useful—it was amazing how the delicately flowered lilies spread and spread. Another of her great successes was the Christmas rose and the later-flowering Lenten rose, both much appreciated by her children.

Mrs Burrows was a keen bee-keeper and she introduced several hives into the garden, thereby much improving the fruit crops through better pollination of the blossom.

The hive-bee is a highly social and successful animal. Much of its success is due to its utility to man, of which it is blissfully unaware. At the time when the Bartons End garden was first started, for example, bees were the main source of sweetening for most families. Sugar made from sugar-cane came to England only in small amounts from North

Africa, Spain and India, and was very expensive.

Bees have the disadvantages of being cold-blooded, of having no tools, no voices (though they have a language of sorts), no finger and thumb, no great intelligence and no reasoning, yet by means of associating together they have produced a highly successful economy, one of utility both to themselves and the outside world. Their main setback at first sight seems to be that they have not been able to prevent men robbing them of half their wealth, their honey and wax. But they may be on their way to dealing with that problem—the race of African killer bees is now advancing from Brazil northwards. If it establishes itself and replaces our present milder race, bee-keeping may become too dangerous to man and vanish.

However, man's use of the bee is not necessarily bad for it. Because of its utility to him the bee is protected, given hives for new nests, and its diseases, predators and parasites studied and controlled. Hive-bees are now more numerous because of man than they would have been without him.

During the summer bees collect pollen and nectar and convert the latter substance to honey by masticating it and driving off some of the water. They then store the honey in the comb. Those persons who, like the fat boy in *The Pickwick Papers*, 'want to make your flesh creep', point out that honey is nectar mixed with bee spittle, vomit and, in the case of fir-tree honey, aphid faeces. Honey is the colony's winter food. If man removes too much of it in the autumn the bees will not survive the winter. Today, of course, most of the honey in a hive is taken by man and the bees given an artificial food, sugar. Honey, which is 76 per cent sugar, sells at a premium over white sugar, on account of its attractive nature, its taste and smell. In terms of sugar content it is about seven times the price of white sugar, so the bee-keeper derives a profit in substituting white sugar for honey as a winter food for his bees.

The queen bee, unlike the queen wasp who has to work hard to establish her first colony, leaves her hive with a group of worker bees—a swarm. The bee-keeper usually follows the swarm, collects it and puts it in an empty hive. The queen then goes into production, laying eggs, slowly at first but increasing the output to a rate which may eventually reach a figure of 2,000 a day. Her fertility has been the result of her mating with several males, because one copulation would not supply enough sperm for her long life. The eggs are laid in the hexagonal wax cells of the comb that her workers have built for her, and which hangs from the roof and sides of the nest. In passing we may note that these cells are so regular, attractive and mysterious that the great French scientist Réaumur suggested to Joseph-Louis Lagrange's commission for designing the metric system in France, early in the nineteenth century, that the width of the bee's hexagonal cell be the new unit of length and thus the basis of the whole system. The proposal was rejected because different races of bees use differently sized cells.

The worker bees are sterile females who spend their lives collecting nectar, pollen and water with which to feed the brood and the queen, building the comb, nursing the young, and defending and cleaning the colony. Workers have sacrificed the possibility of having offspring of their own (and thus of propagating their own particular genes) in order to make it more likely that the queen's offspring survive in greater numbers. That altruism can be seen as a cunning device of the bees' genes to secure even greater chances of survival and increase. The phenomenon of sterile female workers found in the social insects —bees, wasps, ants and termites—means that such groups are far more successful than the solitary species of related genera.

Late in the season, after thousands of normal cells have been built, the workers construct some rather larger cells and persuade the queen to lay unfertilised eggs in them. This results in the production of males, the drones. The males thus carry only their mother's genes, but the mother's genes consist of ones carried down from ancestral males that existed before the haploid (breeding from unpaired chromosomes) type of breeding developed. Thus, though the males only have their mother's genes, those genes can have a varied selection of male-derived factors. That can be seen in the results of the multiple matings of a queen. She may lay eggs giving, say, dark bees and then suddenly start producing light-coloured ones. This is because the sperm of a dark male has been used up and the seed from another mate now comes into action. The dark-making and the light-making eggs carry far distant genes differing in this respect, but these male-derived genes descend through the female.

In a successful hive the population increases very rapidly during the summer and the structure becomes too small for it. The workers then

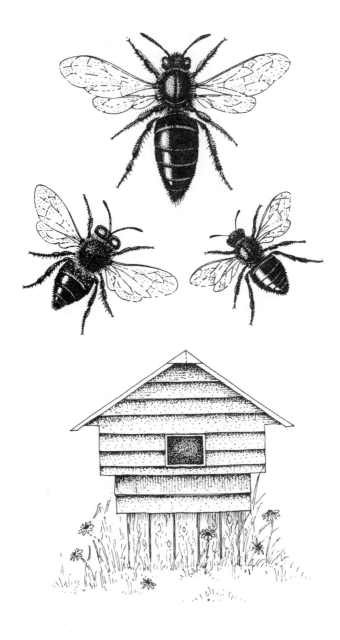

Hive bees, queen, male and worker.

build some special large cells and raise a number of princesses in them by feeding normal female larvae on the famous royal jelly, a substance resembling yoghurt secreted from the bees' pharangial and mandibular glands.

The first princess to emerge from her pupal case usually goes around the hive stinging to death any other princesses. It should be noted that in a soft target, such as a bee larva, a bee can use her sting many times whereas when stinging a tougher surface, such as human skin, the barbed sting cannot be withdrawn. The entrails are torn out and the bee dies. By her death she helps the colony survive.

Having killed her potential rivals, First Princess then goes off on her marriage flight, soaring high into the air, followed by a bevy of eager drones. She mates in the air with several of them and then returns to her hive, collects a band of workers and avoids contact with the reigning queen, who will attempt to kill her young rival. After mating the males die. Their function performed, males once outside the hive are refused re-entry, while those inside are ejected.

If the old queen is still relatively vigorous, but fails to kill the young princess, which failure is usual, the old queen will then gather about half the workers around her and leave the hive, intending to go to a site previously selected by special scouts sent out beforehand. Her escorted departure constitutes the swarm. The swarm first settles on some convenient point near the original colony, prior to going off to the scouts' selected place. It is at this juncture that the bee-keeper steps in; he pours the swarm into a box in order to retain his bees and then transfers it to a new hive, one baited with a little honey and wax. He only effects the transfer successfully if he can find the queen, because once she is in the new quarters the rest of the bees will follow. Just before swarming the bees gorge themselves on honey stored in the comb for winter use. They are then less prone to sting.

However, if man does not intervene, the swarm eventually moves off to one of the selected sites, which may well be an empty hive, because hives—especially modern ones—suit bees very well, or to a hollow tree, a cavity wall, chimney, or a corner of a cupboard or outhouse.

Many of the gardeners at Bartons End kept bees, but up to the time of Mrs Burrows they had all used the old-fashioned straw skep, which usually led to the destruction of the colony when honey was removed from them. Mrs Burrows introduced the movable frame hive. The frames of honey can easily be taken out of the hive and the bees left unharmed, provided food is given to them. It was invented about 1789 by François Huber, the Swiss zoologist who, in spite of his blindness, made profound studies of bees and ants. The new hive did not become much known in Britain until 1851 when the Reverend L. L. Langstroth popularised it. Mrs Burrows was among the first to take advantage of that great improvement.

It was mentioned earlier that bees have a language of sorts, a much disputed point that turns on how one defines 'language'. Bees convey information by means of an elaborate dance, and the basic function of language is to convey information.[34] A scout bee, having found food, returns to the nest and by means of a complicated figure-of-eight dance on the vertical honeycomb indicates to the workers, who crowd round her, the direction in relation to the sun where food can be found and how far away it is. A great economy of effort in getting food is thus secured.

This, at first startling, hypothesis was advanced by Dr von Frisch around 1926 and was received with great scepticism by most scientists. He persuaded such a doubting Englishman, a Mr Thorpe, of its truth in a most convincing way. On holiday in the Tyrol he provided Mr Thorpe with an observation hive with glass sides, and a protractor. Dr von Frisch said, 'I have put out a saucer of honey in the park, which the bees will find. You also will be able to find it, solely from the information the bees give you.' Applying the hypothesis, using his watch and protractor, and watching the dance, Mr Thorpe set out in the direction indicated and at 300 yards almost stepped on the saucer of honey.

Bees pass the winter by getting together in a slowly turning mass, kept at a fairly high temperature, rarely below 55°F, by the consumption of their carefully stored honey, or, if the bee-keeper has taken it, then of the syrup he has provided.

We may well ask what directs a bee to forage, exude wax, make comb, tend the young, swarm and so on, always to the advantage of the colony? The answer seems to be chemicals.

The bees are continually licking each other and exchanging regurgitated food, a process known as trophyllaxis. Pheromones, chemical substances controlling behaviour, secreted by the queen in small amounts are among the food exchanged to the whole colony. The pheromones suppress or lead to certain activities in the workers. For instance, the queen will put out an anti-queen substance which inhibits the production by the workers of the larger queen cells and thus of rival queens. But as the queen gets older and the workers increase in numbers the anti-queen cell substance ceases to be so plentiful and the workers make queen cells. The workers, on the other hand, feed the queen with substances that control her activities.

All this is based on trophyllaxis, the taking of sicked-up substances from neighbours, and of giving them too. Trophyllaxis is not an attractive procedure to us humans, yet we already practise it to a certain extent: at a party, or in a crowded train, every time you smell tobacco smoke you have breathed in some air that has just been in someone else's mouth or lungs.

Bees are highly social animals. Left in isolation a bee is helpless and dies. This has led Chauvin, a French scientist, to postulate, in 1968, that the hive should be regarded as the animal.[16] It is an ingenious proposition and really turns on the definition of an animal, in the same way as the argument about the bees' language turns on the definition of that word.

The creature weighs some nine or eleven pounds and will contain 40,000 to 50,000 bees. The bees, he maintains, are just the cells of the animal, performing different functions, as do our own cells in our hands, hearts and livers but, in the case of the bees, they are cells moving around from time to time and then rejoining the main body. A feature of Chauvin's animal was that, like a mammal, it maintained a constant temperature, of 91–93°F, unlike insects which become the temperature of their environment.

Emmanuel Burrows decided in 1869 that he was too old to continue farming and he retired to a small house in Ashford. The farm was then let to Mr William Daker, a keen naturalist and farmer. He was not married. His mother, Jane Eleanor, ran the house and tried to get her son to help with the garden, but with little success. William's two married sisters, Janet and Julia, lived quite near and, with their children, frequently visited Bartons End. Their protests about the shabby state of the garden were useless, but William loved his nephews and nieces, especially when they took an intelligent interest in natural history.

Besides the bees, there were other social insects in the garden, such as wasps, ants and aphids. At Bartons End, because of the abundance of fruit, two social wasps (*Vespula vulgaris* and *V. germanica*) flourished. Their life style was not as advanced as that of the hive-bees, nor was the help they were giving to man appreciated. Because they sting and, unlike the bee, can sting repeatedly, and because they attack fruit, they were regarded as enemies. Yet they consume large numbers of pest insects. For example, in many areas the summer of 1982 saw a large number of flies, particularly of the little *Drosophila* fruit or vinegar fly, largely because there were so few wasps that season.

In the autumn the queen and princess wasps, after mating, seek hibernation sites, frequently just under roofs, in attics and curtain pelmets. All the other wasps, workers and males, die after an orgy of feeding on any available food, a fact which William Daker had noticed. He had also seen that male wasps, which have no sting, are much attracted to the autumnal ivy flowers, whereas the females (workers and queens) do not seem to like them. Taking a natural history walk with friends and children round the garden he would stop and point out the wasps crowding over the ivy flowers. 'I can charm wasps,' he would say and run his fingers through them, unstung. Great was the surprise. 'You try it,' he would say. Fortunately for his reputation, no one ever did. And unfortunately, at least once when doing this trick, there was also a worker present, which stung him, a mishap he attempted to conceal with the fortitude of a Spartan.

William Daker had another useful device in connection with wasps. When they became too numerous and were attacking his fruit, he would seek out and destroy their nests. His trick was in discovering where the nests were. A little jam on a plate put out in the garden would soon attract some wasps. He had ready some foot-lengths of white cotton, with a loop at one end. Such a noose slipped over a wasp would slow down its flight when it left for home and lead Mr Daker, if not to the acutal nest, at least to its neighbourhood.

Wasps lose all their workers in the autumn, a considerable check to their economy, in contrast to bees which retain workers for next year's use. Moreover, the queen wasp on emerging from hibernation has to find a nest site, make comb, lay eggs and feed the first hatching larvae, a full-time job, again in contrast to the bee, who starts her new nest with a staff of willing helpers.

Another family of social insects, the ants, have an advantage over both bees and wasps. The ants at Bartons End made their nests in the soil, so did not have to expend considerable effort in making the materials for the nest structure and the comb. Admittedly they had to excavate the nest, which required much work, and when mined did not make so secure a home, but on the whole an ant's nest is more easily made than a wasp's.

Ants share their nests with a number of other creatures, commensals and parasites, whilst bees will tolerate no intruders. Even so, the wax moth sometimes got into the hives. Laying eggs on the comb the moth's larvae tunnel into it, feeding on the bee grubs and doing much damage. The *Lomechusa* of the ants was mentioned in Chapter 1.

Ants have lived in the garden from its start to the present. The commonest species was the little black garden ant but three other kinds were also found. They were the yellow lawn ant, a species living almost all its life underground, the small yellow ant, fond of the grass in the orchards and making shallow mounds, and the red-brown ant. There were two ways of identifying this last creature, Mr Daker would explain. The best one was that it stung, a method of identification not appealing to everyone. The second method was to examine it with a hand-lens: its waist (the petiole), joining the abdomen and thorax, had two swellings or scales, whereas the *Lasius* species had only one.

Most of the gardeners at Bartons End thought of the ants as minor pests. A nest might occasionally be made in a lawn and spoil its smoothness, or one might be constructed under a favourite plant and kill it. Only the red ants were regarded as highly undesirable, because of their stinging. But a few of the gardeners, such as Susannah Munroyd, thought them desirable, because they appeared always to be attacking the greenfly on the roses and other plants.

That was a faulty observation. The ants were using the aphids as cattle. When suitably stroked with an ant's antennae an aphid exudes a drop of sugary excrement, usually almost unchanged sap that it has sucked up from a plant. The ant absorbs this drop, goes back to the nest, regurgitates the drop and feeds it to the queen, the larvae, or to another worker ant—the process of food exchange, trophyllaxis, already mentioned in connection with bees.

The ants guard their aphids, drive off predators and parasites, harbour aphid eggs in the ants' nests during winter, move young aphids to new sites, and so on. Mr Daker used to throw great scorn on those people who maintained the ants were killing the greenfly. He used to say, 'If you think that, then you haven't looked at them for more than five seconds. Use your eyes.' He was equally scornful of people who thought that the ladybirds, ravenous feeders on greenfly, were the helpers of those pests, instead of their enemies.

There is thus considerable co-operation between ants and the soft, very vulnerable aphids. By surrendering food the greenfly get protection from many predators, though birds are not deterred by the ants. However, greenfly do have two or three moves they can make against bird attack. Firstly they are very numerous and breed quickly, so that though many may be taken by birds, enough survive to continue the species. Some of them are winged and some wingless, and usually the winged forms appear when the population begins to get very dense. These insects feed by pushing a beak into a plant and sucking up the sap and their second defence method is quickly to withdraw their suction tubes and drop to the ground, climbing or flying back again when the danger is past. A third method is strange as it presupposes some system of communication; when in danger a whole colony of winged aphids on a stem may flap their wings together and frighten away a predator. How they do this in unison is not known.

William Daker did not cut much of the grass in the garden, explaining to his mother and sisters, when they complained, that grass was the food of certain attractive butterflies and moths. He showed them a collection, in a glass case, of a ringlet, three kinds of skippers, the speckled wood, the very handsome marbled white whose caterpillar had a forked tail, and the day-flying tiger moth, and said, 'Surely you would not have me mow the lawn and destroy such beautiful creatures.' Mrs Daker's reply that, yes, she wanted the place looking decent, in no way disturbed him or altered his behaviour. Needless to say he used the same argument for not destroying nettle beds that he employed for not cutting the grass. Ridding the garden of nettles would remove the food of five beautiful butterflies and eighteen attractive moths, he said. Mr Daker withheld

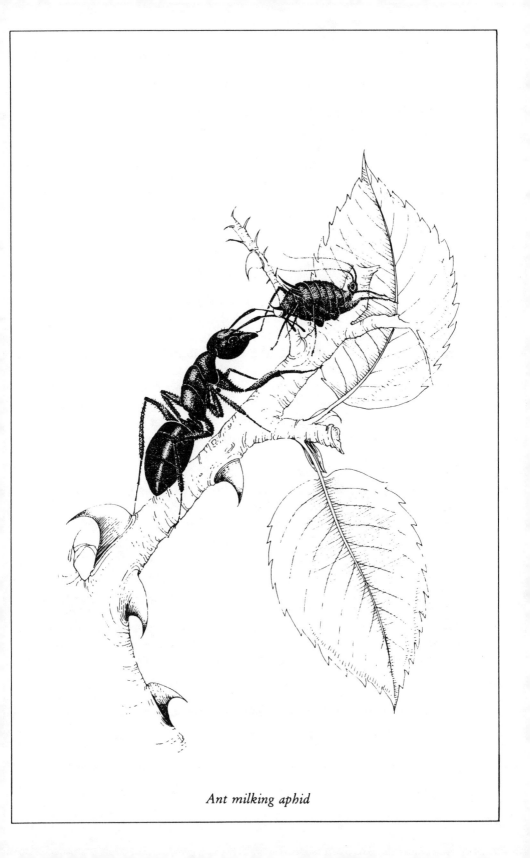

Ant milking aphid

the information that the nettle was the sole food of only three of the butterflies and none of the moths. Admittedly the three exclusively nettle feeders were attractive. They were the small tortoiseshell, the peacock and the red admiral (*Vanessa atalanta*). The name 'admiral' was an error for 'admirable', which mistake somehow became adopted, and the generic name *Vanessa* was used by Linnaeus in memory of Jonathan Swift's companion, the beautiful Esther Vanhomrigh. One of the moths, a creature flying by day, the garden tiger, was also strikingly coloured. Its caterpillar is the hairy 'woolly bear'. The caterpillar tends to be left alone, because the hairs easily come away and are irritant, causing a skin rash.

Sentimental as he was about the Lepidoptera, William Daker drew the line at some of them. The large and small whites caused much damage to his cabbage and turnip crops and he took active measures against them. He chased the adults with a butterlfy net and destroyed them and gave nets to the farm children to do the same thing. He also set the children hand-picking the caterpillars off Brassica plants, teaching them to leave those caterpillars having a dark spot, as this meant the creature was attacked by the Ichneumon parasite *Apantales* and was being consumed by the latter's larvae. These larvae eventually kill the caterpillar, emerge from it and at once spin cocoons from which the adult Ichneumon flies emerge, fly off and attack more caterpillars.

Numerous caterpillars also attacked his trees. Among these pests were the larvae of the lackey moth, protecting themselves with a tent of fine spun silk; the codlin moth, which spoiled many fine apples by boring into them; a tortrix moth (so called because the caterpillars wriggle and twist when disturbed), and the green oak moth which sometimes stripped the trees of leaf.

Another pest of the Brassica crops from the late eighteenth century until around 1910 was the turnip sawfly. The black caterpillars would devastate crops in field and garden alike. Very common, it received a number of names, such as black palmer (the Bible describes caterpillars as palmer-worms), canker, slug, and so on. In 1835, two years after William Hackshaw had purchased Bartons End, scarcely a turnip or cabbage was grown because of the attack of this pest. All the farm children, including the two Hackshaw boys, were set to hand-picking the caterpillars. Curiously, the turnip sawfly is now a rare insect. Why that is so is not known. Perhaps the lesser area of turnips now grown is below the critical area needed for the successful breeding of this insect.

Insects, and related creatures, were not the only pests the garden knew. Diseases of plants, caused mostly by fungi, also took their toll. The most dramatic occurrence of this nature was the potato blight of 1845. William Hackshaw subscribed to *The Gardener's Chronicle and Agricultural Gazette* and in the number for 23 August 1845 he read: 'A fatal malady has broken out among the potato crop. On all sides we hear of the destruction. There is hardly a good sample in Covent Garden.' First the leaves and then the potatoes rotted away. The rot was caused by a fungus (*Phytophora infestans*), but this was not acknowledged for some time in spite of clear proof from the 'fungiferous curate', the Reverend M. J. Berkeley. Some scientific opinion, even that of the distinguished editor of *Gardener's Chronicle*, Dr John Lindley,[56] held that the fungus seen on the leaves was the *result* of the blight, not its cause, and a Mr A. Smee, FRS and surgeon to the Bank of England, published a book in 1846 that tried to prove the cause to be an aphid.[67] Eventually, around 1885, during William Daker's tenancy, the potatoes were sprayed with Bordeaux mixture, a combination of copper sulphate and lime, which enabled much better crops to be obtained.

Old Mrs Daker was not allowed much labour for her garden. She continued to tend the herbaceous border and then she and her grandchildren introduced another labour-saving device, the shrubbery, epitome of the Victorian garden. The Bartons End shrubbery started with the rather dull evergreens beloved of small Victorian gardens: spotted laurel, an early introduction to Britain (1804), the evergreen spindle tree, holly and privet. The last two were native plants and the gardeners soon found two interesting variations, a holly with golden edges to the leaves and yellow berries, and a yellow-leaved privet.

A point Mr Daker made to his nephews and nieces was the strange economy of the holly bush. It had, he said, prickly leaves to stop cattle eating them, but high up in the tree the leaves had no, or very few, prickles. As the cattle could not reach so high there was no point in arming the leaves with thorns.

More decorative shrubs were gradually introduced as the shrubbery was extended. Among them were the butterfly bush (*Buddleia davidii*), a native of China, one much appreciated by Mr Daker as it lived up to its name and attracted masses of butterflies; the mock orange; the flowering, or American, currant; golden bells, a fairly recent arrival in England from China when Mrs Daker planted it; and the rose of Sharon as ground cover. Some American imports, of which they were very proud, were the sumach bushes with their strange growth and brilliant autumn foliage. Finally there were jasmines, honeysuckles, and brooms. They also planted rhododendrons, but without much success, as the soil on the site chosen was not really acid enough for that genus.

William Daker's interest in natural history had led him to become a 'modern' and thus a firm supporter of Charles Darwin. His neglect of the garden was more ecological and financial than due to laziness. He regularly read the works of John Curtis[a] (1791–1862) and Miss Eleanor Ormerod[b] (1826–1901), who had studied the inter-relationships of natural life and, as a result, had practical proposals for the control of pests. Gardening was expensive. He had to make the farm pay in order to meet the 'enormous' rent always hanging over him. And the more he improved the place the higher would that rent go, and the more easily would that great connoisseur, Alfred Hackshaw, live in Venice: nothing like an untidy garden to greet Mr Hackshaw's agent and put a low value on the property! Mr Daker could have been described as a 'dangerous radical'.

In 1898 William Daker was sixty-eight years old; his mother was eighty-nine and still very active for her age. But it was a hard struggle for her to keep the garden tidy. At Michaelmas that year William said to his mother, 'I'm not renewing the lease, Mother. We'll retire to a small house I have my eye on and both of us make a lovely garden. You'll celebrate your hundredth birthday there.' And after eleven years that is what she did, at Michaelmas 1909.

Alfred Hackshaw had just died, leaving Bartons End to his nephew Oscar. The agent said the property would make more if it were sold as two units, the farm and the house. The farm did sell well, but not the house, and as a result the garden was to suffer greatly.

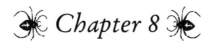

Chapter 8

The Garden Catastrophe, 1899–1910

Parasitic Plants, Spiders, Harvestmen, Mites and Molluscs

IN 1899, when William Daker gave up the lease, Oscar Hackshaw's agents advised him to make Bartons End into two properties and to sell them separately, on the grounds that the Liberals were intent on ruining the country with their Tenants' Compensation Acts. It was a fine state of affairs when an owner could no longer obtain the natural improvements accruing to *his* property at the end of a lease. Get rid of landed property was the advice of the agents.

The farm was easily sold, but the big, old Tudor farmhouse was not the sort of place to appeal to the prosperous, influential middle classes of Victorian England. The rooms were low and there was no gas, and no elegance. Admittedly, there was a fine garden but this presented a problem, for, being the property's main asset, it had to be maintained. To this end the agents appointed one of the farm foremen, Thomas Claridge, as gardener to keep the place tidy, the grass cut and the hedges trimmed for a very small wage, but with the proviso that he could retain for his own use any produce he raised. Thomas Claridge was an intelligent and ambitious man, a descendant of the Thomas Claridge who had been gardener to Mary Barton in 1558. The new Thomas was one of the first to take advantage of the 'whisky money',[a] an Act of Parliament which had given county councils money to spend on technical education. Claridge had attended a valuable course on horticulture at Wye College and with a basic knowledge of the principles was able to raise very good crops of flowers and vegetables. Naturally he spent the minimum of time on keeping the place tidy and the maximum on growing flowers and vegetables for sale, all of which greatly influenced the kind of life in the garden.

The house did not sell. For three years Claridge kept the approach drive and shrubbery reasonably tidy and the grass edges cut and trimmed. The extensive lawns were allowed to grow and were cut for hay, which maintained the Claridge goats during the winter. Mrs Claridge sold her goats' milk well, maintaining that it was a much healthier drink for children than cows' milk; which was correct for that age, as the goats did not carry tuberculosis.

In 1903 Thomas Claridge suffered a heart attack and could no longer do the gardening but his wife, Sarah, persuaded the agents that she could maintain the place on the same terms.

Mrs Claridge was an able woman, the mother of four children, the youngest, Sylvia, born in 1907, named after Sylvia Pankhurst, the suffragette, thus expressing some of Sarah's feelings on the condition of women in her day. Sarah was determined that her children should do well in life, and the disablement of her husband was a serious setback. Obviously she alone, even with the occasional help of the older children, could not maintain the garden in its former state of glory. She was not going to turn her boys into farm labourers, nor unpaid under-gardeners for Mr Oscar Hackshaw's profit. The boys had to study, and it wouldn't do Sylvia any harm to do likewise. She tried to point all this out to the agents, but they could not see their way to giving her—a mere caretaker—a full-time gardener. In fact, they felt they had acted generously in allowing the family to stay on after Mr Claridge's collapse: they had not even reported the event to their client in Venice. 'Just keep the approaches tidy,' they said, 'and when the property is sold we will give you a leaving present.'

Sarah Claridge felt she was being asked to make bricks without straw. Resenting the work-load the agents were piling on her and doubting the value of the proposed present—'A silver watch, I expect'—she, like most caretakers, thought she would be better off staying put for as long as possible. She became an expert in denigrating the place to every potential buyer that came to inspect it. The house was very damp and full of rot and woodworm, she said. The gas would never come there because the soil rotted the pipes. As to this new-fangled electricity, the less said about such dangerous stuff the better. And the rabbits, they ate everything in the place; while at night the owls made so much noise one could not sleep. Only one pump worked and that brought up dirty water. There were bats in the attic, and mould and woodworm too. The place had nearly killed her husband. As for taxation, goodness knows what the arrears were that a new owner would have to pay . . . and the tithes . . .!

Sarah would have made a good actress and she had a wonderful ploy, provided there was a little notice of the arrival of a potential buyer. Mussels were abundant in the Thames estuary and along the coast of the Romney Marsh. The hop-growers used to buy train-loads of them for manure, as the decaying flesh provided nitrogen and the shells lime. The smell of rotting mussels was appalling. The farmer at Bartons End manured his hops to a large extent with mussels: he liked the Claridges and, if asked, would dump a load of mussels near the house the day before a possible buyer was expected. Discreetly spread over the nearer flower beds these were guaranteed to lessen the charm of Bartons End. Mrs Claridge, in displaying the property, never mentioned the smell as a disadvantage, letting it act on its own. In fact, if asked, 'What is that appalling smell?' she would reply, 'What smell?' Rotting mussels were one of her best deterrents.

By 1906 the Claridge family were only cultivating a plot the size of an allotment, and most of the rest of the garden had been allowed to go wild.

The first great change in the decay of the garden from 1899 was seen in the neglected portions of the lawns, a neglect of two kinds, some parts being allowed to grow and then being cut for hay, and others entirely abandoned. In the hayed areas the coarse grasses gradually replaced the fine bents and a number of tap-rooted plants established themselves. At first there were dandelions, docks and sorrels, cats-tails and thistles of various kinds, but soon the dandelions were crowded out and the main weeds of meadow hay—docks, sow thistles, the Scotch thistle, knap-weed and yarrow—established themselves. In passing, it is curious to note that the Scotch thistle is a Mediterranean plant. At the start of this century it was being used to represent the Scottish heraldic thistle though it was not even wild in that country. At Bartons End it throve in the abandoned parts of the garden.

The same process took place in the entirely abandoned lawns, except where the bramble branches grew out from the hedges, touched to the ground and rooted. By the end of 1902 such abandoned lawns had become blackberry thickets, defying entry by anyone other than a determined person clothed in leather and armed with the fiercest of hedging tools. Grass still grew amidst the blackberries and other plants, but it was mostly the coarse couch grass. The blackberries naturally endeavoured to take over the parts of the old lawns set aside for hay, but here they were not so successful because the young plants from rooted tips and seedlings were cut back by the mower when the hay was taken.

The Claridge goats played an important part in keeping down weeds. Shortly after the hay harvest they would be tethered on the land and would eat off the secondary recovery growth the hay weeds were trying to make, killing or setting back such intruders. For many years the tethered goats kept the grass bordering the main drive to the house in reasonable condition and they much facilitated the area's return to a fine garden in later years.

Obviously the new conditions at Bartons End led to a fierce struggle for survival among many life forms, which extended over time. As an example, in the completely abandoned lawns the bramble thickets did not have it entirely their own way; after a few years, tree seedlings pushed up through the blackberry growth. The trees were ash, oak and sycamore, together with bushes of hazel. They weakened the blackberries by depriving them of light and in another twenty years the vegetation climax would have been reached: they would have turned the area back into Wealden forest, with the blackberry as an occasional growth on the forest floor.

Among the plants struggling for dominance and survival were a number of parasites, some having no chlorophyll, and thus being unable to make their own food, and others with chlorophyll but drawing from their hosts the minerals they needed. Such plants find the parasitic way of life easier, though they must not be too successful and extinguish their host altogether.

A chlorophyll-containing parasite which proved advantageous to the Claridges was the mistletoe (*Viscum album*). It grew well on the old

Missel-thrush and mistletoe

neglected apple and on certain forest trees, such as elms and poplars. Boxes of mistletoe sold very well for the Christmas market and the plant needed no expensive cultivation. The numerous missel thrushes did much to propagate that parasite. They liked the sweet, sticky fruit and after eating the pulp cleaned their beaks by wiping them on branches. This left the seed in a good position for germination and so the parasite spread.

Thomas Claridge was intrigued by the nature and mystery of the mistletoe. It seemed to him to be an ancient plant because it had many names besides its best known one; among them were kiss-and-go, churchman's greeting, muslin bush and even *herbe-de-la-Croix* because of the tradition that the Cross was made of its wood. Then there was the belief that the ancient Druids cut the mistletoe from the oak with a golden sickle, and then, so long as the plant was never allowed to touch the ground, the spreading yellow stems had magical powers. If it fell to the ground all its potency was lost. But Thomas was puzzled by two things. He had seen mistletoe growing on many trees but never on an oak and, besides, its branches were fairly tough, a golden sickle would never have cut them. Perhaps its very rarity on oak made it, when it did occur there, of special value and only the ends were cut with the soft gold hook.

Cutting the mistletoe for the Christmas market meant the use of long ladders and climbing into many trees. The Claridges were always careful to catch the falling plant on out-spread sheets or sacking and into each crate packed they put a note, 'This mistletoe has not been allowed to touch the ground.' Did the kisses exchanged under the Claridge mistletoe, an essential Edwardian Christmas tradition, have a more binding effect than those made under less carefully harvested crops?

It was not only the parasitic plants that exploited their neighbours; climbers did so as well, using trees and shrubs to carry their flowers and foliage into the light. Climbers led a semi-parasitic life, thus economising their resources, for making a stiff stem used a lot of plant food. The ivy is the outstanding example of this way of life, but another climber, the honeysuckle, did well in the abandoned lawn area and proved useful to Thomas Claridge.

Because of his heart attack, Mr Claridge was unable to take on hard work in the garden, but he was by no means idle and one of his ways of adding to the family income was to make fancy walking sticks. The honeysuckle, in climbing up one- or two-year-old shoots of trees and bushes, such as ash, hazel and chestnut, gripped them very tightly. As the host shoot grew it tried to expand but the honeysuckle prevented this. The result was a shoot with a spiral twist in it and these Thomas sought out and used for his unusual walking sticks. His great triumph was supplying a very twisted specimen to that great music-hall artist, Harry Lauder. Thomas was told that Mr Lauder used the Claridge stick when he appeared in the command performance before Edward VII in 1908.

In general, in going back to the wild, the garden had lost most of the decorative cultivated plants, showing how important utility or attractiveness to man is in the struggle for survival. But some still grew, often in small patches where conditions particularly suited them. Some survivors might only last a few years, but others came through until the garden was cultivated again.

The buddleia continued to grow and even spread to new points where a seedling managed to get among stones or at the base of a wall. Such a position enabled the young plant to defeat its first enemy, grasses, particularly the couch. Once the seedling was about a foot high it could shade out the grass and in autumn drop its leaves on to its rival, depriving it of light and life. Other survivors were hops, Michaelmas daisies, Japanese anemones, wallflowers, primroses and angelica, but the greatest success of the cultivated plants over the natives was in the shrubbery. The laurels, hollies, *Euonymus* and privets stood up to the ten years' abandonment very well to begin with, though in about thirty years' time they would have been dominated by the forest trees climbing above them, reducing them to weaklings just alive in the shade.

We must now turn to some of the garden's small animals that have not so far been mentioned—spiders, harvestmen, mites and molluscs.

Except for molluscs, these are all Arthropods. The Aranae, or spiders, were numerous. Why they should be so feared by man through the ages is strange, because they are very beneficial to him, killing large numbers of noxious insects. Man's skin is too tough to be bitten by any British spider. Exceptionally, a very soft part might be penetrated by a large

Theridon, but even so the bite would be no worse than a nettle sting. Disliked though spiders are in the house, yet they are seldom deliberately killed by man. Inside a room or shed they will be collected in a duster or tumbler and put outside—a great mistake as they are keeping down flies, clothes moths and furniture beetles, to name but a few of their victims. Perhaps spiders are not destroyed because it is thought to be unlucky to do so, a subconscious realisation of their value to man.

The spider is not an insect: its body is divided into two segments, the cephalothorax and abdomen, not into three as with insects. While insects have six legs, spiders have eight. They have a small mouth and a pair of powerful jaws like curved, hollow fangs. A small hole towards the tip of the maxilla (the fang) allows the spider venom to be injected into the prey, tranquillising and eventually killing it. The venom seems to consist of about six protein-like compounds of which spermine is the most important, and it also contains an enzyme that decomposes carbohydrates.[64] The poison appears to act by stimulating the production of acetylcholine from the nerve endings. This quickly uses up the victim's supply of the substance, a product causing the muscles to relax. In the absence of acetylcholine, nervous impulses cannot cross the synapses (the nerve junctions) and the muscles harden. With the animal half immobilised, the spider soon kills the creature.

A curious feature of spiders and of other venom-using animals, such as bees, wasps and snakes, is their ability to store considerable amounts of powerful poisons within their bodies and suffer no ill effects. Spiders can use their venom to kill other spiders when they fight, so the venom is toxic to spiders if injected in a suitable place. Snakes fighting each other do not use venom, so presumably it is toxic to snakes and there is a mutual agreement to refrain from using this weapon, reminding one of man's restraint, so far, on the use of all-out nuclear warfare. Obviously the poison sacs and canals are lined with a poison-resisting substance, an example of the complicated structures that have evolved in the natural world.

Spiders cannot take solid food; they suck the juices out of any victim or crush and liquify it with digestive secretions before sucking up the nourishing portions. Spiders are entirely carnivorous and usually eat only food they themselves have caught. Such food is mostly insects, those universal providers of the natural world. However, insects in their turn have developed defences against spiders. Some of their potential victims, ladybirds for instance, and woodlice, are heavily armoured or too slippery for the spider to get a grip. One common species of woodlouse (*Porcellio scaber*) at Bartons End could roll itself into a ball and defy the attack of any spider. Other insects, many aphids, for instance, have developed substances in their bodies which make them distasteful to spiders. Another example is the magpie moth; if a spider takes a bite at one of these it will stop, go to the edge of its web and spit out any juice absorbed. One bite does not do the moth much harm and it has the sense to remain still and thus not excite the spider to further activity. The magpie moth's cunning proved a handicap to the garden for, spared from attack from its worst enemy, the spider, it could at times be a severe pest of the gooseberries and currants.

Spiders have much influenced insects. In the early days of the world the many insects running about the earth were wingless and were much preyed on by spiders. By developing wings and taking to the air insects became one up on the spiders, but these latter creatures soon found an answer to that trick. They built the gossamer, almost invisible, web, returning the insects to the condition of main spider food once again.

Spiders have six to eight eyes, according to species, and thus good all-round sight. They have no antennae, as do insects, but their two palps have some of the functions of antennae and also act like hands. For example, when mating, a male uses his palps to place a bag of sperm inside the female. It is fairly well known that male spiders are often eaten by the female after copulation, which can be regarded as a simple provision by Nature for not wasting valuable food—the father literally contributes his substance to his offspring. However, it should be noted that in some species the males have reacted in an understandable way. The legs of some megalomorph spiders carry small hooks on their inner sides. When copulating the male pushes these hooks against the female's jaws, effectively gagging her and much increasing his chances of avoiding the kiss of death when the act is over.[64]

Spiders were important animals on the site of the first garden made at Bartons End; they have been there throughout its history and are in the place to this day. They were, and still are, very numerous. In fields, woods and gardens in summer there can be one or two million spiders present per acre. Spiders do not weigh very much: a garden *Theridon*, for instance, can run from 1 milligram at birth to several hundred milligrams when adult. A curious feature of spiders in Tudor times was that the spider population weighed more than the human one. For instance, 1½ million spiders at 4 milligrams each is 6 million milligrams or 6 kilos per acre, that is 13 lbs. 6 oz. per acre. The human population of England and Wales, having an area of 37 million acres, was then about 2 million people, and at 108 lbs. each they weighed 96,428 tons, equivalent to 5 lbs. 5 oz. per acre. The biomass of humans was, therefore, over the whole countryside, less than half that of spiders. Today the spider weight per acre is much the same, but the human population is now some 52 million, giving a human biomass of 152 lbs. per acre.

Some spiders have a stridulating organ, like grasshoppers. Most of the sound produced is very low and confined to the males, but some spiders can buzz like a bee and others purr like a cat. Either sound, if identified as coming from a spider, would intensify any existing aranaphobia!

The special characteristic of spiders is the production of silk, the main feature leading to their striking success in life. The silk is produced as a liquid in seven different kinds of glands, with some similarity to those producing venom. From the glands the fluid passes to the spinnerets from which it emerges as silk. It is not squeezed out like toothpaste from a tube but has to be drawn out and spiders show great skill in doing this with movements of their legs. Different kinds of silk are produced according to the structure being made or function performed.

Silk is used to bind captured insects, to make nests, egg cocoons, homes and finally webs. Young spiders, standing at an elevation, raise their bodies and emit a silk thread which floats away into the air. When the friction on the soaring line is more than the weight of the spider it mounts into the air and is carried away to new territory. Many such threads are a common summer sight. Pliny noted it: 'In the year that L. Paulus and Claudius Marcellus were consuls [216 BC] it rained wool.'[59] Obviously, a massive flight of Linyphid spiders. Silk is also used as a safety line, allowing a spider to return to base after foraging, or a fall. Finally we have the web.

In building an orb web the first thing the spider does is to establish a bridge thread, either by selecting a spot used by insects in flight and carefully putting a line across it, or just letting a thread sail out on the

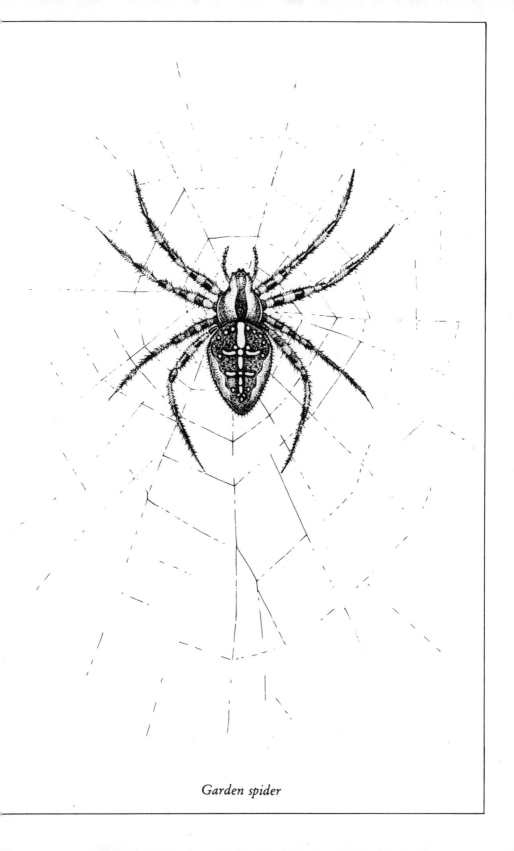

Garden spider

wind and attach itself to something. Once the bridge line is established the spider strengthens it by travelling along it several times, adding a new line as she goes. The framework now starts. Two lines are attached and pulled down below to a central point to make a V. The bottom of the V becomes the web centre and a number of radii of different lengths —because of the irregularity of the surroundings—are added. From the centre the spider then constructs a temporary spiral giving strength to the structure and a foothold for herself as she makes the business part.* Another kind of silk is used for this, fine and sticky; she works from the outside inwards and stretches the silk as she goes. This causes the stickiness to run into tiny drops along the thread, making the trapping of insects easier, but at the same time causing dew to condense on the strands, turning the web into a thing of beauty to us in the early morning, but making it conspicuous, and thus avoidable, to flying insects. However, spiders tend to construct their webs where there is a gentle airflow and insects do not so much fly into them as drift in, rather like fish caught in a net across a current or tidal flow.

After the rings of sticky silk have been applied the web is sufficiently strong to support itself and the spider cuts away the temporary spiral and waits for prey to arrive. The sticky threads are renewed daily.

The remarkable thing about this construction work is the skill of the builder. She manipulates eight legs and two palps on a network of threads swaying in the breeze, avoiding snare lines put in to trap a struggling catch as well as managing a line or two of her own silk and yet never gets caught within her own traps.

The web constructed, the spider waits for a catch. The garden spider stations herself at the centre of the construction. When an insect is caught it struggles and the spider knows, from the kind of vibration set up, what sort of prey is there. If small and desirable the spider will approach and kill it with a poisoned bite. If of medium size she will entangle it in silk until the creature can no longer defend itself. If large and dangerous, such as a wasp, the spider may decide to make the best she can of a bad job and cut the web away to let the creature escape before more damage is done or she herself receives a fatal sting.

Spiders prey on their own kind and some have acquired ingenious

* It is a convention to speak of spiders as female, but, at any rate early in the season, males also make webs.

tricks to enable them to do so. A Mimetid spider will creep gently into a web unnoticed, cut away a portion and then hang down below it with its long forelegs folded up. The Mimetid then pulls on the web, giving a false signal that desirable food has been caught. Down comes the owner to investigate. The intruder shoots out its forelegs, traps its host and gives it the paralysing bite, for the venom used is particularly powerful.

Not all spiders make webs. Some use the silk substance in an ingenious way: they spit a gob of it at an insect, which pins it down, allowing the spider to consume it at leisure. Some spiders even have poor sight and catch their prey by feeling for it with their long legs.

Many harvestmen (*Opiliones*) were found in the garden, especially when it was abandoned. They got the name harvestmen from the fact that they are numerous at that time of year. They can easily be confused with spiders, from which, in reality, they differ considerably. Though, like spiders, harvestmen have four pairs of legs, their bodies are very different. The body is all in one piece instead of two, as in spiders, or three, as in insects. Theodore Savory, the distinguished Arachnicist, writes:[64]

> The harvestmen are, surely, the comedians among Arachnida: animals with rotund bodies, ornamented with little spikes, with two eyes perched atop, back to back, like two faces of a clock tower, with feeble jaws and an undying thirst—a queer assortment of characters, even among a queer folk.

Legs are important to harvestmen. In fact, 'the study of harvestmen is the study of legs'. The second pair of the harvestman's legs is the most important and leads the others. If a leg is lost another grows to replace it, but if one of the second range goes the animal is severely handicapped. If both of the second pair are lost, the harvestman dies.

Harvestmen live on animal food, mostly that universal fountain of life—the insects.

Mites, or Acari, were numerous in the garden throughout its history and were mentioned in Chapter 2 in connection with soil fauna. But mites were also found on plants and animals, often being a considerable nuisance to them and to man himself.

Scientifically the Acari are divided into seven sub-orders, based on their physiology; each group includes mites living in a number of different ways. They can be predators, ecto- and endo-parasites and can live on fungi, litter or growing vegetation.

Among the predacious and parasitic mites found at Bartons End the red poultry mite may be mentioned. It attacked the domestic and wild birds and even humans at times. As this mite attacked at night it was often not seen. The mites of this sub-order, the Notostigmata, got into the body orifices of warm-blooded animals, such as *Ptilonyssus hirsti* on sparrows. But they were not all harmful. *Blattisocius tarsalis* attacked the grain mite, feeding on the grain stored as chicken food in an outhouse. That mite is dangerous in seed corn as it eats out the germ, thus killing the seed.

The ticks are Acari, that is mites, although much bigger than most mites, such as red spiders. They were found from time to time in the garden, attacking mainly the wild and domestic mammals found there; and acting as the vectors of many animal diseases. They have recurved teeth to the hypostane (the mouth), not for the purpose of puncturing the skin of their hosts but for fixing the creature in position. If a tick is just pulled away from a host, say a child's ear, the tick's head will break off and leave its mouth, all bloody, still in place. There it may cause the place to fester and cause a nasty wound. It was maintained by William Daker that the cigarette had been invented for the purpose of ridding the body of ticks. A lighted cigarette put near a swollen tick causes it to withdraw its beak, when it can be easily removed.

A characteristic of female ticks is that they can increase enormously in size as they suck their host's blood. For instance, an unfed adult can measure from 2–6 mm. in diameter; it can be 2 cm. across when gorged on its victim's blood, an increase in size of from three to ten times. Male ticks, on the other hand, either do not feed at all, or take only very small quantities of food.

Many species of ticks live off birds. They stay in the nest and only feed from time to time as the birds come back to roost or sit on eggs. In this way they avoid being picked off as the birds preen themselves.

Other mites troublesome in the orchard and garden were the 'red spiders' of fruit trees, greenhouse plants and occasionally garden plants. They were particularly damaging in the orchard's later years.

When the powerful synthetic insecticides DDT and benzene hexachloride were first introduced, the troublesome fruit tree pests, such as the aphids, suckers, leaf caterpillars and codlin moth were easily and cheaply controlled, but the chemicals did but little harm to the mites. The sprays also killed the predacious arthropods killing the pests, and soon the red spider mite, which sucked the juice out of the leaves, drying them up, became a serious nuisance. Highly toxic sprays, such as parathon, were then introduced to kill the mites. However, races of pests resistant to the sprays began to emerge and yet newer sprays had to be found. Thus the struggle continues, newer and newer pesticides being introduced as the old ones lose their potency.

A new procedure now being used in glasshouses has spread recently to Bartons End. The tomatoes there used to be badly attacked by red spiders and the crops needed expensive sprays to control them. Today a parasitic mite is introduced and keeps the enemy at bay. Such reliance on a predator calls for iron nerve on the part of the gardener, who well knows what great damage red spider can cause. His instinct is to spray as soon as he sees the pest. But if he is going to use biological control he must let the red spider establish itself, so that the predator, when introduced, has something on which to feed.

Many kinds of Eriophyid mites, at least thirty-three, were found at Bartons End, causing malformations in the growth of their hosts, running from large trees, through crops to humble weeds. *Eriophyes fraxinovorus* attacked the ash (distorted growth in the flowers) and *E. squalidus* the scabious (a mass of silky white hairs also on the flowers).

These mites are very small, about 0·1 mm long, blind and with two pairs of legs. As they feed on the plant tissues they inject a plant hormone that induces a gall, or particular kind of growth, to form. The curious thing is that this substance is always applied so that the gall produced is one adapted to the creature in question. The big bud mite on black currants induces the plant to make big buds. The injected hormone produces this neat ball, about half an inch in diameter and not just a mass of random growth. Inside the home the plant has made for them the mites thrive. Although the bud is not entirely destroyed, it will produce no fruit. The mites not only damage the crop but also spread the virus disease known as reversion, so called because the leaves assume a wild appearance and were held, quite erroneously, to have reverted to that state.

A mite of the sub-order Prostigmata was the harvester (*Trombicula autumnalis*), which bites human flesh when it is presented to them on summer lawns and hayfields. The lawns at Bartons End have led, and still do lead, many ladies, who in general have much softer skin than men, to regret sitting on the grass. It is not dampness that is the danger but the Trombicula's irritating attentions.

Many mites of the order Astigmata eat fungi and grain. Others are the feather lice of birds; some Astigmata are parasitic in the ears of dogs and cats, and another (*Sarcoptes scabiei*) was found at Bartons End from time to time on humans suffering from mange. Finally there are the Cryptostigmata, commonly called oribatid and beetle mites. They were common in soil, leaf mould, under stones and on bark, where they look like shiny insect eggs.

Over the garden's history many other plant galls, not caused by mites, were found and created interest. Let us consider two of them.

The bedeguar, moss gall or Robin's pincushion, is caused by the eggs of the gall wasp (*Diplolepis rosae*) in an unopened rose but particularly that of the dog rose. If the eggs hatch, the larvae induce the rose to make them a comfortable home and to feed them as well. Such a growth can easily produce some fifty cells for the larvae, the whole protected by a mass of twisting sticky threads. Bedeguars were found at Bartons End from the start until the present and produced varying reactions in the different gardeners. Some thought them pretty and liked them; others regarded them as pests to be destroyed. Mary Barton valued them for medicinal use; an infusion was a cure for diarrhoea.

The other gall is the oak apple. At least seventeen kinds of gall-wasps cause oak apples to occur.[19] The commonest oak wasp at Bartons End was *Biorhiza pallida*, an insect showing the curious feature of alternative generations, a complex matter.

A female gall-wasp lays eggs at the base of a bud, nearly wrenching it off as she does so. The 'apple' then starts to develop and will have about thirty cells containing grubs. The adults emerge in June, males and females coming from different galls. They mate in July, after which the females bore into the soil and lay eggs on oak rootlets. Root galls then form, each gall housing only one larva, which may live there for sixteen months. The adults emerging at the end of the second winter are all wingless females. They climb the oak trunk and lay eggs in the leaf buds of the branches, giving rise to 'apples' in due course. Thus, one generation is of females and the next is of males and females.

These galls, and those from another Cynipid (*Andricus kollari*), plentiful in the coppice, were collected at Bartons End from the first making of the garden until the Dunchesters bought the place. Their principal use was to make black ink and a black dye.

We now turn to the molluscs found at Bartons End, chiefly snails and slugs, the Gasteropoda. Their numbers rose and fell over the long history of the garden, their depredations frequently causing the gardeners great annoyance. Strangely enough, it was some of the untidiest gardeners, such as Emmanuel Burrows, who suffered the least damage from these creatures. The natural food of many species is decaying vegetation: if the garden beds are kept tidy, if grass cuttings and old leaves are cleared away, there is no natural food for the slugs and they turn to the tender parts of cultivated plants.

The word gasteropod means 'belly foot' and refers to the way snails, like Napoleon's army, walk on their stomachs. The snail's body is in two parts, the visceral hump and the belly. The hump is in the shell and the belly forms the foot, and thus its lower surface is known as the sole. The snail moves forward by secreting slime from glands beneath the head, then each section of the sole is raised and moved forward a little before being put down again. A rhythmic action moves the creature on over the ground.

The head carries one or two pairs of tentacles, which can be withdrawn into the body. Eyes are carried on the ends of the larger pair. The eyes do not give much of an image, but react strongly to variations in light intensity. The tentacles are also sensitive to touch and smell. When much disturbed the snail, in some species, draws its whole body into the shell and closes the entrance with a door or operaculum. The snail's hump is coiled inside the shell and its covering is known as the mantle. The mantle has a swollen edge and secretes the shell, adding ring after ring as time goes on. The shell is in two layers, the outer, giving the colour, is horny, while the inner is just calcium carbonate, smooth and mother-of-pearly. Most snails are dextral, that is, when held upright with the opening facing one, the orifice will be on the right and the tunnel will rise turning to the right. Although most snails are dextral, rare sinistral ones are sometimes found.

The majority of snails are hermaphrodites, each individual carries

Garden snail

male and female organs, but mating is always needed to produce fertile eggs. These molluscs have a radula, a set of ribbon-like teeth with which they rasp their food.

Snails naturally like damp conditions and hide up in the coolest places available during hot weather, a process known as aestivation. Most of these hiding places are under logs and stones and other wet spots, but sometimes the smaller snails are found towards the tops of grass stalks where they avoid the soil surface heated by the sun. Snails with an operaculum use it to close the entrance during a heatwave. When it rains after a dry spell the snails come out in quantity to feed: they are hungry. In the seventeenth century Mark Barton thought they fell with the rain, having been generated from 'corruption' in the dark clouds.

Snails hibernate in sheltered spots, retreating right into their shells and secreting much slime, which hardens into an 'epiphragm' and closes the opening. Such a closure must not be confused with an operaculum. Snails often congregate in masses glued together by their mucus.

The two most troublesome snails in the garden were the garden snail and the strawberry snail. The edible, or Roman, snail was sometimes found at Bartons End, but in fact it is not the only one that can be eaten. In the eighteenth century 'wall fish' (the garden snail) was much relished by labourers and avidly collected. During the Napoleonic wars Charlotte Munroyd's housekeeper took a great interest in the French officer prisoners on parole at a nearby camp, and, under the impression that they fed exclusively on snails and frogs, spent a long time collecting the Helicidae for them so that they should not go hungry; but she drew the line at frogs. She was, said the Frenchmen smilingly, *'une brave type'* and they gave her a little ship they had carved from bone.

Slugs appear to have developed from snails, finding life easier by not having to carry their housing around with them, but they have not entirely lost their shells. Three kinds of slugs were found in the garden, the shelled, the keeled and the round-backed.

The shelled group are mostly carnivorous. They have a small shell on the hinder end of the body. The shelled slug has sharp, curved teeth with which it can firmly grasp its food, consisting of other slugs, snails, millipedes and above all earthworms. It has a cunning trick with these last. The slug catches an earthworm when both are on the surface. The worm seeks safety by withdrawing into its burrow. The slug then allows itself to be drawn in as well, where it remains and consumes the worm undisturbed.

Other slugs have a rudimentary shell under the mantle. In the garden the most damaging mollusc in this category was the grey field slug and in the early days of the garden it was collected and eaten as a delicacy. In 1777 it destroyed most of George Munroyd's garden vegetables in spite of the hand-picking undertaken.

The slug defends itself against attack by exuding large quantities of slime and in time gardeners became aware of this and devised a method of lessening the slug's attacks. Slugs, dusted with an anti-slug powder, such as ashes, lime or copper carbonate, threw off the poison with the slime. It can do this a second time soon afterwards, but not on a third occasion. The answer to the slug problem was three dustings in succession and hand-collection on dark nights.

The grey field slug has a curious method of mating. The pair climb up a bush or on to a branch of a tree and exude a very thick mucus which hangs down and on which they lower themselves, slowly winding round and round each other as they mate. The process can last a couple of hours or more.

The slugs and snails at Bartons End had many natural enemies. Blackbirds and thrushes could often be seen beating a snail against a pet stone until the shell was broken. Moles, shrews, hedgehogs and toads all fed on them.

Today slug control is easier, because a weakness in their constitution has been discovered. They cannot resist the chemical metaldehyde. Mixed with some organic food, such as bran, breadcrumbs, even sawdust, the chemical draws slugs and snails to it and, like the human alcoholic and the whisky bottle, the mollusc is unable to leave until all trace of the attractant has gone. This leaves the slugs exposed to the sun, drying winds and predators, all of which kill them.

The trouble with these effective slug baits is that they attract the molluscs from far and wide. Slugs are killed in the garden, but the metaldehyde also draws them from the surrounding countryside. Once baiting is started, it has to be continued in order to keep the garden safe. Moreover, a slug in a drunken stupor from a heavy dose of the chemical could kill a bird that ate it, and poisoned slug baits may, at times, be eaten directly by birds.

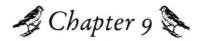

Chapter 9

The Garden of Robert Dunchester and of his Son Robert F. Dunchester, 1910–1958

Birds and Some Other Animals

ROBERT DUNCHESTER was a successful portrait painter with a small private income and was thirty-three in 1903, when he married the young Myfanwy Evans, one of his pupils, aged nineteen. Both of them were artists and, though they wanted to be moderns, circumstances pressed them into being conventional portrait painters. Minor industrialists, who revolted against the mechanism of the camera and could not afford top men such as Sargent and Boldini, would commission a range of lesser-known artists, Robert among them.

The Dunchesters lived in Chelsea and their work proved lucrative. The word 'they' is used because most of the backgrounds of Robert's pictures were done by Myfanwy. Indeed, they developed a particular style by specialising in historical backgrounds, incorporating ancient cradles, Cavalier armour, Empire *chaises-longues* and drapery. At the same time they wanted to paint and record nature and to that end they took up the fashionable and dangerous sport of bicycling. In June 1909 they made a bicycle tour of the Weald of Kent and came across Bartons End with its mysterious and overgrown garden. They asked Sarah Claridge, standing at her cottage gate, for a glass of water. As they did not present an 'order to view' from the agents Sarah did not see them as potential buyers. She gave them glasses of goats' milk and started to chat, but as the cyclists looked round, the danger soon became evident and Sarah went into her routine. She had had no time to get any mussels and every disadvantage she put up seemed to whet the Dunchesters' appetite the more. Dampness? That enormous fireplace would soon dry out the house. Bats? 'How amusing,' said Myfanwy, 'they would keep down the insects,' and she loved owls. Tithes? 'Nonsense,' said Robert, 'this is not a farm, if you have been paying tithes we'll reclaim a vast sum, plus interest.' Rabbits? 'Dogs, lovely dogs, and wire would see to them.'

Robert had just inherited some money from a maiden aunt: he thought no better use could be found for it than saving the old house and garden. And what a background both would make for his portraits.

When Robert made a modest offer for the property Oscar Hackshaw's solicitors laconically passed it on to the owner, at that time in Venice. Oscar, aged sixty-five, was on an extended visit to that city, ostensibly to visit his Uncle Alfred's grave, but also to see if the place attracted him as much as it had his uncle. Oscar had quarrelled with most people, including his lawyers, and so taken aback was he to hear that Bartons End was saleable that he telegraphed back, 'Yes, ha, oui, ja, I accept,' a display of schoolboy erudition that he felt would somehow irritate his agents without actually spoiling the sale. Robert Dunchester, surprised at the ready acceptance of his offer, wished he had named an even lower figure.

The task facing the new gardeners was enormous and they had very little time for natural history for many years after their purchase; gardening took up all their time that was not devoted to the business of portraits. The most important initial step they took was retaining the services of the Claridge family on reasonable terms.

The first decision the Dunchesters made was to get the lawns into good condition. It was comparatively easy to remake the portions that had been cropped as hay. A small Kent balance plough was used on these. This is two ploughs at right angles to each other, one ploughing and the other carried in the air. At the end of a furrow the plough in the air is brought down and cuts the next furrow, going in the opposite direction, thus allowing small awkward areas to be worked. The land was then harrowed, some of it being turfed, and some sown with seed in October 1910.

Elaborate blends were used for seeding in those days. At the Bartons End revival a mixture using eighteen species, at a heavy sowing rate, was used, in contrast to some re-seeding done there recently by Frazer Properties, where a mixture of crested dogstail, rough-stalked meadow grass and wood meadow grass was sown at two ounces per square yard, a third of the Dunchesters' rate, and produced as good or better results.

On the other part of the old lawns, that portion entirely abandoned, the task was much more difficult and Robert Dunchester engaged a special team to strip out the brambles, bushes and saplings. All this brush was piled up and burnt and then the stumps painfully removed, using drag lines, steam winches and tree jacks. Only then could the land be ploughed and sown to grass. It was an expensive undertaking.

Robert next decided to improve the approach to the house and to plant an avenue of trees. As elms did well in the neighbourhood and were quick-growing, he lined the drive with a dozen well-spaced trees. By the time his son, young Robert Dunchester, married Louise Cavanagh in 1935 they had become fine specimens.

Robert senior was spending so much time, effort and money on the garden that he felt it must be made to help in his artistic career. Tudor and Stuart motifs for his portraits were being overdone and he felt a new approach was needed. Should he foster archery or make a lawn tennis court? Archery was too reminiscent of his Tudor period and tennis too modern. Then he remembered and hunted out a book of his father's, *The Game of Sphairistikè*, by Major Walter Wingfield, which had been published in 1876.[76] Sphairistikè was the precursor of modern lawn tennis. He decided to make a sphairistikè court.

The court was hour-glass shaped, 24 feet wide at the centre and 30 feet at the two base lines. It was 58 feet long, and thus rather smaller than the modern lawn tennis court of 36 by 78 feet. The net was 5 feet high at the posts and 4 feet at the centre. Hollow rubber balls, rather like the modern tennis ball, were used and cost five shillings a dozen then. Only the server could score, as in modern squash-rackets. The *Morning Post* had commented that sphairistikè was 'a game at which ladies can display considerable proficiency', as proved to be the case. Myfanwy could usually beat her husband, but she was after all fourteen years younger than he was.

The court was a success: it created great interest locally and the Dunchesters were 'taken up'. With the publicity of the court and his efforts in restoring the house and garden, Robert began to get commissions for portraits from the local gentry, several with a sphairistikè motif. During the First World War the court was at first neglected and then, in 1916, dug up to grow vegetables. The first crop was potatoes and was most unsatisfactory as the resident wireworms, larvae of the *Agriotes* beetles, fed avidly on them. After the war the land was again seeded and became a fine lawn tennis court.

Cultivation for vegetables left the soil in good condition for the rapid establishment of a close sward, but soon the usual broad-leaved weeds began to appear. A new method of dealing with these was now introduced, the use of lawn sand. A mixture of sulphate of ammonia, sulphate of iron and sand was scattered over a weedy patch. The product would fall off the narrow grass foliage and lodge on the weeds' broad leaves, scorching them. The ammonia acted as a fertiliser to the grass and the scorching of the weed foliage, a slight setback, gave the grass an opportunity to squeeze out its rivals. The effect of lawn sand was not as dramatic as today's treatment with hormone herbicides, but nevertheless it helped reduce the labour needed to keep a lawn weed-free.

The re-making of the garden from 1910 onwards was based very largely on the writings and advice of the famous gardener Miss Gertrude Jekyll, though Robert drew the line at her suggestion of tearing down the old house and getting her protégé, the architect Edwin Lutyens, to design a new one, to match a Jekyll garden she would devise, one suitable for such an artist as himself.[48] Mr Dunchester, though susceptible to such heavy flattery, was not rich enough to undertake the plan. Moreover, he liked his Tudor house: such backgrounds were his trademark. He would have a garden on Jekyll principles, not actually Jekyll designed. The lady had pushed a little too hard.

Miss Jekyll considered herself an 'impressionist' gardener and was given to incorporating wild plants and areas in her designs. Bartons End was to have 'glorious but orderly confusion'. At one moment one might gather a moss rose, and a bunch of currants the next. The scent of jasmine and the juice of gooseberries would be interposed and so forth. Such principles gave the garden designer of the time wide scope. He could declare anything unusual he did to be the latest Jekyllism.

The orchard had not been neglected by the Claridges as much as other parts, for the fruit trees gave them good saleable crops, among them the mistletoe already mentioned. Robert Dunchester decided that he would

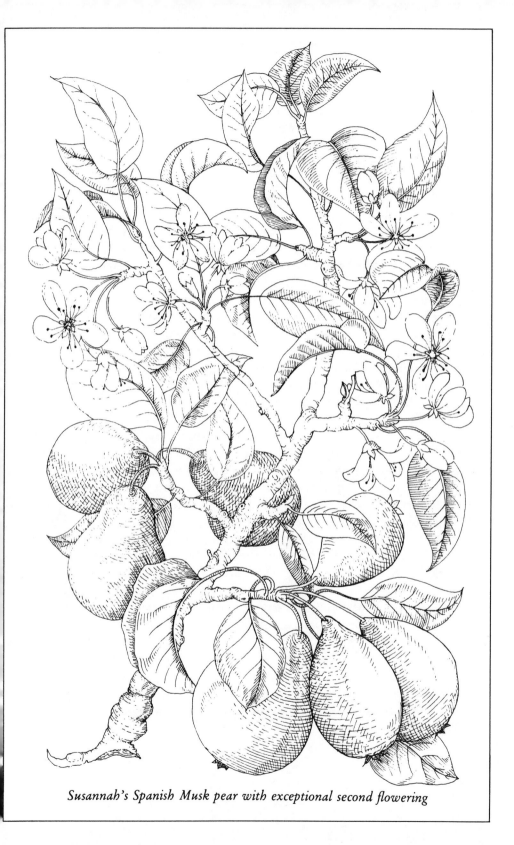

Susannah's Spanish Musk pear with exceptional second flowering

take a particular interest in pears; not only was their blossom beautiful but the fruit was delicious as well. The orchard already had a dozen large standard trees with somewhat vague names, among them Jargonel, Summer Bon Chrétien, Windsor, Bergamot and Cassolet.

Robert decided not only to grow good fruiting varieties but also pears developing other interesting characteristics, and he started to explore the subject, being much helped by W. Robinson's book *The English Flower Garden*.[61] By 1915 he had planted out, as good quality fruiters on the walls, Doyenne de Comice, Beurrée Dumont and William's Bon Chrétien; as tall upright trees, Beurrée Hardy and Duc de Nemours; and as a spreading, drooping bush, Nouvelle Fulvine.

He grew specimens of Delpierre and a Japanese Mikado on account of their beautiful foliage. He planted Marie Guisse because it budded first in the spring and Herbin because it was the last to drop its foliage. He did not neglect the appearance of the bark either. There was the ash-coloured Bési Dubost, the violet Beurrée Giffard, the dark brown Bon Chrétien de Bruxelles and the scarlet-spotted stem of Beurrée Lebrun. Finally there was Poirier de Fosse, now an enormous tree, painstakingly kept alive for its curiosity value. It never did, nor will, produce worthwhile fruit and its crop used to be used for perry, but in the spring it was a fascinating white cloud of blossom. Being grafted mostly on wild pear stocks, instead of quince, the trees grew very large.

The great problem with pears, Dunchester found, was choosing the exact moment to eat them. A pear is left on a shelf to ripen. At first it is hard and unattractive; it next becomes nearly ripe, then perfect, and soon after that rotten. Making this point to his family one day Robert said, 'In fact, a Frenchman has said there is only half an hour in the life of a pear when it is fit to eat. Remember that.' Young Robert, aged twelve, then said, 'To get the right moment, Father, must we have someone watching them all night?' It became a wonderful excuse, the children found, for going to bed late, 'I am just watching the pears, Mother.'

During the First World War, 1914–18, Robert Dunchester was employed by the War Office as a draughtsman and artist. At the outbreak of the Second World War in 1939 both the Robert Dunchesters, the elder being on the Reserve, presented themselves for army service, the reservist—now sixty-nine years old—quipping, 'Nice long leave, Sarge.' Only the younger was accepted.

The lawns once again were dug up and once more the wireworms severely damaged the first crop of potatoes. Louise Dunchester, Robert the younger's wife, was very active during this period, organising the growing of large quantities of vitamin-rich vegetables. She also collected useful materials from the wild, particularly rose hips of all kinds for the children's rose-hip syrup. Her perry was most popular.

In 1944 Kent was on the flying-bomb route to London. One of these bombs fell on to soft ground at the western border of the garden, creating a considerable crater but not causing much damage to the house. Leaded Tudor windows have some give in them, and they bend to a blast that would shatter a solid pane. Louise decided that for the moment nothing much could be done with the crater. Perhaps, after the war, it could be turned into a water garden, or a swimming pool. She made only one proviso about it: it must not be used as a rubbish tip.

The crater developed quite a life of its own. Many seeds will lie dormant in the soil for long periods. Just as in the First World War the poppy was the dominant plant of the turned-up Flanders soil, so in the Second World War, in England, the rosebay willow herb became very common in such places. At least six species of moth caterpillars fed on it. Louise's nephew, Phillip Frazer (born 1937), spent much time with his aunt at Bartons End and was fascinated by the crater, collecting caterpillars from the willow herb and raising them to moths. A success that much pleased the boy was finding the two hawk moths in that patch, the fairly common elephant and the rarer small elephant, a distinction being that the caterpillar of the latter has no horn on its last segment, as do most hawk moth larvae.

The angle shades moth was on the willow herb and from there it spread to the strawberries, hops, and to the tomatoes in the greenhouse. Phillip was set to picking off the caterpillars by hand. He was told he need not destroy them but let them free in the bomb crater, where they could feed on the willow herb, but whether a caterpillar raised on, say, tomatoes, would change its food so easily is difficult to say.

A great feature of gardening during this post-war period was the discovery by the Jealott's Hill Research Station of the selective weed-killers. These were a range of hormone-like substances which tended to kill dicotyledonous plants and hardly to affect the monocotyledons.[a] Moreover, they were very powerful chemicals and only small amounts were needed to get this result. This meant that about half a pound of MCPA, dissolved in water and sprayed over an acre field of wheat, would set back all the charlock and similar weeds without affecting the corn plants, which then smothered the weeds. The new herbicides worked in the opposite way to the then-known chemical weedkillers, such as sodium chlorate and arsenicals, which actually poisoned and killed the plants. The new selective weedkillers acted as plant hormones and stimulated vegetative growth in the broad-leaved plants sprayed, but the extra growth was irregular, twisted and abnormal, so the affected plant did not thrive. The monocotyledons, scarcely affected by the new compounds, then grew and choked out the weeds.

Chlorate and arsenic killed all vegetation and needed considerable amounts to do so. To kill all the growth on a grass tennis court would need the application of about 16 lbs. of sodium chlorate: a similar weight of MCPA (hormone) weedkiller would treat about 32 acres of grass.

The same substances were soon being used on lawns. The chemicals killed the daisies, plantains, clovers, cat's ears and similar plants and left a sward of fine, thriving grass. The saving of labour was enormous and the beautiful, green, weed-free lawn became commonplace.

The use of these products on lawns naturally affected the life there. For instance, it was the practice of many gardeners to scatter grass cuttings over the soil in herbaceous borders, in order to suppress weeds. If, however, the grass had been cut shortly after a hormone weedkiller treatment, the residues left in the mowings would affect, or even kill, sensitive plants, such as wallflowers and vines. So care had to be exercised that lawn mowings taken soon after a dressing of weedkiller should be rotted down in special bins, compost from which was only used on grass lawns.

Naturally certain insects, such as aphids living on lawn plants—dandelions and plantains for example—were eliminated in the new, weed-free swards. On the whole the weedkillers tended to increase the number of earthworms as well as insects feeding on grass roots, wireworms and daddy-long-legs among them. By the time young Robert died the Bartons End lawns were all hormone treated and had become fine stretches of soft green grass.

Rosebay willow herb and elephant hawk moth

One of the difficulties of gardening throughout the ages has been coping with the weather and one of the reasons why it never seems to be right for the professional gardener is that conditions that suit one kind of plant will not suit another equally esteemed species. For instance, warm, damp summer weather can be splendid for lawns, lettuce and cabbage, and fatal for potatoes, because that climate is then just right for the devastating blight.

During the first third of the nineteenth century most gardeners expected that hard winter weather would kill the new and exciting plants being introduced from abroad, unappreciative of the fact that many came from countries with far more severe winters than were found in Britain. William Hackshaw was agreeably surprised to find that his big magnolia was not harmed by the hard frosts of the winter of 1837–38. A strawberry tree at Bartons also lived through that season, though it did succumb about a hundred years later, by which time it was very old and not so resilient. Obviously severe winters damage plants, but often not as much as has been expected, and apparently dead bushes are often found to sprout from the roots again during the following summer, or even later.

Similarly, summer droughts set back and kill choice specimens. Just as frost often causes less harm than was expected, damage, or at any rate loss of crop or growth, due to drought is often more than is commonly noticed: that is to say, water shortage is frequent, even in the allegedly rain-soaked England.

The winters of 1708–9 and 1739–40 were long and severe and each in its turn set back the gardens of Joseph Munroyd and of the young Charles Munroyd, just as the latter had started his campaign of family improvement. However, his garden survived: the marriage took place, and was not quenched by the terribly wet spring and summer of 1756. The following year, 1757, was famous for its very hot summer, for a record crop of sweet grapes in the vineyard, the flowering for the first time at Bartons End of the South African aloes, and for the capture of Calcutta by Clive of India.

Charles's son, George Munroyd, saw the very severe winter of 1794–95 and the death of some of the garden's prized plants, such as a number of promising young strawberry trees and a sweet bay hedge. Apart from frost the *Arbutus* had another enemy, the rhododendron, whose seedlings smothered the young strawberry trees and prevented natural regeneration. However, the Munroyds and their successors, nothing daunted, replanted their lost plants and did so again after similar setbacks in 1800, 1812–13 (the year when the weather defeated Napoleon in Russia), 1916–17, 1940–41 and 1973–74.

1873–75 saw bad weather for three gardening summers in succession. The winters were not particularly hard but the summers were wet and largely overcast. They gave point to William Daker's neglect of the garden. 'What can you do in such weather?' he would say.

In both world wars the Bartons End garden suffered severely from winter frosts. The famous gardener E. A. Bowles made a study of the first of these unhappy events,[10] listing the effects of the weather in the winter of 1916–17 on some 1,570 species of plants growing in seventy-six gardens up and down the country. At Bartons End the frost was bad; in the screen the temperature fell to 17°F and to 7°F on the grass. In Britain the winter of 1940–41 was very hard and the frost probably did more economic damage than Hitler's bombs. Ice accumulated on tree branches and on power and telephone cables and the weight broke many of them. A whole range of plants was destroyed at Bartons End; among them may be mentioned a number of prized shrubs, such as *Abelia floribunda* with no common name, the tree of heaven, the Katswa tree, the Californian lilac, the sweet bay and some delicate buddleias (*B. asiatica* and *B. auriculata*), although the common butterfly tree survived. The rhododendrons did not grow well at Bartons End, nevertheless they all stood up to the frost.

Let us now consider an interesting phylum of animals found during the whole history of the garden—the birds. They fall into two classes, visitors and residents, the latter being more numerous and themselves divided into wild birds and domestic ones, such as ducks, geese, pigeons and, at one period, hawks and peacocks.

When the garden was first started wild bird life in the area was changing considerably, because the forests were disappearing. New farms were being made all the time, but the main need for trees was as fuel for iron smelting. The discovery of America, and a rising population, had led to a constant demand for tools, guns, bolts, nails, armour and so forth. Kent supplied iron ore, and charcoal was needed to smelt it, so the forests were felled. The woodland birds, such as jays, nightingales, blue tits and woodpeckers were giving way in the sixteenth century to those of the forest edge and meadows: skylarks, warblers, blackcaps, blackbirds, song thrushes, chaffinches, and other tits.

Birds are plastic animals and throw off new kinds able to adapt themselves to altered circumstances very readily. Large numbers of species are extant because of their very adaptability over the aeons of evolution.

The flight of birds has always fascinated man: they have a vivid life and usually a fast death, points which greatly impressed W. H. Hudson:

> Yesterday he lived and moved, responsive to a thousand external influences, reflecting earth and sky in his small, brilliant brain as in a looking glass; also he had a various language, the inherited knowledge of his race, and the faculty of flight, by means of which he could shoot, meteor-like, across the sky and pass swiftly from place to place; and with it such perfect control over all his organs, such marvellous certitude in all his motions, as to be able to drop himself plumb down from the tallest tree-top or out of the void air, on to a slender spray and scarcely cause its leaves to tremble.[41]

Birds are warm blooded and mostly comparatively small. Their weights are low compared to their surface area, which means they must eat considerable amounts of food in order to keep warm. For instance, an unfledged bird must consume its own weight of food daily to maintain existence and to grow—it is no wonder that parent birds are very busy all the time their young are around. Most of the food the young bird takes is used to maintain its temperature, but by the time it is adult it has feathers and these reduce the heat loss considerably. The feathers trap little pockets of air, which is a good insulator if the bird cannot move. When it begins to feel cold it fluffs up its feathers and looks bigger. It is increasing the number and size of the insulating air pockets. When we put on a woollen jersey we are doing much the same thing, covering ourselves with a layer of trapped air pockets.

In addition to the lightness of its feathers a bird's body has other weight-saving devices. Many of its bones are 'pneumatic', with hollow, air-filled pockets in them. A bird's respiratory system includes both lungs and the air-filled spaces in the bones. This allows a rapid transfer of oxygen into the blood when the animal is very active, such as when in full and difficult flight. The spaces often have cross-struts, as in aeroplane wings, to give strength. Female birds, in spite of the large numbers of eggs laid by many species, have only one ovary, another saving of weight. In the formation of an egg, the yolk comes first; it passes down the egg-tube and then is coated with the albuminous white and the shell, composed mostly of calcium carbonate. The egg then moves into the cloaca and out of the vent.

Inside the egg the young bird develops a hard knob on its beak which enables it to break the shell and escape. Some kinds of birds, the domestic hen, for example, have precocious young, able to feed themselves at once, while most of the wild birds have nestlings who need to be fed by their parents for some time.

Bird life has many strange sides to it: at times birds seem able to do things we require elaborate apparatus to achieve. At others they seem unable to solve simple problems. For example, the house martins at Bartons End have migrated for centuries to the other side of the world for the winter and returned to their own nests in the late spring, using no scientific apparatus at all, no sextant, marine almanac or magnetic compass. How do they find their way? But a bird will batter away at a closed window for a long time, quite failing to notice an open door behind it by which it could escape.

What happened to certain species of birds in winter, such as cuckoos and swallows, has intrigued mankind for a long time. Charles Munroyd (1716–64) felt he ought not to disagree with such an authority as Dr Samuel Johnson, who wrote:

> Swallows certainly sleep all the winter. A number of them conglobate together by flying round and round, and then all in a heap throw themselves under water and lie in the bed of a river.[9]

The magic of that word 'conglobate' seemed to mask the fact that not only had no one ever seen that plunge, but neither had anyone ever dug up a cache of wintering swallows. It was gradually accepted, as swallows and similar migrants were found in alternative sites in the world, that long migrations took place. Finally, putting numbered rings on birds, particularly fledglings, led to definite knowledge of their movements.

Such extraordinary feats of navigation are still not fully explained. It is fairly obvious that birds and other migrating animals use factors that we are scarcely aware of and they may well combine many systems in order to achieve their aim. Moreover we notice the birds that do return but we fail to take account of those that are lost on the journey, due to bad weather or predators—not the least of which is man in countries such as Italy, where migrant birds are trapped by the thousand and eaten.

Man finds his way around the world by using what is known as a bi-coordination system of navigation. Basically the two reference points needed are the place's latitude and longitude. Using a sextant, compass and chronometer he can identify his position, go to a desired locality and return home as he wishes. Such a calculation is beyond the powers of a migrating bird.

Among the factors that possibly help birds to find their way are the position and movement of the sun and moon, an appreciation of the passage of time, terrestial magnetism, inertia navigation, changes in the magnetic field, temperature gradients, odour changes, the north/south variation in the strength of gravity and remembrance of the outward journey. It is possible to raise objections to all of the above, for instance, remembrance of the outward journey: juvenile birds can successfully navigate a route they have never traversed previously, and in the autumn the first swallows to leave are the juveniles. As regards variations in the strength of gravity, though different places have different gravities the variations are very small. If the birds can detect them they must possess a very delicate organ to that end. The fact remains that birds have a mysterious power of navigation which we do not fully understand.

The domestic birds resident in the garden at Bartons End varied considerably. The first were common chickens and ducks (*Anatidae*), introduced by the Bartons from the start and maintained in greater or lesser quantities to the present. More unusual birds, in today's terms, were introduced by John Barton. He kept a pair of goshawks for, being of but moderate social status, he could not aspire to the aristocratic peregrine.

Mary Barton would often accompany her husband, carrying a sparrow-hawk. These hawks caught more game than the noble falcons and peregrines which soar high in the air, well above their prey, and 'stoop' on it, that is, dive at immense speed—estimates of 180 miles per hour have been made[14]—striking it dead with one blow of the talons or grappling with it and falling to earth where the victim is quickly despatched. It was an exciting thing to see one's favourite bird kill in such a decisive way a victim one had shown it.

The goshawks and sparrow-hawks do not rise high in the air and so are less spectacular to watch than falcons, but they fly direct and rapidly at the game. The kill is not as clean and rapid as with the peregrines. merlins and kestrels, but is just as effective in the end.

The Bartons were fascinated by hawking and added quite a bit of food to their larder in that way. Lark pie was a favourite dish; sparrows were not despised. Wood pigeons, then comparatively rare, were a great prize; the hawks were not flown at domestic pigeons as these were more easily obtained from the garden's pigeon loft. But keeping and training hawks was time-consuming, and the sport had died out at Bartons End by about 1620.

It should be noted that the numerous wild raptorial birds around when the garden was being made meant that many pest animals, such as mice, rats, voles, sparrows and certain insects, were kept under control. When gamekeepers began to destroy kestrels, merlins and owls they greatly increased the populations of mice, voles, grasshoppers and beetles, the birds' favourite food.

An unusual and much later addition to the garden was peacocks, introduced by Charles Munroyd as part of his social improvement campaign. They were as good or better than watchdogs, he maintained, making a great noise if a strange man or beast came by.

Charles was more successful in getting his peacocks to display their tails than many neighbouring Pavophiles because his collection consisted of four cocks and two hens. If there is a solitary male, or just a pair, there will be no or very little display. In their native Indian forests the peacocks gather on a special site, both cocks and hens. The males spread their tails into the well-known colourful fan, rattle their plumes and quiver their wings in front of the females. Each peahen can then compare the efforts of a number of males and make a choice. She moves to the front of the one selected, who then, coyly, turns his back. Eventually mating takes place. As those males with the most attractive display mate the most often, the genes making for good displays are strengthened in the species.

Male great tit singing to defend his territory

It is not only the gaudy birds, such as the peacocks, that use displays. Nearly all birds use it to a greater or lesser extent, the amount of display possible being balanced by the amount of concealment needed. Display may be needed to secure copulation even more than actual pair-formation, or marriage, if such an anthropomorphic term may be used. For instance, the migratory warblers' males arrive in Kent in spring, ahead of the females, and search for nesting sites, probably having fights to obtain and retain them. A cock warbler, having found a site, awaits the arrival of the females, spending the time feeding and singing. The hens arrive and search out the songsters. A female, having found a male with a nest that suits her, adopts the male, possibly having to fight another female for him. No displays are indulged in up to this point. The birds form the association for one brood only, not for life as do some birds such as pigeons.

After the pair-formation, with the nest ready, the male display starts, its objective being to induce the female to mate. Though the warblers are dull-coloured, yet they do their best: they spread their wings, fan out their tails and bristle up the feathers on their heads and necks. The males may also select pieces of nesting material and present them to their partners. In due course the display induces the right hormone flow in the hen and mating takes place. Soon afterwards the eggs are laid. The garden warbler, found at times at Bartons End, would also use the display procedure to frighten away predators trying to attack the young in the nest.

One of the features of the early garden was a pigeon loft, set on the top of a tall pole in the centre of a grass plot. It was a useful source of fresh food during winter, or in an emergency at any time, and was the equivalent of today's deep freeze. One could always make a pigeon pie at a few hours' notice. The pigeons were of the rock pigeon species, *Colomba livia*. The bird is named from the livid or lead colour so many of them have. There were, and still are, some five races of this species: the rock pigeon, nesting on cliffs and rocks, now fairly rare; dovecote pigeons, semi-domesticated birds, exploited for food and dung, but not confined; feral pigeons, birds living in a free or ownerless state, now found in large numbers in towns, exploiting their charm for man and getting him to feed them in public squares; domestic pigeons, birds kept under a greater degree of control and selectively bred by man, mostly for exhibition purposes; and finally racing pigeons, now a very popular kind and bred in large numbers.

Robert Dunchester, with an eye for a good publicity measure, kept some homing pigeons and would give one to a person sitting to him for a portrait, saying, 'Take this bird home and release it when you are ready for another sitting.' It was more romantic than the halfpenny postcard and secured an earlier sitting, too, because the recipient, not knowing how to feed and hold the pigeon, released it as soon as possible.

Bird song was one of the attractions of the garden from the earliest days. The songsters ran from the melodious nightingale to the discordant starling. Nightingales used the garden from its start and are still found there in summer, though today they are rare birds. They are migrants from Africa who like woodlands with a dense ground cover, such as brambles and blackthorn. When a coppice is cut nightingales lose a favourite habitat.

From the time of John and Mary Barton onwards nightingales were prized for their song, gentle flute-like trills, on a still night, starting softly and building up to an orchestra of sound. For gardeners the birds had practical uses too, as they fed mainly on ground insects, cockchafers, wireworms and rose chafers. Of course, nightingales sing by day as well as by night; when George Munroyd had the house (1764–1808) there were so many in the copse, defending their territories with song at night, that Sophia complained she could not sleep.

Song is an important feature of bird life. Birds do not sing for the purpose of providing inspiration or pleasure for man, as many poets and writers imply. All the nightingale's song is really saying is, 'Keep off my territory, or you'll rue it.'

As far as song goes, birds are almost uninfluenced by man, and that the song may be attractive to him or not is but incidental. It can have some slight importance because a song attractive to man can have a survival value for the bird when habitats are under pressure. Because of it photographers, radio engineers and TV producers may be drawn in to protect a species which otherwise might have vanished from many habitats.

In the spring the male of most species of bird has to acquire and maintain a territory, to which he invites a female. Here they mate, breed and raise their young. Song is used both to secure territory and to hold it; this last function being neatly expressed by David Attenborough's comment, 'Trespassers will be sung at.'[6]

Song is also used to convey information, such as 'I am cock of this walk; would any lady within earshot care to inspect this desirable property?' Once the pair-bond is formed the territory is more easily held.

Territory is advertised by the proclamation song, such as the blackbird's from a tall tree or telephone pole. Proclamations have to be such that they proclaim the species: it is no good a blackbird singing a song that will bring in a thrush. When the pair is formed the song must be sufficiently individual to identify the singer, enabling the mate to return to the nest if lost or confused. The great tits have a species song and great individual diversity within it. In musical terms they employ variations on a theme. Rival males, each on the edge of his territory, will sing vigorously at each other, especially in the early mornings, when conditions are not good for foraging. Fights between rival males are seldom to the death. At a certain point one or other of the contestants gives up, making a recognised surrender gesture or call.

Naturally, the song is also heard by predators and parasites, such as cuckoos, so that the advantages of singing must be balanced against the risk of giving away the position of the nest. For this reason song may be limited to certain seasons or times of day and some song patterns are such that predators have difficulty in locating the exact position of the songster. It is a common experience among bird-watchers not to be able immediately to focus their binoculars on a singing bird, particularly a cuckoo. Robert and Sloane Dunchester as children knew this. Playing hide and seek they would call 'Cuckoo', as the sound least likely to reveal the exact hiding place.

Alarm calls are part of song and obviously serve to alert birds to the approach of danger. Sound is also used to keep the flock, or a pair's fledglings, together. The clucking of a hen keeps her chicks around her, and they run beneath her at the approach of danger. Sound can also be used to drive off enemies: the reed warbler will scream at and drive off a cuckoo trying to lay an egg in the warbler's nest, while the mobbing of an owl by smaller birds is accompanied by a cacophony of sound.

Nests, eggs and sitting birds are vulnerable to predators, and various measures are taken to reduce that risk. Nests, such as those of chaffinches and dunnocks, can be well hidden in a dense thicket or hedge. The goldfinch may choose the end of a fragile branch that would not support the weight of a predator. Spotted woodpeckers and nuthatches seek the protection of a hollow tree. To prevent the entrance of predators, which are usually larger than the prey, birds, like the nuthatch, may reduce the size of the entrance hole by partly closing it with mud. The wren for the same reason constructs a ball-like nest, with only a small entrance.

House martins built their nests under the eaves of the house and its outbuildings from the start of the garden. Possession of these nests is often disputed by house sparrows who tend to take them over after the martins have migrated and the following year the migrants have to spend a lot of energy making new nests. However, it is not such a serious loss as might at first appear. The nests can be full of feather-lice awaiting the return of their hosts, and a new nest avoids reinfection by lice at an early stage in the season.

By the time Robert F. Dunchester died in 1958 the commonest birds in the garden were chaffinches, robins, swallows, pied wagtails, spotted flycatchers, blackbirds, dunnocks, song thrushes, blue tits, goldfinches, house martins, starlings, house sparrows and wrens.

Chapter 10

The Garden of Sloane Frazer, her Children, and of Frazer Properties Ltd., 1958–1984

ROBERT F. DUNCHESTER died comparatively young, when he was forty-eight years old. He left the property to his wife Louise for her lifetime, or until her remarriage, when the estate would revert to his nephew, Phillip, and two nieces, Caroline and Myfanwy Frazer, the children of his sister, Sloane Frazer. Louise was very fond of them and the two ladies decided to divide the house and garden into two parts of unequal size, the larger being for the Frazers and the smaller for Louise.

Dividing the house presented considerable difficulties, and was delayed, but splitting up the garden was comparatively easy and a start was made on that, the bomb crater falling to the particular care of Phillip, now twenty-one years old.

About the time the Frazers were disposing of their own house in 1960 and extensive alterations and additions were about to be made to the old farmhouse, Louise announced she was going to marry an old admirer and consequently the property would then be the children's. She also said that as James Endicott, her fiancé, was reasonably wealthy, had a flat in Paris and a house in Worcester, she would not, as she might have done, contest her deceased husband's will. She would hand the house over, and vacate it so that the Frazers could move in whenever they liked. The Frazers were delighted. Sloane insisted on making a generous settlement, some £10,000, on Louise, and the family situation was happily resolved.

In 1960 Phillip Frazer was about to become a solicitor. Caroline was studying medicine and Myfanwy II was reading horticulture at Wye College, now part of London University. They were in no position to maintain the house and garden and left the property in the hands of their mother Sloane who, at forty-eight, was still comparatively young. In 1961 a young American, Desirée Barton of Duxbury, Mass., called at Bartons End saying she was tracing her English ancestors. Phillip Frazer offered to help her: they fell in love and in 1962 they were married.

Running the old house and garden had proved to be a considerable strain and expense to Sloane Frazer, yet the family were loathe to give it up and canvassed various schemes to make Bartons End a paying proposition. It could have been turned into an hotel, a country club or offices for some international company, but in the end the family decided to make it into a home for the elderly; needless to say, for the well-off elderly. To this end, in 1965, the three children formed a company, 'Frazer Properties Ltd.', and appointed their mother as Managing Director. Caroline Frazer had graduated MD, was interested in geriatrics and became the resident doctor. Myfanwy II was head gardener and Phillip their legal adviser.

Extensive additions to the buildings had to be made (*see* plan p. 223). The old barn was turned into an assembly hall. The house itself contained kitchen, dining-room, and lounges. The old stables, cow byres and pigstyes became extensive living quarters for the patients. The old dower house, a pleasant eighteenth-century building, more or less continued its original function as it became the manager's residence and Sloane Frazer was the manager. A sickbay and staff quarters were also built. The old hop oast became a library and reading room.

It was decided by the shareholders that a fine garden should be the main attraction of the Home, and thus Sloane and her daughter Myfanwy faced considerable responsibilities. In 1967 Myfanwy II married a local farmer, Giles Thompson. She had three children in due course, but continued to run the Bartons End garden, a hard task since a balance had to be kept between expense and attractiveness. It is as true today as in Tudor times that the beauty of a garden depends on how much time, or money—in the long run much the same thing—is spent on it. The garden not only had to be liked by the patients and their friends but also, at any rate at first, it needed to draw attention to itself for publicity purposes. Myfanwy II unblushingly devised a number of what she called 'stunts' and opened files for them, such as 'Stunt 1. Camomile lawns', 'Stunt 2. Sphairistikè'. Her mother agreed with the idea but thought the word stunts provocative and unworthy of Bartons End, and substituted the words 'New Projects'.

The garden was also set to grow fresh vegetables and fruit, both of which presented opportunities for 'stunting'. An eye had to be kept on labour costs and every advantage taken of labour-saving devices, such as selective herbicides, no-digging techniques, and avoidance of expensive pesticides by using biological control and disease-resistant varieties.

The first of the New Projects was the camomile lawn. *Anthemis nobilis*, the common camomile, was used—the vigorous, branching non-flowering Treneague variety being most planted. Apart from its stunt value it had several other advantages: it needed little or no mowing, it was fragrant when walked upon and it looked most attractive, and it got talked about and mentioned in the weekly papers. A small lawn was also made with the common flowering camomile whose white daisy-like flowers appeared from time to time in the summer. Myfanwy II rather regretted she had planted it, because the patients liked it so much that, led by the retired Indian botanist, Dr Dhusti, they began to ask for daisies in the grass lawns.

> Daisies, those pearled Arcturi of the earth,
> The constellated flower that never sets.[66]

To bring the daisy back to the grass lawns would have been expensive. It would mean stopping the use of selective weedkillers, hand-weeding out plantains and dandelions and leaving a judicious quantity of daisy plants. From where could she get the labour? As for paying for it . . . What to do? Then Dr Dhusti came to her aid. He explained that, not being a player of games on turf, though once he had been a cricketer, he too liked a lawn with daisy flowers on it, but he knew it was an expensive luxury. He would call a meeting, 'Daisies and Lawns', and explain the situation. Miss Frazer would give up the use of weedkiller on the grass if they, the patients, would keep down the weeds, on their hands and knees with knives, during the summer. Or, if they would not do that, then pay for it. It would only cost each of them another £5 or £10 a week.

A meeting was called and the scheme for increasing the fees quickly rejected. Dr Dhusti then called for volunteer hand weeders; he recruited six and that allowed a scheme to be adopted for the daisies to come back on a quite substantial lawn in front of the house. Myfanwy II arranged for a big letter D on the lawn to be treated with weedkiller, in honour of Dr Dhusti's plan. The green D stood out prominently among the white daisies, showing, to Myfanwy's satisfaction, that the daisies were there deliberately and not through neglect. Dr Dhusti became very proud of his D.

The replacement of grass by camomile naturally changed some of the insect life in the area. A striking caterpillar sometimes found on the new lawn was the camomile shark (*Cucullia chamomillae*); it was about two inches long when full-grown, yellowish-green in colour with transverse bands of red and oblique streaks of olive-green. Its common name is curious: there does not appear to be anything particularly shark-like in either the larva or adult. *Cucullus*, in Latin, means a hood, a reference to the structure of the adult moth.

Another, smaller, caterpillar found on the camomile also had a strange common name, the vestal. It was a migrant from France and a Geometer, that is, a caterpillar with only four false legs instead of the ten most families of Lepidoptera have. All have six true legs. In the Geometers two of the false legs are on the thirteenth or rear, ring of the caterpillar and two on the tenth section. The caterpillar walks by drawing its rear pair of legs up towards the pair on the tenth section, arching the body in the air as it does so. The first to tenth rings are then moved forward and the loop flattened, whilst the legs on the thirteenth, known as the anal claspers, hold tight to the surface on which the creature is walking. The process is repeated, another loop being formed as the rear legs are brought up to the tenth ring. The name Geometer arises from the apparent measuring activities of the caterpillars.

New Project 2 was the revival of the old sphairistikè court, and a great find in one of the attics was a number of the old racquets. Phillip Frazer presented a cup, which was competed for each year and again attracted notice in the press.

A New Project which was a great success was the provision of small raised beds enabling such patients as wished it to indulge in gardening without a lot of stooping. They were brick bins about 2 ft. 6 ins. high, 4 ft. long and 2 ft. wide. The bottom of the bed was filled with coarse stone and gravel and the top foot was soil. A pipe came up inside the bin with a metal rose-top a few inches below the surface so that internal irrigation could be given, although at times the rose got blocked, and later on a porous earthenware cap was substituted. Most of the bins were filled with the common weald loam, slightly acid garden soil, but a few beds were filled with other kinds of mould, such as acidic peats for alpines, alkaline soils for ornamental cruciferae and other lime-lovers and one very chalky soil as a challenge to a Mr Dumbarton, one of the patients, who maintained he loved a chalk garden. This calciphile took on the contest, but cheated by liberally sprinkling his bed with sulphur and peat, which gradually increased the acidity; he then planted pelargoniums.

Some of the beds were lower, so that patients in wheelchairs could tend them. All this construction was expensive, but the patients really appreciated the possibilities of easy gardening. The scheme was a great success and some very specialised crops and plants were grown. For instance, on her raised bed a Miss Simmons, from Saffron Walden in Essex, decided to grow the plant for which her town was once famous, the saffron crocus, and to produce yellow saffron for cakes and the true Valencian paella which, by arrangement, she proposed to make in the Home's kitchen. Miss Simmons had spent much of her life in Spain and knew and loved the saffron fields around Valencia.

Saffron is an interesting plant and needs a lot of tender care. The soil was dug and manured with good compost, firstly in March and then again at the beginning of May. In the middle of June Miss Simmons planted the corms she had obtained from Spain, using the traditional way. She dug out two flat-bottomed trenches, about eighteen inches wide and four inches deep, the length of her bed and put in a double row of corms some two inches apart, so roughly a hundred corms were used. The saffron crocus blooms in the autumn, before most of the leaves appear, and thus is similar, but quite a different species from, the autumn crocus whose wonders will be considered below.

The patients eagerly awaited the flowering of the saffron and, learning that 'at harvesting time abundant labour is required',[46] Miss Simmons received many offers of help. However, she graciously declined, saying she thought she could handle her small bed, but that when she and Mrs

Thompson (Myfanwy II) were making a fortune out of the five acres they would eventually plant, then the offer would be greatly appreciated.

The saffron flower is a rich purple-red in colour, about four inches high. In the centre is the pistil which is an orange bulb containing a few seeds. A slender stalk springs from the ovary, the pale yellow style; it is about an inch long and divides into a three-lobed stigma, orange-red in colour, an inch to an inch and a half long. The dried stigma, with a little of the style attached, is the saffron of commerce.

In the autumn of her first year Miss Simmons picked her crocus flowers day by day as they opened and at once cut out the long red stigmas, putting them into the sun to dry. As they dried the growths twisted together: in this state they were known as 'hay'. The final drying was done on a piece of silk stretched over an embroidery frame and put above a radiator, for, as she explained, in Spain the stove-dried saffron was considered to be superior to sun-dried.

Miss Simmons produced a very good sample of saffron, but not much of it, only about half an ounce! However, it was enough for one magnificent paella which she and the cook made for the enthusiastic appreciation of the patients. The toast 'Simmons and Saffron' was eagerly drunk in wine from the Bartons End vines. Plans were made to extend the saffron area in the following season.

Inspired by the raised beds, many of the patients took up gardening and great rivalry prevailed in keeping the beds tidy and producing attractive or novel plots. The enthusiasm spread beyond the beds themselves and soon portions of flower borders were being put under the care of individuals. Cheap labour, said Sloane Frazer to her daughter, but Myfanwy doubted it, because goodness knows what some of them might do in their enthusiasm. For instance, only recently old Mr Nicholls had carefully hoed out a bed recently planted with antirrhinums.

As a rival to saffron a comfrey bed was produced and later extended to one of the flower beds against the house. It was a pretty plant and one that in olden times was much valued by the herbalists. At least three species were found at Bartons End, *Symphytum asperrimum*, *S. perigrinum* and *S. officinale*. Lawrence D. Hills, at the Doubleday Research Station in 1976, found that certain strains of comfrey would

Saffron crocus

produce great weights of fodder per acre: Bocking No. 14, for instance, averaged well over 33 tons per acre (85 tonnes per hectare). Not that the gardeners had cattle to feed, but great mounds of comfrey produced a splendid, dark-coloured compost. And, as a rival to the saffronists, it made a pleasant tea: at least the Symphytophiles so described it, in contrast to the Saffronists, who derided the possibility.

The midribs of the big comfrey leaves were cut away by a band of devoted ladies. 'Come and see our strippers at work,' was a jest of the day, as it still is in a cigar factory. After the ribs were stripped out the leaves were cut up into small portions and dried in the sun on wire frames. At tea-time each table was provided with three teapots, dispensing Indian, China and comfrey tea. Comfrey also made delicious fritters, while heads of comfrey were hung in the deep-litter chicken houses and the birds loved it.

Another exercise on the somewhat esoteric home-food front was a patient's cultivation in his raised bed of the alhagi (*A. maurorum*), a legume from the Near East. It excretes a white gum, which solidifies into small lumps and is reputed to be the manna that sustained the Children of Israel in the desert. At Bartons End it was grown in pots as it had to be taken indoors for the winter. The resulting manna was quite pleasant to eat. 'But,' said the grower, 'if I were going to rely on it as my main food I'd need about twenty acres. No wonder the Israelites took so long on their journey!'

Many of the raised beds grew alpines and rock plants. One container held a collection of indigenous or nearly indigenous stonecrops, its gardener maintaining, in accordance with the self-sufficiency schemes sweeping Bartons End at that time, that a substitute for pepper was *Sedum acre*, or wallpepper. The cook, however, was not impressed. Other stonecrops growing there were the midsummer men, or rose-root especially imported from Scotland—the name arises from the fact that the roots smell like roses. It is an annual and had to be encouraged, in order to persist, by allowing the young seedlings room to develop in the spring. Of course the orpine was there, long a favourite in cottage gardens, and one or two sedum as well, such as the rare *S. anglicum* and the thick-leaved *S. dasyphyllum*. A house-leek hung over one end of the bed.

One of the keener gardeners made a gentian bed, growing one plant of the large *Gentiana lutea* in the middle and surrounding it with some attractive and more difficult species, such as the spring gentian (*G. verna*), 'Angulosa', the summer China (*G. gracilipes*) and the autumn *G. sino-ornata*.

A rather lazier individual took the easy way and planted his bed with a ground-cover plant, carefully choosing an unusual one, namely *Dryas octopetala*, which has white, saucer-shaped flowers with eight petals. The mysterious death of a bed of calceolarias was put down officially to lightning and, privately, to the sprinkling of a handful of chlorate by a rather spiteful Mrs Edwards.

The peat raised beds were popular and had a wide variety of plants. One had a collection of trilliums, distinguished by having everything in threes, leaves, sepals and petals. A clump of wake-robin eventually occupied the centre of the bed, with specimens of the painted wood-lily at the ends. They were difficult plants to establish and the trilliums were regarded as something of a triumph.

Amidst all this rivalry the most unusual raised bed was that of Dr Dhusti. As a tropical botanist great things were expected of him, but he was never seen to work on his patch. 'Perhaps I work, all alone, for secrecy, before breakfast,' he would say. In the spring some seedlings started to come through the rather rain-washed surface of Dr Dhusti's bed. What could they be? They were carefully watched. Slowly the dreadful truth emerged. Dr Dhusti had done absolutely nothing to his plot!

Tackled on this woeful state of affairs the learned gentleman explained it was deliberate. He needed to know what the natural vegetation would be. Without that information he had no measure of the efforts they had made in cultivating the different parcels. He was recording all the plants that came up, how they grew, which triumphed and which failed, what their weights were and so on. His was to be a nature garden in microcosm and would lead to endless correspondence in *Nature*.

'But it will spread weeds to all our plots, dear Dr Dhusti, spare us that. And it looks so terrible,' said a spokeswoman.

'No,' said Dr Dhusti, 'you can now look at these wonderful plants close to. How beautiful is the dandelion seed head. How pretty the groundsel.' In the end he agreed not to let the seeds ripen on his plot and, after he made his records, to grow some nice Indian plants for next year.

The indignation died down, but some fears persisted as to just what the doctor might plant, as he declared he was expecting some roots of the mandrake from India. 'It shrieks, you know, as you dig it from the ground. A most interesting plant. It usually mysteriously kills the person,' he continued, 'who digs it up. In India, of course, one gets an untouchable to do it and it doesn't matter.' One never knew when Dr Dhusti was serious.

In fact, though, the mandrake is a solanaceous, Mediterranean plant and by no means Asiatic, as the Indian botanist was well aware. Its mystic reputation grew out of the fact that its root is often forked and slightly resembles a human form. The carrot at times produces a forked root, but that has only led to Voltaire's slighting dictum on man, but a 'forked carrot', on the face of it not a very great insult.

Frazer Properties Ltd. were anxious to have a fine garden at Bartons End, but nevertheless had to keep the costs of running it to a reasonable figure, which meant they needed to use labour-saving devices wherever they could. One or two such strategies have already been mentioned, such as the use of weedkillers on lawns and the mulching of flower beds with lawn mowings and composts. But modern herbicides have a far wider application in the garden than just the treatment of lawns, and Myfanwy II had a range at her disposal, though nearly all were complex organic chemicals and thus expensive. Myfanwy was interested to see how far the enthusiasm among the patients for the hand-weeding of one of the lawns would persist. On the whole she did not think she would get a lot of free labour from them. She also had to balance the cost of chemical weedkilling against the expense of hand-hoeing. Theoretically the herbicide manufacturers would put a price on their compounds which would make them just a little cheaper than mechanical methods. She would watch and see if this was so.

The main products Myfanwy used, according to different circumstances and weeds, were: alloxidim-sodium which killed grass weeds among ornamental plants during the summer; paraquat and diquat which killed all green foliage they touched and were at once inactivated when they entered the soil. They did not affect bushes and trees that had bark on them, so were most useful in the orchard; simazine was applied 'pre-emergence' and killed annual weeds as they came through the soil; it could be used in the herbaceous border provided the flowers were well established and the dose carefully calculated.

There are many cases of plants being brought from abroad as a garden novelty that have taken enthusiastically to their new environment and have become troublesome weeds, known as 'garden escapes'. A recent example at Bartons End, and in many other parts of Britain as well, is the Japanese knotgrass (*Polygonum cuspidatum*). A curious feature is that it was imported in 1825 and was grown in a few gardens to fill odd corners: not being a particularly attractive plant it was not very popular. When it 'escaped' from the garden is difficult to say, but it is only within the last thirty or so years that it has been causing noticeable trouble. Today railway cuttings, roadsides and waste ground are often found growing vast clumps of Japanese knotgrass, and it continually spreads.

At Bartons End it appeared in the orchard in 1972. By 1975 a big clump grew up each year and took no notice of being cut down once or twice during the season. Soon it had established itself in hedges and many odd corners, growing each year to a height of ten feet or more. 'If something is not done soon,' thought Myfanwy II, 'we will have a mono-culture of *Polygonum cuspidatum*.' What could be done? To encourage beetles and caterpillars that fed on the plant might be a solution, especially an insect that fed only on the weed. It would be difficult to attack an indigenous weed with biological enemies, as the plants would be so well-established and have closely related plants of value. But the Japanese knotgrass was an introduced plant, quite another matter.

Had not the Australians got rid of a garden escape, a cactus that had ruined millions of acres of pasture, by importing a moth from Argentina? And more recently, in the USA, the introduced St John's wort which had become a troublesome weed, had been controlled by the introduction of two beetles, an *Agrilus* and a *Chrysolina*.

Owen S. Wilson had listed in his book *The Larvae of the British Lepidoptera* in 1880 twenty-four Lepidoptera that fed on *Polygonum aviculare*, a common, indigenous and very different kind of plant: would some of them do? Weed research bodies in Britain were not very interested in this approach; as far as they were concerned weeds were meant to be controlled by the use of herbicides. Myfanwy decided she would make some experiments with Lepidoptera. She had noticed the weed leaves were sometimes eaten, mostly she thought, by slugs. She tried the grass wave, found on some broom, and the satin wave, without any marked success. While looking into the fauna records for Japan she decided in the meantime to use herbicides. The plant was very resistant to chemicals: the roots and rhizomes persisted, breaking up concrete and filling drains, but she found sprays of bromacil greatly weakened the stand in the first year of application and killed it in the second if another treatment was given, while allowing a cover growth of grasses and speedwell to appear.

In the past gardeners had advocated the thorough digging of gardens for the purpose of improving the soil structure and destroying weeds. But in fact, while the incorporation of organic matter, farmyard manure or compost, will improve the soil, it is doubtful if digging, *per se*, does much for the structure, or for weed control, unless very careful sorting of the soil is done as the digging goes on, to remove roots of perennials, such as couch grass and bindweed—a most laborious task. Earthworms are the great soil improvers and there usually are more worms in undug than in dug soil. Moreover, plant seed can lie dormant in the lower layers of the soil for a long time and be brought to the surface by digging, there to germinate. For instance, seeds of fat hen have been known to persist in a deep soil for forty years. Soil covered with a mulch two inches deep will not allow seeds to germinate, but some mulches, such as grass mowings and compost, may contain weed seeds which naturally take advantage of the opportunity and germinate when spread on a suitable surface.

At retail prices Myfanwy found her herbicides for weed control cost from a penny to four pence per square yard for the chemicals alone, but she soon negotiated trade terms for the considerable supplies she needed. The weedkillers were cheaper than a paid gardener's hand-hoeing, but what about the volunteers among the patients? Could they be trusted to do shallow hoeing only? It was important not to cut the roots of the young growing plants, as deep hoeing would do. Somehow her guests did not take kindly to the idea of 'chemicals'. 'We're all a bunch of chemicals,' she would cry. 'There's nothing wrong with chemicals provided they are properly used.'

Some 'no dig' gardening was tried quite successfully at Bartons End on plots troubled mostly with annual weeds. In the spring the weed growth would be killed with an application of paraquat, then a row shallowly hoed and opened, and seed, such as peas or beans, sown. It was also found that much could be done with weedkillers by directing the spray to the weeds and protecting the crop with shields of glass or plastic.

Paths were treated with 'total weedkillers'; Myfanwy II used a mixture of aminotriazole, M C P A and simazine, as being the cheapest treatment she had found. The herbicides were applied either through a low pressure spraying machine or a 'dribble bar' fixed to the spout of a watering can. Some products, such as Propachlor were in granules, which made for very easy application, but usually granules were more expensive than liquids. A great deal of the beauty of the Bartons End garden was through the skilled use of weedkillers.

Around 1970 the garden suffered a setback due to the combined activities of an insect and a fungus, namely the Dutch elm disease. The avenue of large English elms had reached perfection in the 1960s and made a dignified approach to the old house.

Many wood-boring beetles cannot feed on the wood itself and enlist the aid of a fungus. Some Scolytid beetles (*Scolytus scolytus, S. multistriatus* and *S. laevis*) introduce a fungus into the network of tunnels they make just under the bark of elms, and the fungus breaks down the excavated wood, enabling the insects to eat it. In return the beetles always carry a bit of the fungus to any new mine they open. Such co-operation has gone on for a very long time. A little damage was caused to the tops of elms from time to time by this activity, but nothing serious.

However, the co-operating pair, beetle and fungus, emigrated from Europe. One of the places in which they then throve was Canada, where the fungus mutated and produced a fast-growing, virulent strain. This new variety, once introduced into an elm, grew rapidly through its tissues and blocked the water-carrying tubes, killing the tree, whereupon the fungus, regardless of its obligation to the beetle, feasted on a mass of dead wood.

By mistake, this new strain of fungus was imported into Britain from

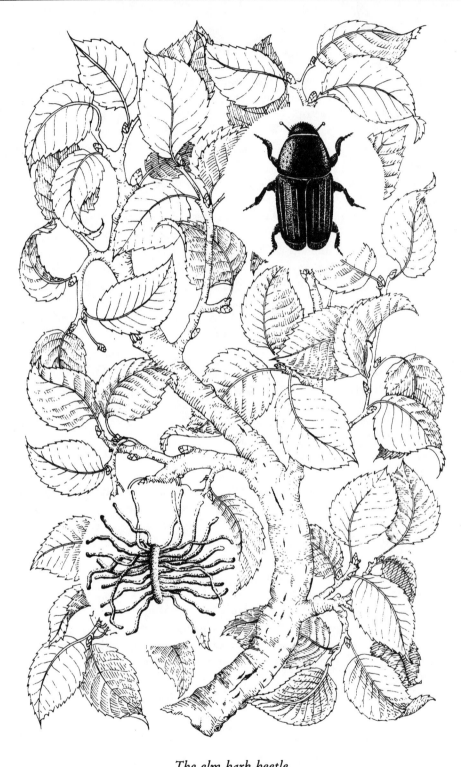

The elm bark beetle

Canada in inadequately de-barked timber. Soon it was killing elms all over the country and continues to do so.

At Bartons End, attempts were made to save the elm avenue by injecting an organic fungicide into the trees. It had to be done every year and was difficult because the chemical, naturally, had to reach every part the beetle was likely to attack. Holes were bored into the tree with an auger around the base of the trunk. Hollow tubes were connected to a pipe and pump, which fed in the fungicide solution. But the pump pressure was not the main means of distribution of the chemical in the tree—the suction of the leaves transpiring water was far more important. A sunny day with a light breeze after a night of rain was ideal for the treatment. The leaves were then transpiring rapidly and drawing up readily available water from the roots, which had a plentiful supply. As the water moved up the tree it mixed with the fungicide which then killed the malignant growth.

The process was laborious and costly; Myfanwy II decided she would only attempt to keep the two elms at the entrance to the drive, and felled the others. Treated regularly the two trees are still alive, but not flourishing—a victory for the beetle and fungus. In the meantime a search for an elm resistant to the new fungus strain continues.

Today the gardener is constantly being tempted by the nursery trade with ever more new plants, proclaimed as larger, more brilliant and most striking, and all at premium prices. Whereas old-established dahlias, such as Garden Wonder, sold at a price equivalent of, say, an index figure of 100, new dahlias such as Ming Pygmy and Otto Trill, respectively small and large, were on offer at 144. The increase in price, some 44 per cent, is a considerable gain for the nurseryman. Undoubtedly Otto Thrill is a nice dahlia, but is it 44 per cent better than Garden Wonder?

Roses naturally show the same tendency. Bobby Charlton at an index figure of 121 looks very like Fragrant Cloud at 100, but possibly the association with the great footballer is worth the premium of about 20 per cent, even though the cheaper bush has the advantage of being scented.

Myfanwy II thought a lot of money could be wasted on a craze for novelty. Trying to keep up with the latest issue of hundreds of cultivars was like trying to keep a collection of postage stamps up to date. She took a few new plants in, but mostly grew the tried and true cheaper cultivars. 'What's wrong with Dorothy Perkins as a climbing rose?' she would ask and get an enthusiastic response. It must be remembered, though, that an old cultivar such as Dorothy Perkins could be carrying a virus disease which a new variety did not have, the stock not yet having been infected.

New varieties are produced by cross-breeding species and sub-species and by the use of colchicine. This is an alkaloid obtained from autumn crocus (*Colchicum autumnale*). It is very poisonous, though used in small doses as a medicine for gout, and is soluble in water, alcohol and chloroform, and breaks down if exposed to light. The chemical has the strange property of reacting on the genetic make-up of plants. If seeds are soaked for a few days in a weak solution of colchicine and then sown, the resulting seedlings are dwarfed and malformed. But their descendants will often have the number of chromosomes in pollen and ovary doubled, resulting in larger and often doubled flowers. Many of today's double flowers have been produced by means of colchicine and quite a number of the people at Bartons End, now enthusiastic about 'nature gardening', looked on doubles as 'monstrosities' and referred in indignation to 'colchicine torturing' of plants. They did not mind a double rose, provided the scent had not been taken out in the process, as, they said, was usually the case.

In many double flowers, such as double snowdrops, daffodils, nasturtiums, clarkias and kerrias, the flowers are aborted and useless for reproductive purposes. The stamens have been replaced by additional petals which makes them blossom more conspicuously and last longer, usually because they cannot produce seed. But as far as the beauty of the plant is concerned, often the increase in size is counterbalanced by a loss in the grace and form of the flower. It looks artificial. Kerrias (bachelor's buttons) today are mostly double-flowered and can only be propagated by means of cuttings, the seed not being viable.

Roses and carnations are two of the fine flowers which have kept an attractive shape in their double state, but, even so, most people cut roses for the flower vase before they are fully open, suggesting that, unconsciously, they acknowledge that the attractiveness of the flower is more in its single than its doubled condition.

However, this is not to say that useless flowers do not occur under natural conditions. Many inflorescences, such as those of the cornflower and guelder rose, have a central group of fertile florets in each head, surrounded by a ring of sterile ones. The outer, sterile ring is there to make the inflorescence more conspicuous and to attract insects.

Garden seeds had always been important at Bartons End and the great improvement in seed condition is an enormous asset to the modern gardener. In the 1860s Mr and Mrs Burrows were somewhat at the mercy of unscrupulous seedsmen who would add dead seeds to the stocks they were selling. The dead seed might be old stock with a poor germinating capacity or seeds of other species similar in appearance to the kind of seed being sold. In any case, before being used to dilute the good seed, it was killed, usually by heating. The dead seed did not germinate and, unless the amount was large, was not noticed by the customer. It was somewhat akin to adding sand to sugar.

The outcry against poor seed led to an Act of Parliament, the Adulteration of Seeds Act 1869, which much improved matters for farmers, market-gardeners and gardeners, though it did not affect Bartons End immediately because that was the time at which the garden was much neglected.

Today seed novelties are almost as numerous as ever, but the situation is regulated by a number of national and Common Market regulations, some of which result in the withdrawal of a few long-loved cultivars, such as the onion Up-to-date and the German Black Kale. However, seed sanctuaries have been established in many parts of Europe where 'prohibited' cultivars are maintained. They are a gene bank for genetic material that could be of future use to plant breeders.

Today the nursery trade performs a valuable service in the provision of hybrid seed. Hybrids, crosses between two different species or sub-species of plants, often have valuable properties, such as greater vigour, resistance to disease or other desirable qualities possessed by neither of their parents. The seed produced by hybrids, even if it is not sterile, will not 'breed true'. Some seedlings will be like one parent, some another, some mixtures of both and some like the hybrid itself. Thus, to secure the advantages of hybridisation the hybrid seed must be made anew every year. This is a task for the professional nurseryman, and several successful hybrids are now grown at Bartons End, for instance Brussels sprouts Peer Gynt and Perfect Line, winter cabbage Celtic, and bush tomatoes Slegford Abundance and Alfresco.

A lot of Myfanwy II's work lay in making out her seed order. Seedsmen naturally orientate their business towards the needs of the commercial grower. The farmer wants a crop of sprouts ripening all the same time and all the same size, one that can be mechanically harvested, so he buys expensive F1 seed, that is hybrids, with their traditional vigour; flavour is not a priority. Bartons End wants a crop giving a succession of tasty produce over an extended period, and Myfanwy grew Early-half-tall and Winter Harvest. Did the saving of labour in growing Golden Self-blanching celery make up for a lack of certain qualities found in the labour-intensive, trenched Giant White? It was a moot point.

Watering in summer had long been practised in the garden. An 'engine', that is, a portable, hand-operated, pump, with which choice plants could be sprayed and kept moist, had been introduced by the great Bartons End improver, Charles Munroyd, in 1751. At first the engine was used to apply just water but soon tobacco extract and soap were being sprayed on to vegetables and flowers to kill the insect pests. By 1806 Charles's son, George, had purchased a barrow-engine from Messrs Chieslie and Yowle of London, a much improved machine.

Most gardeners think they know when plants need water, but many errors are made. Myfanwy II, having studied the matter, used a scientific approach, the water balance sheet.

The rainfall in Kent is usually between 20 and 30 inches a year, much of it falling at the wrong time. Plants take in water through their roots and, in some rare cases of high humidity, through their leaves as well. Plants get rid of water through the stomata of the leaves; in short, they sweat. All goes well as long as the root uptake exceeds or is equal to the leaf disposal. But if the transpiration is greater than the uptake, the life of the plant is slowed down, growth is stopped and eventually the plant wilts and the gardener suffers a loss. The soil scientist, such as Myfanwy II, postulates a concept, the 'root constant', that is the greatest soil water deficit that can exist in a soil without checking plant transpiration.

At a certain depth in the soil is a water table, which rises and falls according to season. Above this level water exists in the soil in two forms: in the air in between the soil particles and as a skin of water around each particle. During heavy rain the air is driven out and replaced by water and unless this water can drain away the plants will die from drowning, the soil being waterlogged. A garden soil usually drains: if it did not it would not be a garden. But a good soil needs to be water retentive as well, hence the importance of humus in it.

Under dry conditions the plant roots draw in water existing in the soil spaces and from some of the water in the skin round the particles, but if the drought continues eventually the soil refuses to yield any more water and the plants wilt. This is by no means the point where the soil is bone dry. It is when the surface tension holding the water to the particles is greater than the power of the roots wanting to extract it. That is to say, a soil is at optimum condition for plant health when, following drainage, it is holding all the water it can against the pull of gravity seeking to drain it away. Such a soil is then said to be at 'field capacity'.

The gardener's aim is to maintain his soil at field capacity. Rain helps him do this, but there are forces working against him, firstly the amount of transpiration, secondly the weather and season and finally the amount of vegetation present.

To maintain optimum water conditions (the soil at field capacity) the gardener needs to know, first, the monthly loss of water due to transpiration and second, the rainfall (including dew). The second taken away from the first shows the deficit that should be made up by watering.

It is quite easy to measure rainfall and this Myfanwy II did by taking daily records in a rain-gauge; whilst she was at it she also recorded temperatures and sunshine. It was more difficult to record transpiration but she used the figures of long-term averages supplied by the Meteorological Office which, for Kent, in inches per month are April 2·00, May 3·25, June 4·00, July 4·05, August 3·3, September 1·80, a total of 18·4 inches. For instance, in the hot dry summer of 1976 she applied 4 inches of water over three acres of her garden because of deficiency. An inch of rain is a lot of water: it is equal to 22,622 gallons per acre. In that year Myfanwy II pumped her water from the old Bartons End wells. The mains supply would have been far too expensive.

Toad

Of course, in a wet season rainfall can exceed transpiration and there is not much the gardener can do, but Myfanwy obtained some relief by hoeing out shallow channels to conduct surface water away from the beds as the soaking rain fell, as it did in the summer of 1982.

Toads had always found the cellar of the old house attractive and consequently the garden as well. They are still there, having been encouraged by the bomb crater, now a water garden. Occasionally newts and frogs were found there too.

Toads and frogs are Anoura, and are remarkable for two things. First, they breathe by means of gills when young and lungs when adult, a striking change to be made in the middle of a life. Second, they show a great attachment to their place of birth.

At the end of the war the bomb crater was very ragged and untidy, full of water in the winter and dry, cracked and a mass of willow herb in the summer. Robert Dunchester, in late 1946, conceived the idea that, as a war memorial, it would make a good water garden. He lined the pit with puddled Kentish clay, which only held the water for a couple of years. The explosion had left stresses in the subsoil and the clay lining opened during dry weather. Persisting with his scheme Mr Dunchester eventually fitted a plastic liner, with great success. One spring he threw in a cupful of toad spawn. It produced a number of toads, some of which always returned to their native pond in successive springs. They appeared to find their way by smelling their particular, native water and obviously thought there was nothing like it anywhere else as good.

Some human visitors also came back to the garden, at times a considerable weight of them. At Myfanwy Frazer's wedding reception in June 1967, about 220 people, guests and staff, weighing some twelve tons, were in and out of a marquee erected on the lawn. The tent, food, drink and tables added another three tons, all pressing on that patch of about 1,620 square feet. This sounds a lot, yet in terms of ground consolidation it is not. It is only 0·14 pounds per square inch, considerably less than the pressure in an average motor car tyre.

Plants grow well when the roots can easily penetrate an open, uncompacted soil, and the weight of Myfanwy's party did not directly much affect it. What did, though, was the moving about of the guests. Walking over a garden plot exerts considerable pressure on the bits stepped on. At the end of a step the toe of one foot, about 1·5 sq. ins. in area, is supporting the person's whole weight, say 10 stone for a man, equal to 93 lbs. per sq. in., a considerable pressure. Women, usually lighter than men, tend to exert more pressure because they have smaller feet. This is what damaged the lawn.

The lawn at Bartons End suffered considerably from the wedding. The fine grasses were suffocated and tap-rooted weeds, daisies, plantains and cat's ear started to take over. However, the gardening staff immediately applied remedial measures, 'spiking' and an application of hormone weedkiller. Spiking, as now done, by a small machine, is the driving into the turf of small, hollow tines which extract a core of earth, thus opening up the soil. The machine is not as effective as earthworms but much better than using solid tines, such as driving in a garden fork, as this only further compresses the soil. An autumn application of selective weedkiller then restored the lawn almost to perfection.

Today the gardeners at Bartons End are aware of the dangers of soil consolidation and avoid walking on the beds by using narrow bridges of six-inch planking, which span the beds and allow the land to be worked without stepping on the earth itself. The pressure is thus transferred to the path and there helps suppress weeds.

Myfanwy Thompson seems to be devoted to her garden. Her husband Giles tolerates it well, as befits a Kentish farmer, and it is not unprofitable. Her sister Caroline is fascinated by it and her sister-in-law, Desirée, still takes an interest in the subject, though from afar.

As to the next generation, Myfanwy and Giles have three children. Whilst it is too soon to say what they will become, or make of Bartons End, yet Phillip, the eldest, aged fourteen, seems to be interested in fruit farming. Caroline shows promise of artistic ability and Sloane Myfanwy, aged eleven and named after her maternal grandmother and mother, will perhaps be a gardener. She already carefully tends a bed of her own special primroses. The prospects of the garden at Bartons End continuing to thrive are good.

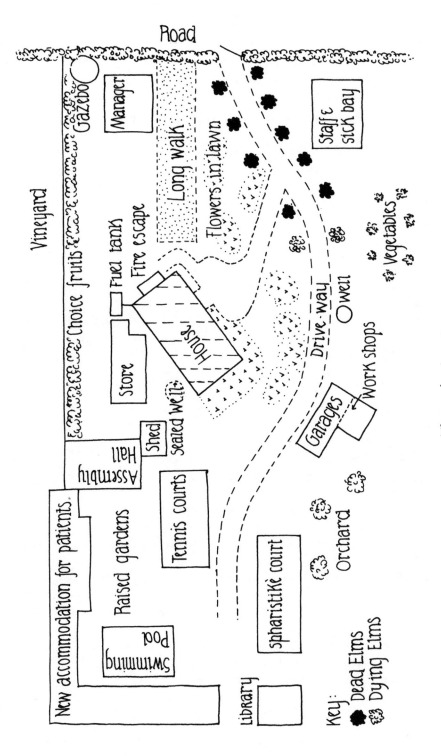

The garden in 1984

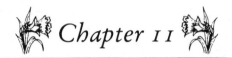

Chapter 11

Reflections on Four Centuries of Gardening at Bartons End

THE GARDEN at Bartons End, started in a very small way in 1556, has now become a large and very pleasant place. In the course of its 428 years, there have naturally been a great many changes in the life found there. Even so it is interesting to list some of the things that have not altered.

In the first place the biomass produced per acre then and now is very similar and many of the animals and plants originally found on the site are still there today. There are the earthworms and other soil fauna, a considerable collection of trees and bushes, and many wild plants mostly regarded as weeds: dandelions, buttercups and groundsel, for example. There are also the animals living on these plants. Within the five acres that now make up the garden the struggle for existence has persisted. Many life forms have enlisted the help of man to obtain success. Without his attention most of the garden plants disappear after a few generations, but there are some notable exceptions, including garden escapes such as the Japanese knotgrass. Other deliberate imports have escaped long ago and have become naturalised, among them the Scotch thistle, the cherry laurel and the sweet chestnut, as well as countless weeds.

Some of the motives leading man to his kindly intervention on behalf of plants have been recorded in this book. At first it was utility. Garden plants at Bartons were grown for their actual or supposed medicinal properties, next for their culinary uses. Herbs added flavour to a monotonous diet of beef, mutton and brown bread. Next came strewing-herbs—sweet-smelling plants to counteract the foul smells arising around most houses and farms. Here we see various selective factors at work. Plants useful to man, particularly laxatives and anti-diarrhoea herbs, were promoted; then came the influence of beauty. Flowers were welcomed, such as the wild white violets, and new and rarish kinds sought for and protected.

By the end of the sixteenth century cultivated plants had quite an advantage over wild ones, and had induced the Bartons, in one way or another, to give them some protection. The process continued and is stronger than ever today, when salesmanship, science, colchicine and genetic engineering are all brought into play to produce a stream of novelties and valuable F1 hybrids.

How is it that garden life was able to project itself so successfully and on such a large scale? The plants in the seedsmen's catalogues today are sold to an eager public and represent an enormous weight of vegetation grown every year.

The motives are various: plants, of course, are essential for the production of human food, but this is only one reason for the existence of garden plants in Britain. They are also grown for the aesthetic pleasure they give and the feeling of co-operating with the natural world that gardening creates. Mixed with that is the feeling of getting something for nothing. A handful of bean seeds, put into suitable soil, produces, some ten weeks later, a fine crop of a delicious vegetable, which—if the gardener costed it in rent and his time—could have been purchased at half the price as a tinned import from Texas. However, home production now does several things for the gardener that are difficult to cost. He or she has produced something, and something of a kind that commerce may well no longer supply, such as the delicious Royal Sovereign strawberry or the gourmet potato that was grown at Bartons End and called May Queen, though it was too poor a cropper to be commercially viable.

Another powerful reason for gardening has been the advancement of science, the desire to understand the natural world and the inter-relationship of life. Scientists explored the world for this purpose and their expeditions were usually combined with the commercial advantages of supplying the nurseryman with novelties.

Another motive for gardening throughout the history of Bartons End was keeping up with the Joneses, or even surpassing them. Gardens offer exceptional opportunities of displaying social superiority —'Goodness gracious! Are you still growing those old Mrs Sankeys? Let me give you some of my Jet Set and Royal Flush sweet peas, so much prettier.'

For this man-plant co-operation to succeed, both gardener and gardenee make sacrifices. The gardener's are obvious—time, sweat and money. The plants' are the sacrifice of flowers, seed, tubers and so on to man, together with hybrid sterility and other man-induced artificial conditions.

If we think of life in a garden like Bartons End as a whole, there is an element of chance in what succeeds and what does not. Had Robert Dunchester turned his bicycle to the right at the fork in the lane that day in 1909, instead of to the left, he would not have discovered Bartons End. The neglect of the garden would have continued and in all probability it would have gone back to Wealden copse or forest, with the house eventually falling down. If the fungus *Ceratocystis ulmi* had not produced a virulent strain in Canada, which then crossed to England, the elm avenue would still be there.

Throughout human history the explorer or conqueror nearly always took his native seeds with him and always brought back strange and possibly useful plants. Lucullus (110–56 BC), the vanquisher of Mithridates, was a great gourmet and gardener and brought back the cherry from Cerasus, near the Black Sea. It flourished in Italy where it was eagerly eaten by man and cockchafer, the latter much to the general's annoyance.[a]

One of the big surges of plant introduction to Britain was during the reign of George III (1760–1820) when Britain's overseas empire was growing rapidly. It is said that 7,000 new plants were introduced to the country during that time.[42] During the latter half of the nineteenth century the plant introductions were yet more numerous, stimulated by increasing prosperity, the steamship and the Ward Case, all making the transport of living plants much easier.

But at Bartons End after 1825, except for strict utility purposes, gardening was in decline: the property was occupied by tenant farmers or caretakers, and thus escaped the main pressures of the nursery trade launching its bewildering succession of novelties. When Robert Dunchester purchased the property there was a tremendous leeway to be made up.

In the course of writing this book I have once or twice shown that poets, pointing to the beauty and peace of a garden, were mistaken as to the latter, unless the matter is considered from the human, anthropocentric, point of view. The poet is right: the garden is, usually, beautiful, calming and consoling to man, but the poet should dig a little deeper. He might then see the reverse of the coin: the utility, if not the beauty, of man to the plant. For, just as man uses plants, so do plants use him. Because of their utility as food, fascination for, or beauty to him, there are today, for example, far more plants of wheat, tobacco, cocaine, poppy, and more varieties of roses growing in the world than there would have been had those species not developed their particular qualities.

Throughout its existence the garden at Bartons End has given tremendous satisfaction to a large number of people in a variety of ways—even today gardening has greatly improved and prolonged the lives of many people there. Probably the chief satisfaction has always been the fulfilling of the creative urge. The gardener, like the artist, has brought something he believes in, something new and desirable, into the world, and gardeners will make sacrifices to achieve this, forgoing other pleasures for the garden's sake.[b] Some gardeners will even sacrifice a crop to birds because of the asset of their song. Joseph Addison wrote: 'I value my garden more for being full of blackbirds than of cherries, and very frankly give them fruit for their songs.'[2]

The word 'garden' comes from the Hebrew and means 'a pleasant place', and it is to this Eden that each gardener, after his or her fashion, strives to return.

Notes

Chapter 1

a   C. E. Raven (*English Naturalists from Neckham to Ray*, CUP 1947) remarks, 'A Church of England canon said that Gerard was a rogue . . . but like many such he was a pleasant fellow . . . moreover, botanically speaking he was . . . a comparatively ignorant rogue.'

Most of Gerard's *Herball* was taken, without acknowledgement, from the collected works of the great Belgian botanist, Rambert Dodoens. Mrs Gerard put in a paragraph here and there to make the work appeal to women. It was a popular book.

A strange thing about the 1597 *Herball* is that his portrait shows Gerard holding a spray of the potato plant, flower, leaf and berry: it was but a *curiosa* at that time.

b   Hyll's book was also published with the title of *The Profitable Arte of Gardening (in three books), now the third time set forth . . . to this annexed two Proper Treatises, the one entitlted the Marveilous government of the bees . . . the other the yerely Conjectures meete for the husbandman to know.* (1568). This is the earliest edition in the British Library, but not the first edition.

c   Sir Francis Drake is said to have been playing bowls on a camomile lawn on the famous occasion when he was advised of the approach of the Spanish Armada.

d   What are called ant eggs and sold as fish food are really ant pupae.

e   The diet, of course, varied with the social class and the time of year: in spring and summer the Bartons would have had a salad from time to time and in summer and autumn they would have taken stewed and baked fruit. Fresh fruit was considered dangerous. Labourers rarely ate beef or mutton; their 'white meat' was dairy produce. A chicken was an occasional luxury. Salted fish was taken, but was despised.

Chapter 2

a   Brewer's *Dictionary of Phrase and Fable*, London, Cassell.

b   The Cox's Orange Pippin was bred by a Mr Cox, gardener to the Duke of Devonshire at Chatsworth, in about 1860. Mr Cox raised hundreds of seedlings by crossing promising fruits and eventually produced the famous apple to which his name was given.

c   The East Malling Research Station has also produced a number of apple rootstocks, named with the prefix Merton, which are resistant to the woolly aphis (*Eriosoma lanigerum*).

d In spite of the name, the mites are not really parasites but harmless commensals. They live in bumblebee nests, feed on pollen, faeces and debris and do a certain amount of cleaning up.

e One ton of coal per hour per miner is an accepted figure. A 70-kilo man thus cuts $\frac{1000}{70 \times 3}$ kg. $= 4.762$ his own weight in 20 minutes.

Chapter 3

a The term 'daisy-cutter' in the 1850s was applied to a low-travelling ball in cricket, and is still used; though no modern groundsman would allow a daisy to appear on the pitch.

b See Jonathan Schell, 'The Fate of the Earth' in the *New Yorker*, 1st, 8th and 15th February 1982. According to this author, after a large-scale nuclear war, because of excessive ultra-violet radiation, the only life likely to survive would be grasses and a few insects. The struggle for existence would then probably be between couch grass and perennial ryegrass. I would back the former to win.

Chapter 4

a These hellebores should not be confused with the once popular botanical insecticide called hellebore, which was prepared from the poisonous white and green veratrums (*V. album* and *V. viridis*) in the 1840s. *Viridis* is an American plant.

b The name arises from the corruption of the Spanish '*girasol*', or 'sun-turner'. The plant is a kind of sunflower and its flowers always turn to face the sun. It was grown by the Indians in north-eastern America, hence the name Canadian potato.

c During Pizarro's conquest of Peru the Spanish army starved rather than eat potatoes. The flowers look like those of deadly nightshade.

d The Devil's bit is so called because the short tap-root seems to have been bitten off below ground level by some mysterious denizen. Many of the obscure diseases that plagued mankind were said to be cured by this root. Incensed by this, the Devil bites the root off. Fortunately he does not destroy it entirely.

e William Lawson's book *The New Orchard and Garden* 1618, went to nine editions by 1683. Of the gardener he wrote:

> Such a gardener will conscionably, quietly and patiently travell in your orchard, God shall crowne the labors of his hands with joyfulnesse, and make the clouds drop fatnesse upon your Trees, he will provoke your love, and earne his Wages, and Fees belonging to his place: the House being served, fallen fruit, superfluity of herbes, and flours, grasses and sets besides other offal, that fruit which your bountifull hand shall award him withall: will much augment his Wages and the profit of your bees will pay you back again.

Chapter 5

a The great philosopher J-J Rousseau (1712–78), in addition to his political and philosophical writings, composed a book on botany, explaining Linnaeus's system of nomenclature, in use to this day. Walking one day with Mme de Warens in her garden, the lady remarked that the periwinkle was in flower, but Rousseau was too short-sighted to see it. Thirty years later, when doing his botany book, he found the periwinkle and exclaimed, '*Voilà de la pervanche*', hence its name 'the pleasures of memory'.

b Addison, some years previously, had also attacked topiary. Under the signature 'O' in the *Spectator* (25 June 1712, Paper IV) he wrote:

> The works of nature are more pleasant than any artificial show . . . Our British gardeners, on the contrary, instead of humouring nature, love to deviate from it as much as possible. We see marks of the scissors on every plant and bush . . . for my own part I would rather look upon a tree in all its luxuriating and diffusion of boughs, than when it is thus cut and trimmed into a mathematical figure.

c In 1657 opium was 8s. per lb., scammony 12s. and rhubarb 16s. (J. G. L. Burnby, 'John Sherwen and Drug Cultivation in Endfield', *Edmonton Historical Society*, Occasional Paper No. 2, 1973).

d John Rose, Charles II's gardener, dedicated his book *The English Vineyard Vindicated* (1666, London) to 'The Prince of Plants to the Prince of Planters'. The King greatly encouraged the 'plantations', the colonies overseas.

e Champagne is made mostly from black grapes.

Chapter 6

a The final link in this chain, the maiden ladies, it must be admitted, is only 'attributed' to Darwin. It does not occur in the *Origin of Species*, 1st edn. 1859.

b The advice of James Hales, lord of Winstanley, to his son illustrates this theme. At first the son was told to 'grow as much corn as he could for it is ready money and cometh once a year'. But by 1610 Hales had changed his mind and bade his son grow no more corn than was needed for his household. He had 'been much hindered by the keeping of servants. They care not whether the task go forward, so that they have meat, drink and wages. Small fear of God is in servants.' (S. Banks, *The Memorandum Book*.)

See also Shakespeare, *As You Like It*, III, 3. Old Adam, the servant, proposes to follow Orlando into exile, leading Orlando to comment, in surprise:

> 'O good old man, how well in thee appears
> The constant service of the antique world . . .
> Thou art not for the fashion of these times
> Where none will sweat but for promotion.'

Chapter 7

a John Curtis (1791–1862) was an able entomologist, artist and engraver. A poor man, he was one of Britain's first professional scientists and contributed much to the control of pests in the garden and farm.

b Miss Eleanor Ormerod was a wealthy woman, the last of ten children of a rich coal-mine owner, who also had a Gloucestershire property. 'The extent,' to use Miss Ormerod's words, 'was not very great, only about 800 acres.' She became an authority on pest control and published many books and, at her own expense, an annual report on the subject.

Chapter 8

a The term 'whisky money' arose from a change in the laws governing the running and opening of public houses. In the 1890s the Liberals maintained that there were too many pubs open for too long every day. Legislation was brought in, closing some licensed houses, and regulating hours during which liquor could be sold. The brewers and distillers naturally complained at this threat to their business and a million or so was voted as compensation for them. In the event, before any compensation was paid, it was found that just about as much liquor was sold after the Act was in force as before and, with fewer premises to manage and for shorter time, the brewers' profits greatly increased. The Government dared not pay out the compensation fund, and to get rid of this embarrassing sum, decided to spend it on technical education, much of it in agriculture, hence its name the 'whisky money'.

Chapter 9

a Monocotyledons are plants such as grasses and bulbs, pushing up one seed leaf as seedlings. Dicotyledons have two seed leaves, usually containing a reserve of food which helps the seedling establish itself. Beans are an example.

Chapter 11

a One of the reasons I find it difficult to believe in pre-Colombian landings of Europeans in America is that such explorers would surely not have failed to take wheat, oats and barley with them, nor to have brought back maize, potatoes and artichokes, all plants confined respectively to the eastern and western sides of the Atlantic before the Colombian adventure.

b *The Art of Gardening:*

> 'In this the artist who lays out the work, and devises a garment for a piece of ground, has the delight of seeing his work live and grow hour by hour; and, while it is growing, he is able to polish, cut and carve, to fill up here and there, to hope and to love.'
>
> Albert, Prince Consort of England

Appendix

The Names of the Life in the Garden

In the eighteenth century the great Swedish naturalist Linnaeus (1707–83) devised a system of naming plants and animals that did away with much confusion and is in use to this day. It is a binomial method; the first word is the genus and the second the species, and usually these words are derived from Latin or Greek roots. In an age when a knowledge of those tongues was more widely diffused the names told something about the plant or creature named, but today classical languages are much less generally understood and to most people scientific names mean nothing.

Below is a list of the 'trivial' (English) and the scientific names of the plants and animals mentioned in this book, together with certain meanings that can be given to the Graeco-Latin names.

PLANTS

English Name	Scientific Name	Meaning
Abelia	*Abelia floribunda*	Dr Abel's many-flowered plant
Achillea	*Achillea millefolium*	Achilles's thousand-leaved plant
Caspian	*A. cupatorium*	Achilles's Caspian plant
Silver milfoil	*A. clavannae*	Achilles's cloven plant
Sneezewort	*A. ptarmica*	Achilles's sneezing plant
Aconite *or* Monkshood	*Aconitum napellus*	Turnip-rooted dart
Adam and Eve in the bower *see* Nettle, dead		
Agrimony	*Agrimonia eupatoria*	
Alexander	*Smyrnium olusatrum*	The helper of man
Alhagi	*Alhagi maurorum*	The Moor's alhagi
Allheal	*see* Valerian	

Aloe, African	*Aloe ferox*	The fierce aloe
Amaranthus	*Amaranthus tricolor*	The unfading three-coloured plant
Anemone, wood	*Anemone nemorosa*	The wind house of open glades
star	*A. hortensis*	The wind house of gardens
Apple	*Pyrus malus*	The pear apple
Artichoke, Jerusalem	*Helianthus tuberosus*	The tuberous sunflower
Arum	*Arum maculatum*	The spotted fiery plant
Ash	*Fraxinus excelsior*	The taller ash
Asparagus	*Asparagus officinalis*	The prickly plant of shops
Auricula	*Primula auricula*	The first ear-like leaf
Bachelor's buttons	*Ranunculus asiaticus*	The asiatic frog-like plant
Bay	*Laurus nobilis*	The green noble plant
Beans, broad	*Vicia faba*	The clinging bean
runner *or* French	*Phaseolus coccineus*	The scarlet little boat
Bedeguar	*Diplolepis rosae*	Double-scaled rose
Beet	*Beta vulgaris*	The common beet
Bindweed	*Convolvulus*	The entwiners
Blackberry	*Rubus fruticosus*	The red-fruited plant
Black currant	*Ribes nigrum*	The black (Arabian) currant
Borage	*Borago officinalis*	The rough-leaved shop plant
Box	*Buxus sempervirens*	The evergreen box
Broom	*Cytisus spp.*	The shrubby plants
Broomrape	*Orobanche hederae*	The ivy throttler
—	*O. rapum-genisteae*	The broom turnip throttler
—	*O. minor*	The lesser throttler
Buddleia	*Buddleia davidii*	The Revd Buddle's David
—	*B. asiatica*	The Revd Buddle's Asiatic plant
—	*B. auriculata*	The Revd Buddle's golden plant

Burning bush	*Dictamnus albus*	Mount Dicte's white plant
American	*Kohleria amabilis*	Kohl's lovely plant
Buttercup	*Ranunculus*	Plants living in frog's territory
Butterfly bush	*see* Buddleia	
Cabbage	*Brassica capitata*	The headed cabbage
Camomile	*Anthemis nobilis*	The noble camomile
Campanula, clustered	*Campanula glomerata*	The clustered bell-flower
rampion	*C. rapunculus*	The little turnip bell-flower
Canadian potato	*see* Artichoke	
Canterbury bell	*see* Campanula	
Carnation	*Dianthus prolifer*	The divine flower
German carthusian	*D. carthusianorum*	The Carthusians' divine flower
clove	*D. caryophillus*	The divine dove flower
Carrot	*Daucus carota*	Red-rooted carrot
Catalpa	*Catalpa bignonioides*	The Indian (American) bignonia-like tree
Cat's ear	*Hypochoeris radicata*	The under-rooted elegant plant
Cauliflower	*Brassica botrytis*	The bunched cabbage
Charlock	*Sinapis arvensis*	The cabbage-like plant of the fields
Cherry	*Cerasus vulgaris*	The common tree from Cerasus
Chervil	*Anthriscus cerefolium*	The wax-leaved anthriscus
Chestnut	*Castanea sativa*	The cultivated chestnut
Chives	*Allium schoenoprasum*	The pungent leek
Christmas rose	*Helleborus niger*	The black hellebore The black, killing food
—	*H. orientalis*	The Eastern, killing food
Chrysanthemum	*Chrysanthemum coronarium*	The crowned gold flower
Cineraria	*Senecio cruentus*	The blood-red, old man's plant
Clover, wild white	*Trifolium repens*	The three-leaved creeper

Coca (Cocaine Plant)	*Erythroxlum coca*	The red-wooded coca plant
Coffee	*Coffea arabica*	The Arabian coffee plant
Coltsfoot	*Tussilago farfara*	Farfara's cough cure
Columbine	*Aquilegia canadensis*	The Canadian eagle's claw
Granny's bonnet	*Aquilegia vulgaris*	The common eagle's claw
Comfrey	*Symphytum asperrimum*	The healing roughest
—	*S. perigrinum*	The spreading healer
—	*S. officinale*	The shop healer
Coriander	*Coriandrum sativum*	The bug-smell, cultivated plant
Cornflower, common	*Centaurea cyanus*	The blue, centaur plant
big-flowered	*C. macrocephala*	The centaur's big-headed plant
Sweet sultan	*C. moschata*	The centaur's musky plant
Cowslip	*Primula officinalis*	The first-flowering shop plant
Creeping thistle	*Cirsium arvense*	The injurious field plant
Crocus, autumn	*Colchicum autumnale*	The autumn colchis
Currant, flowering	*Ribes sanguineum*	The blood-red currant
Cyclamen, round-leaved	*Cyclamen coum*	The circular plant from Kos
common	*C. europaeum*	The circular European plant
Cumin	*Cuminum cyminum*	Cumin cumin
Daffodil	*Narcissus pseudo-narcissus*	Narcissus false narcissus
Dahlia	*Dahlia spp.*	Mr Andreas Dahl's plants
Daisy, ox-eye	*Bellis perennis*	The pretty perennial
Dandelion	*Taraxacum officinale*	The night disturber of the shops
Death-cap fungus	*Amanita phalloides*	The phallus-like fungus
Delphinium *or* Larkspur	*Delphinium spp.*	The dolphin-like plant
Devil's bit	*Scabiosa succisa*	The bitten itch-cure plant

Dill	*Anethum graveolens*	The strong-smelling upward-growing plant
Dittany	*see* Burning bush	
Dock	*Rumex spp.*	The dock
Dog's tail	*Cynosurus spp.*	The dark blue plants
Dogwood	*Cornus sanguinea*	The bloody horn
Dryas *or* Mountain Avens	*Dryas octopetala*	The eight-petalled wood nymph's plant
Dumb cane	*Dieffenbachia seguine*	Dr Dieffenbach's seguine
Eelworm fungus	*Arthrobotrys*	Bunched jointer with few spores
Eglantine	*see* Sweetbriar	
Elcampane	*Inula Helenium*	Helen's plant
Elder	*Sambucus nigra*	The black flute
Elm	*Ulmus campestris*	The field elm
Elm fungus	*Ceratocystis ulmi*	The wax-bladder of the elm
Epilobium *or* Willow herb	*Epilobium hirsutum*	Hairy pods
Evening primrose	*Oenothera biennis*	The biennial wine inducer
Eyebright	*Euophrasia officinalis*	Plant in the shop bringing light
Fairy ring fungus	*Marasmius oreades*	The nymph Oreas's fungus
Fat hen	*Chenopodium album*	The white plant with goose-foot leaves
Fennel	*Foeniculum vulgare*	The common hay-smelling plant
Feverfew	*Chrysanthemum parthenium*	The golden flower of Parthenium
Flax	*Linum usitatissum*	The most common flax plant
Forget-me-not	*Myosotis spp.*	The mouse-eared plants
Forsythia	*Forsythia suspensa*	Forsyth's hanging plants
Foxglove	*Digitalis purpurea*	The purple finger of a glove
Fraxinella	*see* Burning bush	

Furze	*Ulex europaeus*	The European prickly shrub
Fustic	*Rhus cotinus*	The wild olive-like roos
Gentian	*Gentiana spp.*	King Gentian's plants
Gillyflower	*see* Mullein *and* Wallflower	
Globe flower	*Trollius europaeus*	The European round flower
Globe thistle	*Echinops banaticus*	The Banat hedgehog-like plant
—	*E. sphaerocephalus*	The round-headed hedgehog-like plants
Gloxinia	*Gloxinia maculata*	Mr Gloxin's spotted plant
Golden ball	*Edgeworthia chrysantha*	Mr Edgeworth's golden plant
Golden bells	*see* Forsythia	
Golden rod	*Solidago canadensis*	The Canadian healer
Goldilocks	*Chrysocoma linosyris*	The golden-haired flax-leaved plant
Gooseberry	*Ribes grossularia*	The rough, acid plant
Grass, Common bent	*Agrostis tenuis*	The thin plant of the fields
Creeping bent	*A. stolonifera*	The stolon-bearing field plant
Crested dog's tail	*Cynosurus cristatus*	The crested dog's tail
Fescue, red	*Festuca rubra*	The red blade
Meadow grass	*Poa trivialis*	The common grass
smooth stalked	*P. nemoralis*	The sylvan grass
bulbous	*P. bulbosa*	The bulbous grass
Perennial ryegrass	*Lolium perenne*	The perennial darnel-like plant
Guelder rose	*Viburnum opulus*	The guelder rose-tieing shoots
Hawthorn	*Crataegus oxycantha*	The strong-wooded thorn
Hazel	*Corylus avellana*	The Avellana helmet
Heartsease	*see* Pansy	
Hedge *or* stone parsley	*Sison amomum*	The fragrant Sison
Hellebore, green	*Helleborus viridis*	The green hellebore

stinking *or* bear's foot	*H. foetidus*	The stinking hellebore
Holly	*Ilex aquifolium*	The pointed-leaved oak-loving plant
Hollyhock	*Althaea officinalis*	The healing shop plant
fig-leaved	*A. ficifolia*	The healing fig-leaved plant
Honesty	*Lunaria annua*	The annual moon plant
Honeysuckle	*Lonicera spp.*	Herr Lonicer's plants
Honeyworth *or* wax-plant	*Cerinthe major*	The larger wax flower
Hop	*Humulus lupulus*	The trailing wolf-like plant
House-leek	*Sempervivum tectorum*	The ever-living roof plant
Iris	*Iris spp.*	The rainbow plants
Japanese knotgrass	*Polygonum cuspidatum*	The many-jointed sharp-pointed plant
Jasmin	*Jasminum*	The *ymyn* (Arabic) plants
Jerusalem cross	*Lychnis chalcedonica*	The Chalcedonian lamp
Juniper	*Juniperus communis*	The common juniper
Katswa tree	*Cercidiphyllum japonicum*	The Japanese tree with Judas-tree leaves
Knapweed	*Centaurea scabiosa*	The centaur's wound and scabies healer
—	*C. nigra*	The centaur's black plant
Laburnum	*Laburnum vulgare*	The common laburnum
Larkspur	*Delphinium ajacis*	Dolphin head with AIAI mark
Laurel, spotted	*Aucuba japonica*	The Japanese aucuba
Lavender	*Lavandula officinalis*	The washing plant of the shops
Leek	*Allium porrum*	The garlic-like leek
Lemon	*Citrus limonia*	The orange lemon
Lent lily	*see* Daffodil	
Leopard's bane	*Doronicum pardalianches*	The Doronigi panther-strangler
—	*D. plantagineum*	The plantain-leaved Doronigi

Lilac, common	*Syringa vulgaris*	The common tube-like plant
Californian	*Ceanothus thrysiflorus*	The ceanothus with thryses flower heads
Lily, white	*Lilium candidum*	The white lily
Turk's cap	*L. martagon*	The Martagon lily
wood	*Trillium spp.*	Triple
Lily-of-the-valley	*Convallaria majalis*	The May-flowering valley plant
Liquorice	*Glycyrrhiza glabra*	The smooth, sweet-root plant
Lobelia	*Lobelia linnaeoides*	Matthias de Lobel's plant like Linnaeus
Lords and ladies	*see* Arum	
Lovage, wild	*Ligustrum vulgare*	The common binding plant
Love apple	*see* Tomato	
Lucerne	*Medicago sativa*	The cultivated healing plant
Lupin	*Lupinus spp.*	The wolf (destroyer) plants
Madwort	*Asperugo procumbens*	The low-growing, rough plant
Magnolia	*Magnolia grandiflora*	Magnol's big flower
Mallow, round-leaved	*Malva rotundi folia*	The soothing round-leaved plant
curled	*M. crispa*	The curled, soothing plant
musk	*M. moschata*	The fragrant, soothing plant
Mandrake	*Mandragora officinalis*	The shop mandrake
Marguerite	*Felicia pappei*	The happy plant or Herr Felix's plant
—	*F. amelloides*	The amellus-like happy plant
Marigold, French	*Tagetes patula*	Tages's spreading plant
'African'	*T. erecta*	Tages's upright plant
Marjoram	*Origanum onites*	The Onites plant from the beautiful mountain
Marrow	*Cucumis pepo*	The cucumber-like plant
Melancholy gentleman	*Hesperis tristis*	The sad evening

Michaelmas daisy	*Aster ericoides*	The star plant like heather
Mint	*Mentha spp.*	Mint
—	*A. novae-angliae*	The New England star
Mistletoe	*Viscum album*	The white mistletoe
Mock orange	*Philadelphus coronarius*	King Ptolemy Philadephus's wreathed plant
Mullein	*Verbascum thapsus*	The hairy plant from Thapsus (Tunisia)
Nasturtium	*Tropaeolum majus*	The climbing helmet-like plant
Nettle, dead	*Lamium album*	The white, throated flower
Nightshade, deadly	*Atropa belladonna*	Atropos's beautiful lady
None-so-pretty	*see* St Patrick's cabbage	
Oak	*Quercus pedunculata*	The long-stalked oak
Onion	*Allium sativum*	The cultivated garlic-like plant
Orach	*Atriplex hortensis*	The black-woven garden plant
Orange	*Citrus sinensis*	The China orange
bitter	*C. aurantium*	The golden orange
Orpine	*Sedum telephium*	Telephus's healing plant
Paeony	*Paeonia officinalis*	Dr Paeon's shop plant
Paigle	*see* Cowslip	
Pansy	*Viola tricolor*	The three-coloured violet
Parsley	*Petroselinum crispum*	The crested rock plant
Parsnip	*Peucedanum sativum*	The cultivated parsnip
Pasque flower	*Anemone pulsatilla*	The shaking wind living plant
Pawpaw	*Carica papaya*	The papaya from Carica
Peach	*Prunus persica*	The Persian plum
Pear	*Pyrus communis*	The common pear
Peas	*Pisum sativum*	The cultivated pea
Pennyroyal	*Mentha pulegium*	The flea-destroying mint
Peppermint	*Mentha piperita*	The pepper-like mint
Periwinkle	*Vinca major*	The greater binder

—	*V. minor*	The lesser binder
Phlox	*Phlox spp.*	The burning flower
Pinks	see Carnation	
Plantain	*Plantago spp.*	The flat-leaved plant
Pocket-handkerchief tree	*Davidia involucrata*	The Abbé David's involucrated plant
Poplar	*Populus alba*	The people's white tree
Poppy, wild	*Papaver rhoeas*	The pomegranate-like poppy
opium or garden	*P. somniferum*	The sleep-inducing poppy
Potato	*Solanum tuberosum*	The tuberous solacing plant
sweet	*Ipomoea batata*	The bindweed-like batata
Primrose	*Primula spp.*	The first-flowering
Privet	*Ligustrum vulgare*	The common privet
Pumpkin	*Cucurbita maxima*	The largest gourd
Purple medick	see Lucerne	
Purslane	*Portulaca oleracea*	The milky juice pot herb
Quamash	*Camassia esculenta*	The edible quamash
Quince	*Cydonia vulgaris*	The common plant from Cydon
Ragwort	*Senecio jacobaea*	Old man naked
Raspberry	*Rubus idaeus*	The red raspberry
Red-ink plant	*Phytolacea americana*	The American red plant
Rhododendron	*Rhododendron ponticum*	The rose-tree from Pontus
—	*R. anthopogon*	The Anthopogon rose-tree
—	*R. arboreum*	The tree rose-tree
—	*R. campanulatum*	The bell-shaped rose-tree
—	*R. chrysanthemum*	The golden rose-tree
—	*R. dauricum*	The Daurian rose-tree
Rhubarb	*Rheum rhaponticum*	The Volga rhubarb plant
—	*R. palmatum*	The palmate rhubarb
Robin's pincushion	see Bedeguar	

Rose		
Damask	*R. damascena*	The Damascus rose
dog	*R. canina*	The dog rose
Evergreen	*R. sempervirens*	The everliving rose
Frankfurt	*R. turbinata*	The top-shaped rose
French	*R. gallica*	The French rose
Provence or cabbage	*R. centifolia*	The hundred-petalled rose
White, of York	*Rosa alba*	The white rose
Rue	*Ruta graveolens*	The strong-smelling rue
Saffron	*Crocus sativus*	The cultivated thread
Sage	*Salvia officinalis*	The saving plant of the shops
St John's wort	*Hypericum perforatum*	The perforated heath plant
St Patrick's cabbage	*Saxifraga spathularis*	The spoon-shaped rock breaker
Savory, winter	*Satureja montana*	The mountain savory
summer	*S. hortensis*	The garden savory
Scabious	*Scabiosa spp.*	The scabies-curing plant
Sedum	*Sedum spp.*	The assuaging (healing) plants
Self-heal	*Prunella vulgaris*	The common quinsy-cure
Sensitive plant	*Mimosa pudica*	The obedient mimic
Shavanese salad	*Hydrophyllum virginicum*	The Virginian water-leaf
Shepherd's club	*see* Mullein	
Shepherd's purse	*Capsella bursa-pastoris*	The shepherd's purse
Skirret	*Sium sisarum*	Water skirret
Snapdragon	*Antirrhinum spp.*	The snout-like flower
Snowdrop	*Galanthus nivalis*	The snow-white milky flower
Soapwort	*Saponaria officinalis*	Soap plant of the shops
Spiderwort	*Tradescantia virginiana*	John Tradescant's Virginia plant
Spinach	*Spinacea oleracea*	The prickly pot herb
Spindle tree	*Euonymus japonicus*	The Japanese plant of good repute

Spotted orchid	*Orchis morio*	The testicular buffoon
Star of Bethlehem	*Ornithogalum umbellatum*	The umbelled bird's milk plant
Stock, night-scented	*Matthiola incana*	Piero Matthioli's hoary plant
Virginia	*Malcolmia maritima*	Malcolm's sea plant
Strawberry, wild	*Fragaria vesca*	The weak strawberry
Chile	*F. chiloensis*	The Chile strawberry
Hautbois	*F. elatior*	The taller strawberry
Strawberry tree	*Arbutus unedo*	The rough-fruited, eat-one tree
Sugar	*Saccharum spontaneum*	The spontaneous sugar plant
Sumach	*see* Fustic	
Sundew	*Drosera spp.*	Dewy plants
Sunflower	*Helianthus annuus*	The annual sunflower
Sweetbriar	*Rosa rubiginosa*	The rusty rose
Sweet pea	*Lathyrus odorata*	The fragrant legume
Sweet William	*Dianthus barbatus*	The bearded divine flower
Sycamore	*Acer pseudo-platanus*	The hard false plane tree
Thistle, blessed	*Cnicus benedictus*	The blessed safflower
sow	*Sonchus arvensis*	The field thistle
Scotch	*Onopordon acanthium*	The plant eaten by donkeys from Acanthium
Thyme	*Thymus spp.*	The perfumed plant
Tobacco	*Nicotiana tabacum*	Jean Nicot's tobacco
Tomato	*Lycopersicum esculentum*	The edible wolf-peach
Torch thistle	*Cereus jamacaru*	The wax plant from Jamacaru (Brazil)
Tree of heaven, downy	*Ailanthus vilmoriana*	Vilmorin's ailanthus
common	*A. altissima*	The very high ailanthus
Tulip, common	*Tulipa sylvestris*	The wood tulip
narrow-leaved	*T. turcica*	The Turkish tulip
Clusius's or lady's	*T. clusiana*	Clusius's tulip
Turnip	*Brassica rapa*	The rape cabbage

Valerian	*Valeriana officinalis*	Dr Valerius's shop plant
Verbascum	*see* Mullein	
Vetch, yellow purple	*Lathyrus spp.*	Legume
Vine	*Vitis vinifera*	The wine-making vine
Violet	*Viola odorata*	Sweet-smelling violet
—	*V. canina*	Dog violet
Wake-Robin	*see* Arum	
Wallflower	*Cheiranthus cheiri*	Cheiri's hand flower
Wild white clover	*Trifolium repens*	Three-leaved creeper
Willow herb, rosebay	*Epilobium angustifolium*	The narrow-leaved upon the pod plant
Windflower	*see* Anemone	
Yellow rattle	*Rhinanthus christagalli*	The cock's-crest nose-like flower
Yew	*Taxus baccata*	The berried yew
Zinnia	*Zinnia elegans*	Professor Zinn's elegant plant

ANIMALS
Arthropods, insects

Angle shades moth	*Phlogophora meticulosa*	The timid flame carrier
Ant, garden	*Lasius niger*	The black hair
lawn	*Lasius umbratus*	The shady hair
red	*Myrmica scabrinodis*	The scratching ant
—	*M. laevinodis*	The left-hand ant
red-brown	*Myrmica ruginoides*	The reddish ant
wood	*Formica rufa*	The red ant
Apantales fly	*Apantales spp.*	Of the all-grasping
Aphids, apple	*Aphis pomi*	The lavish apple creature
Apple sucker	*Psylla mali*	The apple flea
Bee, hive	*Apis mellifera*	The honey-making bee
bumble	*Bombus spp.*	Bee
Beetle borers	*Scolytus spp.*	The shortened creatures
Brimstone butterfly	*Gonepteryx rhamni*	The Rhamnus angle wing
Cabbage white butterfly, large	*Pieris brassicae*	Cabbage Pieris
small	*P. rapae*	Turnip Pieris

Camomile shark moth	*Cucullia chamomillae*	The hood camomile creature
Cockchafer	*Melolontha spp.*	The cockchafer
Codlin moth	*Cydia pomonella*	The apple Cydia
Crane fly	*see* Daddy-long-legs	
Cutworms	*Graphiphora pronuba*	The bridesmaid carrying writing
Daddy-long-legs	*Tipula paludosa*	The marsh crane fly
—	*T. maxima*	The biggest crane fly
Flea beetle	*Phyllotreta*	The leaf piercer
Hawk moth, common elephant	*Deilephila elpenor*	The god-loving elephant
small elephant	*D. porcellus*	The god-loving pig
Hop aphid	*Phorodon humuli*	The hop carrier
Lace border	*Acidalia ornata*	The sour, ornamented creature
Lackey moth	*Malacosoma neustria*	The soft-mouthed nerved creature
Large blue butterfly	*Maculinea arion*	Arion's spotted, lined creature
Large white butterfly	*Pieris brassicae*	The muse of cabbages
Lomechusa beetle	*L. cava*	Fringed cave creature
Magpie moth	*Abraxus grossulariata*	The shaver of the gooseberry
Mealworm	*Tenebrio obscurus*	Dark lover of darkness
Oak apple wasp	*Biorhiza pallida*	The pale root-liver
—	*Andricus kollari*	Kollar's hermaphrodite
Oak moth, green	*Tortrix viridiana*	The green twister
Peacock butterfly	*Nymphalis io*	The nymph-like Io
Red admiral butterfly	*Vanessa atalanta*	Vanessa Atalanta
Rose chafer	*Cetonia aurata*	The golden seton
Small tortoiseshell butterfly	*Aglais urticae*	Aglais of the nettles
Springtails	*Collembola*	The gum maker
Springtail, yellow	*Sminthuris viridis*	The green Apollo
Turnip sawfly	*Athalia colibri*	The withering creature
Vestal moth	*Rhodometra sacraria*	The sacred red-measurer
Vinegar fly	*Drosophila*	The dew bearer
Ware moth	*Aspillatus strigillium*	The destroying scraper

Wasp, common	*Vespula vulgaris*	Common wasp
German	*V. germanica*	German wasp
Wax moth	*Galleria mellonella*	The honey gallery
Wild thyme bug	*Eupithecia constricta*	The good trickster
Winter moth	*Cheimatobia brumata*	The winter monster-like creature

Arthropods, other

Bee mite	*Parasitus fucorum*	The bee's parasite
Centipede	*Geophilus longicornis*	The long-horned earth-lover
Harvestmen	*Opiliones*	Shepherds
Millipede	*Blanjulus pulchellus*	The beautiful gentle creature
Mites		
ash	*Eriophyes fraxinus*	The ash woolmaker
currant big bud	*E. ribis*	The currant woolmaker
grain	*Acarus siro*	The granary mite
harvester	*Trombicula autumnalis*	The autumn timid one
mange	*Sarcoptes scabiei*	The rough flesh eater
parasitic	*Blattisocius tarsalis*	The moth comrade of the Tarsus
red poultry	*Dermanyssus gallinae*	The skin-liver of chickens
scabious	*E. squalidus*	The rough woolmaker
sparrow	*Ptilonyssus hirsti*	The sparrow wing-pricker
Red spider mites	*Panonychus ulmi*	The web-maker of the elm
Spiders, large garden	*Theridion spp.*	The little wild animal
garden	*Epeira diademeta*	The bold diadem bearer
Woodlouse	*Porcellio scaber*	The rough woodlouse

Birds

Blackbird	*Turdus merula*	The blackbird thrush
Blackcap	*Sylvia atricapilla*	Sylvia's hair room
Blue tit	*Parus caeruleus*	The blue tit
Chaffinch	*Fringilla coelebs*	The single little finch

Chickens, domestic	*Gallus gallus domesticus*	The domestic hen hen
Duck	*Anas spp.*	Ducks
Dunnock	*Prunella modularis*	The measured little plum
Flycatcher, spotted	*Muscicapa striata*	The striped catcher of flies
Goldfinch	*Carduelis carduelis*	Thistle user
Hawk, sparrow	*Accipiter nisus*	Nisus's hawk
House martin	*Delicon urbica*	The delight of the city
Jay	*Garrulus glandarius*	The talkative acorn seeker
Kestrel	*Falco tinnunculus*	The belled falcon
Mistle thrush	*Turdus viscovorus*	The mistletoe-eating thrush
Nightingale	*Luscinia megarhynchos*	The big-beaked Lucina
Nuthatch	*Sitta europaea*	The European nuthatch
Owl	*Asio spp.*	Owl
Peacock	*Pavo cristatus*	The tufted peacock
Pigeon	*Colomba livia*	Lead-coloured pigeon
wood	*C. palumbus*	The wood pigeon
Ruff	*Philomachus pugnax*	The fight-loving fierce creature
Sparrow	*Passer domesticus*	The domestic sparrow
Starling	*Sternus vulgaris*	The common sputterer
Skylark	*Alauda arvensis*	The lark of the fields
Thrush, song	*Turdos philomelos*	The singing thrush
Wagtail, pied	*Motacilla alba yarrellii*	Yarrell's white tail-mover
Warbler, garden	*Sylvia borin*	Sylvia's north creature
reed	*Aerocephalus scirpaceus*	The head-in-air creature of the reeds
Woodpecker	*Dendrocopos spp.*	Woodpecker
Wren	*Troglodytes troglodytes*	Cave dweller

Mammals

Badger	*Meles taxus*	The yew badger
Bat, noctule	*Nyctalus noctula*	Drowsy night creature
pipistrelle	*Pipistrellus pipistrellus*	Little-bat, little-bat

Cat	*Felis maniculata*	Small-handed cat
Dog	*Canis familiaris*	Domestic dog
Dormouse, edible	*Glis glis*	Dormouse dormouse
Fox	*Vulpes vulpes crucigera*	The tormenting fox fox
Hedgehog	*Erinaceus europeus*	The European bog creature
Horse	*Equus caballus*	The horse horse
Man	*Homo sapiens*	The wise man
Mole	*Talpa europaea*	The European mole
Mouse, domestic	*Mus musculus*	Little mouse mouse
field	*Apodemus sylvaticus sylvaticus*	The body creature of the woods
Rabbit	*Oryctolagus cùniculus*	The rabbit and digging creature
Shrew	*Sorex spp.*	Shrew
Squirrel, red	*Sciurus vulgaris*	The common squirrel
grey	*S. carolinensis*	The Carolina squirrel
Stoat	*Mustela erminea stabilis*	The steadfast ermine weasel
Vole	*Microtus agrestis*	The small country creature
Weasel	*Mustela nivalis nivalis*	The snow-white weasel

Molluscs

River limpet	*Ancylastrum fluviatile*	The river star-shield creature
Slug, grey, field	*Agriolimax agrestis*	The country field file
shelled	*Testacella haliotidea*	The breath, shell-house
Snail, garden	*Helix aspersa*	The rough winder
strawberry	*Hygromia rufescene*	The red-making wet creature
edible	*Helix pomatia*	The fruit winder
Wall fish	see Snail, garden	

Reptiles, snakes, amphibians

Adder	*Vipera berus*	The viper of Beroë
Newt	*Lissotriton toenatus*	The rattling, smooth Triton
Toad	*Bufo vulgaris*	The common toad

Worms

Earthworms	*Lombricus terrestris*	The earth worm
—	*Allolophora longa*	The long other creature
—	*A. nocturna*	The night other creature
Eelworms	*Pratylenchus pratensis*	The meadow creature
Tapeworms	*Amoebo-tania*	The shape-changing Tania

Bibliography

1 ABEL, W., trans O. Ordish, *Agricultural Fluctuations in Europe*, 1980, London, Methuen, p. 168
2 ADDISON, J., *Spectator*, 477, 1712
3 ALFORD, D. V., *Bumblebees*, 1975, London, Davis-Poynter, pp. 90–2
4 ANON, *The Black Book*, 1820, London, Fairburn, pp. 425–45
5 ARNOLD, G., 'Les variations annuelles dans l'effet de groupe chez l'abeille ...' *Insectes Sociaux*, 1978, Paris, 25. 1, pp. 39–51
6 ATTENBOROUGH, D., 'Bird song', *BBC Radio 4*, 30 March 1981
7 AUSTEN, R., *A Dialogue between the Husbandman and Fruit Trees*, 1676, London
8 BOLAND, M. AND B., *Old Wives' Lore for Gardeners*, 1980, London, Bodley Head
9 BOSWELL, J., *The Life of Samuel Johnson*, 1826, Oxford, Talboys and Wheeler, vol. II, p. 46
10 BOWLES, E. A., 'The effects of the frosts of the winter of 1916–17 on vegetation'; *Journal of the Royal Horticultural Society*, Feb. 1919, London, vol. XLIII, pp. 388–461
11 BRAMBELL, F. W. R., 'The reproduction of the wild rabbit', *Proceedings of the Zoological Society, London*, 1936, vol. 114, pp. 1–45
12 BRISTOWE, W. S., *The Comity of Spiders*, 1941, London, Ray Society
13 BUFFON, G. I. L., trans. W. Smellie, *Natural History*, 1812, London, Cadell & Davies, V. p. 358
14 BURTON, P. S. K., GILLMOR, R., GINN, H., PARMENTER, T. W., PARSLOW, J., WALKER, C. A., AND WALLACE, D. I. M., *Field Guide to the Birds of Britain*, 1981, London, Reader's Digest
15 CAVENDISH, MARGARET, DUCHESS OF NEWCASTLE, 'Hampton Court', *Poems and Fancies*, 1635, London
16 CHAUVIN, R., trans. G. Ordish, *Animal Societies*, 1968, London, Gollancz, pp. 69, 91
17 CORREA DE SERRA, J., 'Notes respecting several Vegetables used as Esculents in North America', *Trans. Horticultural Society*, 4, LXVII, 17 July 1821, pp. 443–6
18 CULPEPPER, N., *Complete Herbal and English Physician*, reprint of 1826 edn., Manchester, J. Gleave, London, Harvey Sales, 1981
19 DARLINGTON, A., *Pocket Encyclopaedia of Plant Galls*, 1968, London, Blandford, p. 150
20 DARWIN, C., *On the Origin of Species by Means of Natural Selection*, 1859, London, Murray
21 DARWIN, C., *The Formation of Vegetable Mould Through the Action of*

Worms with Observations of their Habits, 1881, London, Murray
22 DAWKINS, R., *The Selfish Gene*, 1976, OUP, p. ix
23 DICKSON, T., 'Observations on the Disease in the Potato, generally called the Curl; pointing out the most probable method of preventing it; with an account of the results of a few experiments made on the subject', *Mems. Caledonian Horticultural Society*, 1814, Edinburgh, vol. I, pp. 49–59
24 DZIERZON, I., 'Ueber die Fortpflanzung der Bienen', *Eichstadt Bienenzeitung*, 1845, vol. I, p. 113
25 EDWARDS, R., *Social Wasps*, 1980, Rentokil, East Grinstead, p. 46
26 EMERSON, R. W., *Essays*, 1883, London, Macmillan
27 ERASMUS, D., *Convivium Religiosum*, 1664, Leyden and Rotterdam, Hackiana
28 ERNLE, LORD, *English Farming Past and Present*, 1961, 6th edn. London, Heinemann
29 EVANS, A. C., *Proceedings Zoological Society of London*, 1948, pp. 118, 156
30 EVELYN, J., *Sylva, or a Discourse of Forest Trees . . . Calendarum hortense*, 1664, London
31 FITZHERBERT, SIR A., *Boke of husbandrie*, 1552, 5th edn. London, John Waller
32 FORSYTH, A. A., 'British Poisonous Plants', *Bulletin No. 161, Ministry of Agriculture, Fish, Food*, 1954, reprint 1956, HMSO, London, pp. 51, 93
33 FOSTER, JOHN, *England's Happiness Increased, or a sure and Easie Remedy against all succeeding Dear Years: by a plantation of the Roots called Potatoes*, 1664, London
34 FRISCH, K. VON, trans. Dora Ilse, *The Dancing Bees*, 1954, London, Methuen
35 GERARD, J., *Herball, or general Historie of Plantes*, 1597, London
36 HADFIELD, MILES, *A History of British Gardening*, 1960, rev. edn. London, Hamlyn
37 HAMILTON, W. D., 'The evolution of altruistic behaviour', 1963, *Amateur Naturalist*, 97, pp. 354–6
38 HAWES, S., *Passetyme of Pleasure, or Historie of graunde Amoure and la belle Pucelle*, 1554, London
39 HILLS, L. D., *Comfrey*, 1976, London, Faber
40 HORSLEY, J. W., *Our British Snails*, 1915, London, Society for the Promotion Christian Knowledge
41 HUDSON, W. H., *Birds in a Village*, 1921, London, Dent
42 HYAMS, E., *The English Garden*, 1966, London, Thames & Hudson, p. 111
43 HYLL, THOMAS, *A most Briefe and Pleasante Treatyse*, 1563, London, John Day
44 HYLL, THOMAS, *The Profitable Arte of Gardening (in three books), now the third time set forth . . . to this annexed two Proper Treatises, the one entitled The Marvelous government of the bees . . . and the other the yerely conjectures, meete for the husbandman to know*, 1563, London, Marsh

45 HYLL, THOMAS, *Anti-prognosticon contra inutiles astrologorum praedic-tiones Nostrodami*, 1566, London

46 INGRAM, JEAN S., 'Saffron (*Crocus sativus* L.)', *Tropical Science*, 1969, XI.3, pp. 177–84

47 JAMES THE FIRST, KING, *A Counterblast to Tobacco* (1604), London, English Reprints, 1871, Southgate

48 JEKYLL, G., *Wood and Garden*, 1899, facsimile 1981, Woodbridge, Suffolk, Baron

49 KIRBY, W. AND SPENCE, W., *An Introduction to Entomology*, 5 vols., 1818, 3rd edn. Longman, London.

50 LAWSON, W., *The New Orchard and Garden with the Country Housewifes Garden*, 1618, London, Jackson

51 MACKINTOSH, N., 'Learning' in *The Oxford Companion to Animal Behaviour*, ed. D. McFarland, 1981, OUP

52 MATTHEWS, L. H., *British Mammals*, 1968, 2nd edn., London, Collins

53 MELLANBY, K., *The Mole*, 1971, London, Collins

54 NIELSON, O., *Natura Jutlandica*, vol. 4, 1949

55 ORDISH, G., *The Living House*, 1959, London, Hart-Davis, New York, Lippincott

56 ORDISH, G., *The Constant Pest*, 1976, London, Peter Davies

57 PELOILLE, M., 'Hypomycetes prédateurs de nématodes dans un prairie de Limosin', *Entomophaga*, 26.1.1981, pp. 91–8

58 PHILLIPS, H., *Pomarum Britanicum*, 1823, London, Henry Colburn, p. 283

59 PLINIUS SECUNDUS, *The History of the World*, 1635, London, Islip, LVI, 28

60 POPE, A., *The Guardian*, No. 173, 29 Sept. 1729

61 ROBINSON, W., *The English Flower Garden and Home Grounds*, 1907, 10th edn., London, Murray

62 ROSE, JOHN, *The English Vineyard Vindicated*, 1666, London

62A ROUSSEAU, J-J, trans. T. Martyn, *Letters on the Elements of Botany*, 1794, 4th edn. London, B. J. White, p. 503

63 RUSSELL, SIR JOHN E., *The World of the Soil*, 1971, 5th edn., London, Collins, p. 111

64 SAVORY, T., *Arachnida*, 1977, 2nd edn., London, Academic Press

65 SCOT, REYNOLDS (REGINALD), *A Perfite Platforme of a Hoppe Garden*, 1574, London, Henrie Derham

66 SHELLEY, P. B., 'The Question', *Oxford Book of English Verse*

67 SMEE, A., *The Potatoe Plant, its Uses and Properties together with the Cause of the Present Malady*, 1846, London, Longman, Brown, Green

68 SOUTHERN, H. N., *The Handbook of British Mammals*, reprint 1965, Oxford, Blackwell, p. 71

69 TURNER, W., *New Herball*, 1551, London

70 TUSSER, T., *Five Hundreth good Pointes of Husbandry, united to as many of*

good Housewifery, 1573, London

71 WARD, N. B., *On the Growth of Plants in Closely Glazed Cases*, 1836, London

72 WHEELER, JAMES., *The Botanist's and Gardener's New Dictionary*, 1763, London, p. 50

73 WILDE, O., *The Importance of Being Ernest*, 1899, London, Act III

74 WHITE, GILBERT, *The Natural History of Selborne*, 1822, London, J. & A. Arch, Letter 35

75 WILSON, OWEN S., *The Larvae of the British Lepidoptera*, 1880, London, Reeve

76 WINGFIELD, W., *The Game of Sphairistikè*, 1876, 5th edn., London, Harrison

77 WORDSWORTH, W., 'Lines written in early spring', *The Golden Treasury*, 1924, OUP, p. 282

Index